Thai Cinema Uncensored

# Thai Cinema Uncensored

## Matthew Hunt

Silkworm Books

ISBN 978-616-215-169-9

First published in 2020 by
Silkworm Books
430/58 M. 7, T. Mae Hia, Chiang Mai 50100, Thailand
info@silkwormbooks.com
www.silkwormbooks.com

Typeset in Minion Pro 11 pt. by Silk Type

# CONTENTS

# PART TWO: INTERVIEWS WITH DIRECTORS

# ACKNOWLEDGMENTS

I am very grateful to Apichatpong Weerasethakul, Pen-ek Ratana-ruang, Chulayarnnon Siriphol, Nontawat Numbenchapol, Thunska Pansittivorakul, Surasak Pongson, Tanwarin Sukkhapisit, Kannitha Kwunyoo, Yuthlert Sippapak, and Ing Kanjanavanit for agreeing to be interviewed. Without their cooperation, this book would not have been possible. I would also like to thank Prabda Yoon, Manit Sriwanichpoom, Tom Waller, and an anonymous source for answering additional questions.

Witcha Suyara (Hawk Natpacal) facilitated the interview with Tanwarin, which is much appreciated. Sumit Rungsuriyakorn translated the interview with Kannitha, for which I am very grateful. I would like to thank Nopadol Chinapirom for his role as interpreter during the interview with Surasak. Thank you also to Jit Phokaew, Kong Rithdee, Worapol Preechakriangkrai, Pasakorn Pramoolwong, Chalida Uabumrungjit, David Streckfuss, Vasan Sitthiket, Regis Madec, Puangthong R. Pawakapan, Kong Pahurak, Diethard Ande, Titipol Phakdeewanich, Pachara Aungsusuknarumol, Kriengkrai Tantijinda, Panu Aree, Harit Srikhao, Surat Tomornsak, and Amy Iamphunghorn for support and assistance.

# THAI TRANSCRIPTION

Transliteration from Thai to English is notoriously inconsistent, though the Royal Thai General System of Transcription (RTGS) has been adopted to Romanize Thai words and phrases. Considerable care has been taken to verify the accurate English renderings of Thai names, using the preferred spelling of each person concerned. For Thai films and publications, official English-language titles are used wherever possible. When no official English title exists, an uncapitalized English translation is provided. RTGS has not been used for titles. Instead, original titles in Thai script appear in the Filmography.

# INTRODUCTION

*"Censorship is the order of the day in this society."*[1]

After a campaign by the film community, protesting against the arbitrary censorship of Apichatpong Weerasethakul's *Syndromes and a Century* (2006), the Film and Video Act (2008) introduced a rating system to Thai cinemas for the first time. Since then, there have been nine further censorship controversies: Thunska Pansittivorakul's *This Area Is Under Quarantine* (2008), Tanwarin Sukkhapisit's *Insects in the Backyard* (2010), Ing Kanjanavanit's *Shakespeare Must Die* (2012), Nontawat Numbenchapol's *Boundary* (2013), Yuthlert Sippapak's *Fatherland* (2013), Pen-ek Ratanaruang's *Paradoxocracy* (2013), Kannitha Kwunyoo's *Karma* (2015), Surasak Pongson's *Thibaan: The Series 2.2* (2018), and Chulayarnnon Siriphol's short film *Birth of Golden Snail* (2018).

*Thai Cinema Uncensored* includes interviews with each of these directors, who represent a diverse cross section of the Thai film industry. Apichatpong is based in Chiang Mai and Surasak is from the Isaan region, while the other directors work in Bangkok. Thunska and Ing are both political filmmakers, though they occupy opposite ends of the political spectrum. Apichatpong, Pen-ek, and Yuthlert are industry veterans, while Nontawat and Kannitha discuss their debut films. Apichatpong, Thunska, and Ing are independent directors; Pen-ek, Surasak, Yuthlert, and Kannitha work within the studio system; and Tanwarin and Nontawat have a foot in both camps. Nontawat, Kanittha, and Surasak's films appeal to Thai millennials, whereas Apichatpong, Pen-ek, and Thunska are more prominent on the international film festival circuit. Chulayarnnon and Apichatpong are primarily video artists, while the others focus mainly or entirely on narrative features. The directors' responses to censorship were also different: Pen-ek, Nontawat, Surasak, and Kannitha cut their films to secure a release; Thunska, Apichatpong, Yuthlert, and Chulayarnnon withheld their films from distribution; and Tanwarin and Ing took the censors to court.

Thai film censorship has not been thoroughly examined in an English-language publication before, and the few Thai-language accounts of the subject are largely outdated or limited in scope.[2] Therefore, *Thai Cinema Uncensored* provides an overview of the history of film regulation in Thailand and the ideology underpinning it, and an assessment of the films cut or banned under the rating system. It examines how Thai filmmakers approach culturally sensitive topics, and how their films have been censored as a result. The focus is on sex, religion, and politics, as these issues have all led to Thai films being banned.

The Film Act (1930) established the first Thai film censorship system, preventing the depiction of sex or graphic nudity. Traditional values were also upheld by a paternalistic state and conservative society. However, the rating system relaxed some of these restrictions, and more explicit independent films, especially works dealing with gay sexuality, have occasionally slipped under the censors' radar.

The depiction of Buddhism in Thai films is strictly controlled, and seemingly innocuous acts have been censored in films featuring monks. There have also been protests by religious groups against films perceived as blasphemous. Violence is not generally a major concern for Thai censors, though misdeeds performed by characters in monks' robes are far more controversial.

The twenty-first century has been a period of social polarization and political crisis in Thailand, with street protests and military coups. Equally seismic episodes from Thailand's political history have inspired both fiction and nonfiction films. A collective political awakening experienced by a new generation of filmmakers coincided with increasingly widespread enforcement of the draconian *lèse-majesté* law, leading to an atmosphere of reluctant though necessary self-censorship.

Part One

# Thai Film Censorship

Chapter 1

# A History of Thai Film Censorship

*"Censorship has been intertwined with the*
*Thai film industry since moving pictures were invented."*[3]

## Saving Face

The first feature film made in Thailand, the romantic melodrama *Suvarna of Siam* (1923), was also the first instance of Thai film censorship. King Vajiravudh had granted an American crew permission to film in the country, and he made numerous resources available to the production, perhaps aware that *Suvarna of Siam* could serve as a promotional vehicle for Thailand itself.[4] Thailand's modern infrastructure was a source of particular pride at the time, and in an early example of cinema as soft power, *Suvarna of Siam* showcased the country's development. However, amongst the glittering palaces and steam trains, the director also captured a somewhat less laudable scene: he filmed a prisoner being executed in Chiang Mai.

This led to complaints that the inclusion of such a sequence would damage the country's international image. Chalida Uabumrungjit, head of the Thai Film Foundation, notes the "concerns among the Thai aristocracy that some scenes in this film would create a bad

7

image of Siam"[5] and a newspaper editorial criticized the decision to allow the filmmakers to record the execution: "I would like to blame the local officer who did not save the honor of the country by forbidding them to do so. The execution will represent the barbarism of Siam."[6] The scene was cut before *Suvarna of Siam*'s release, and Scot Barmé demonstrates that at the time, cinema was, for the state, a vehicle to (literally) project only positive images of the country:

> Concern and anxiety about how Siamese society appeared to foreigners, especially Europeans, was intense. In 1921, for example, when a Captain Harold Holland arrived in Bangkok "for the purpose of taking photographs and preparing scenarios in connection with an important cinematograph film production," Prince Dhani, one of King Chulalongkorn's younger brothers, wrote to other high-ranking state officials saying precautions needed to be taken to ensure that he did not film anything that would reflect badly on the country.[7]

Film censorship persists partly to ensure that unsavory aspects of Thai society are not reflected in its cinematic output. This results in mainstream films that present a rose-tinted view, rather than holding a mirror up to society. Apichatpong Weerasethakul has commented on this notion of using cinema to 'save face' by suppressing depictions of social problems: "In our DNA we have this saving face thing, and the media is still the mask. We have prostitution and all these things going on, but we cannot do it in the media." In the eyes of the censors, Apichatpong's films are unpatriotic, and they claimed that *Syndromes and a Century* (2006) "shamefully presents a negative image of Thai society for foreign audiences."[8] Thunska Pansittivorakul's films linger defiantly on forbidden images, precisely because they are forbidden, to counteract the sanitized state-sanctioned narrative: "to keep making movies like this is my fight, as long as the authority doesn't accept reality—as long as they refuse to admit that there are prostitutes in this country and that not everything is as clean and beautiful as they'd like us to think."[9]

The Thailand International Film Destination Festival is perhaps the most clear-cut contemporary example of face-saving censorship. *Happy Hour in Paradise* (2015) and *Detective Chinatown* (2015)— Swedish and Chinese comedies, respectively—were withdrawn from the event in 2016 because they "depicted Thailand's dark side."[10] (For the same reason, Euthana Mukdasanit's film *Bar 21* was censored in 1978 to remove shots of slum dwellings.) In *Happy Hour in Paradise*, a Swedish priest indulges in alcohol, gambling, and casual sex in the Thai resort of Phuket, and the depiction of the town as a hedonist's haven was unacceptable to the Festival organizers. *Detective Chinatown*'s caricature of Bangkok's police officers as bungling and incompetent was also deemed objectionable.

Prior to the 1932 transition to a constitutional monarchy, the king's prerogative included approving (or rejecting) the release of all films shown in Thai cinemas. In 1927, for example, King Prajadhipok found the depiction of prostitution and the criminal underworld in a film about 'dark forces' distasteful. As with *Suvarna of Siam*, the country's international reputation was the paramount consideration, as Prajadhipok "saw it as presenting a negative, damaging image of Siam to the outside world."[11]

When the film's producers petitioned the monarch, he authorized its release on the condition that all prints were destroyed after the limited theatrical run. The police department then insisted that the film be censored and retitled, and cuts were duly made. The controversy continued, however, presenting cinema owners with a dilemma: they were legally permitted to show the film, as its release had royal approval, though if they did so they would be screening a film that the king found offensive. Major Bangkok cinemas ultimately declined to show the film, forcing the distributor to organize screenings at smaller provincial venues instead.

## The Film Act

In 1923, a few months before the release of *Suvarna of Siam*, a Bangkok newspaper observed that there was "practically no film censorship" in the country.[12] This was true in the sense that outright bans were rare, one exception being *The Light of Asia* (1925), an Indo-German film about the life of the Buddha. However, the 'dark forces' case demonstrates that a film's distribution could be curtailed even without a formal ban. It also shows that, if state censorship is entrusted to a single individual, a film's release can depend on the interpretation of any ambiguities in his or her comments. Furthermore, if that individual is the reigning monarch, actions construed as counter to his or her wishes could constitute *lèse-majesté*.

The Film Act, the first legal regulation of the Thai film industry, was passed in 1930. The Act's prohibitions were sufficiently broad that they could be used as a pretext to cut almost any potentially objectionable material, and its main stipulations were as follows:

> It is prohibited to produce, show, or display at any theater, films or placards which violate or may disturb the public peace and jeopardize the public morale or that has a tendency to cause such

a result. Films or placards produced in this Kingdom which contain such characteristics are prohibited to be exported.[13]

The inclusion of a ban on the exporting of problematic films is another indicator of the importance of 'saving face,' constructing and maintaining a wholesome national image through officially sanctioned films shown to international audiences. In 1991, for example, authorities at Bangkok's Don Mueang airport detained three films with gay themes—*The Last Song* (1985), *Anguished Love* (1987), and *I Am a Man* (1987)—to prevent them being shown at an LGBT film festival in Amsterdam. Also, in 2003 the Thai embassy intervened to prevent a screening of Thunska Pansittivorakul's short film *Sigh* (2002) in Hong Kong.

Whereas film censorship had previously been the purview of the king and a select group of his advisers, the Film Act established a censorship committee comprised of government bureaucrats and senior police officers to take over this responsibility. The Act remained in force for three-quarters of a century, though there were periodic revisions to the film censorship system during that time, reflecting both ideological and technological changes. The Act was first revised in 1936, to include a list of specific prohibitions drawn up by the Ministry of the Interior:

Films would be banned should they (1) contain any unsuitable depiction of the king, the queen, or any member of the royal family, the government, or civil service; (2) ridicule the monarchy or royal persons directly or indirectly; (3) depict political events in such a way as to arouse public disorder, loss of faith in the government, or improper social behavior; (4) be sacrilegious or insult any religion;

(5) promote ill-will between nations or individuals; (6) depict evil persons in an attractive manner or suggest emulation of improper ways; (7) depict the life of a famous criminal or criminals; (8) show unusual criminal methods or devices that might inspire the viewer with criminal ideas; (9) depict gory murders or executions; (10) depict inhuman treatment of animals or people; or (11) depict or suggest lasciviousness or show sexual relations.[14]

In 1962, the film censorship board was divided into two. The existing committee, comprising thirteen bureaucrats and police officers, was redesignated as an appeals board. Initial censorship decisions were henceforth taken by a new fifteen-member committee, which included representatives of the film industry in addition to bureaucrats from numerous government ministries. Both groups expanded substantially, with many members treating the film censorship board as a cushy quango. In fact, Rebecca Townsend quotes an internal censors' memorandum complaining that "some official representatives like to go to screenings only for entertaining films. Any film that they are not interested in will not have representatives attend."[15]

In 1970, the Ministry of Education issued its own film censorship regulations. This list of twenty-one items prohibited all nudity, violence towards people or animals, disrespectful portrayals of the monarchy, the Buddha, or the monkhood, and "the depiction of gangsters, drug addicts, or criminals in a favourable light."[16] The new rules also reflected social changes, albeit by suppressing rather than embracing them: depictions of homosexuality and unruly student behavior were also banned. These interdepartmental guidelines added multiple levels of bureaucracy to the censorship process, as Boonrak Boonyaketmala explained:

> The enforcement of this law was highly complicated, at one point involving some 177 members from the Prime Minister's Office, the Defense Ministry, the Interior Ministry, the Education Ministry, the Police Department, the Office of the Attorney General, and the Religion Department, among many others. Given all the confusion, there was always room for some to gain personal income in return for their "special services."[17]

That last point, a suggestion that the officials were susceptible to bribery, is echoed by Apichatpong Weerasethakul. After the censors demanded cuts to *Syndromes and a Century* (2006), he speculated: "Maybe they wanted some money under the table." For the avoidance of doubt, a notice proclaiming a 'BRIBE-FREE ZONE' greets visitors to the censors' office, as shown in Ing Kanjanavanit's fly-on-the-wall documentary *Censor Must Die* (2013).

In 1971, political censorship intensified after military prime minister Thanom Kittikachorn staged a coup on the pretext of suppressing Communist infiltration. His junta issued new film censorship rules in 1972, prohibiting any film "that might cause contempt for government or nation" and banning any political content that could "adversely affect governance or incite the creation of disquietude in the country."[18] At the same time, Thanom placed film censorship under the jurisdiction of the chief of police, giving him the authority to appoint all members of the censorship and appeals committees.

Once the police began supervising the film censorship process, crime dramas received particular scrutiny, to the extent that

"Bangkok simply doesn't have movies about corrupt cops, so familiar in Hollywood."[19] The 'dirty cop,' a cliché in American police procedurals, is largely absent from Thai thrillers, eliminated at the script stage to avoid inevitable police censorship. Thus, the endemic problem of Thai police corruption is whitewashed from Thai screens. Exceptionally, a 1994 *lakhon* [soap opera] featured a crusading police officer exposing corruption within the police force, though it began with a full-screen disclaimer to reassure viewers that the plot was entirely fictional. The series was also prematurely pulled from the television schedules following complaints from the police.[20] Similarly, director Pen-ek Ratanaruang was required to insert a caption after the credits of *6ixtynin9* (1999), reassuring the audience that the film's protagonist had been arrested: "We were asked by the police to put the rolling credit saying that she was caught and went to jail."[21] The police's justification for this addition was not the usual crime-does-not-pay moral lesson; rather, it was a face-saving motive, to uphold the police department's own reputation for law enforcement. As Pen-ek explains: "I thought the reason would be that you might corrupt the young minds of the country, as they always say, that you can kill people and get away with it. But that's not the reason at all. The reason was that, if the girl could do this, the police look bad. They look stupid."

After another coup, in 1976, the regulations were revised again, consolidated by the police department into four prohibitions: depiction of sexual abuse, cruelty to humans or animals, political issues, and violation of "established moral, cultural, and social values."[22] The Ministry of the Interior then issued new censorship guidelines in 1991 which, as in 1976, sought to preserve the state's proscriptive definition of traditional Thai culture. David Streckfuss lists the Ministry's revised restrictions:

> The three areas of violation were "noble morality, culture, and traditions of the nation," "peace and order and security of the nation," and "politics and governance related to foreign relations." In the first two areas, items in a movie which do the following were forbidden: "1.1 show contempt or insult to things of worship, through any action that is false or distorted toward religious principles, and would cause bad feelings toward any religion; 1.2 matters which are obscene; 1.3 actions of cruelty toward any person or animal…. 2.1 to ridicule, mock, scorn, or insult the institution of the Thai monarchy, or any action which is capable [of] or could be the cause of such feelings of ridicule or scorn and insult; 2.2 clear expression in the nature of insult to the state or nation or government, or inciting to cause disquietude in the land; 2.3 matters which are felt will serve as an example in instilling bad traits, leading people to evil behaviour."[23]

## Thai New Waves

After World War II, the Thai film industry had been almost exclusively devoted to producing formulaic silent films shot on 16mm, with dialogue performed by live dubbers at each screening.[24] This mode of production, initiated by the commercial success of *Criminal Without Sin* (1949), sharply declined after 1970 with the release of two major 35mm sound films. The first was the musical *Monrak Luk Thung*, a romantic evocation of Thailand's rural heritage starring Mitr Chaibancha and Petchara Chaowarat, which Chalida Uabumrungjit describes as "the most popular Thai film ever made."[25] In *A Century of Thai Cinema*, Dome Sukwong calls Mitr "the greatest star in the history of Thai films."[26] The second significant film from 1970 was altogether different. *A Man Called Tone* introduced a more modern approach to characterization, acting, narrative, and cinematography. As Anchalee Chaiworaporn explains, *A Man Called Tone* represented "a key transitional point in the history of the Thai movie."[27]

The shift to 35mm production coincided with a period of anti-establishment activism in the 1970s. University students organized a series of pro-democracy demonstrations, which were violently suppressed by successive military governments. Anti-establishment sentiment and the questioning of authority also found expression in a 'new wave' of Thai films dealing with realistic social issues, led by director Chatrichalerm Yukol.

In particular, Chatrichalerm's film *His Name Is Karn* (1973) was groundbreaking in its depiction of state corruption, as the eponymous Karn is an idealistic doctor whose work is undermined by a local protection racket and ineffective police. (In a downbeat ending that distinguishes it from escapist Thai films of the period, Karn is ultimately killed by the corrupt officials he had been struggling against.) This caused the censors to block its release, though Chatrichalerm, a minor royal, was in a position to bypass the censorship committee and obtain personal approval from the military prime minister, Thanom Kittikachorn. *His Name Is Karn* is one of several radical early films by Chatrichalerm, though he subsequently directed lavish historical epics such as *The Legend of Suriyothai* (2001) that are effectively state-sponsored propaganda.

A few months after the release of *His Name Is Karn*, the Hollywood thriller *Serpico* (1973) also exposed local corruption in Thailand, in a rather unorthodox fashion. Live dubbing was still practiced in provincial cinemas, and one voice-over artist, Sirichai Duangphatra, used the technique "to address the day's top political scandals, both at the national and local level. And corrupt politicians were his number one target."[28] When *Serpico* was released in Thailand, Sirichai saw an ideal opportunity for political expression. As Philip Jablon explains in *Thailand's Movie Theatres*:

> With *Serpico*, making political satire for Sirichai was like shooting fish in a barrel; it turned out to be his voice-over magnum opus. The crooked cops in the film were all given names corresponding to Nakhon Si Thammarat's most notorious lawmen. The crowd, well aware of who was who among the police ne'er-do-wells, reacted with cheers and hysterical laughter.... From the rank-and-file right up to the top brass, no corrupt member of the local police department was spared Sirichai's adaptive lampoonery.[29]

A confluence of events in 1997 triggered a second and more sustained Thai New Wave. In that year, Pen-ek Ratanaruang showed his first film, *Fun Bar Karaoke*, at the Berlinale. Another debut, Nonzee Nimibutr's *Dang Bireley's and Young Gangsters* [*sic*], broke domestic box office records. Also, two new film festivals, the Short Film and Video Festival and the Bangkok Experimental Film Festival, provided outlets for independent filmmakers.

Nonzee broke his own box office record with his next film, *Nang Nak* (1999). (In 2013, *Pee Mak*, a horror parody inspired by *Nang Nak*, became Thailand's first film to gross THB 1 billion, making it the country's most commercially successful film by far.) Wisit Sasanatieng, the screenwriter of *Dang Bireley* and *Nang Nak*, made his directorial debut with *Tears of the Black Tiger* (2000). The final director in the New Wave quartet, Apichatpong Weerasethakul, is Thailand's leading independent filmmaker. His critical acclaim culminated in his winning the Palme d'Or at Cannes for *Uncle Boonmee Who Can Recall His Past Lives* (2010).

The year 1997 also marked the promulgation of Thailand's most progressive constitution. This 'people's charter' was relatively democratic in nature (establishing the country's first elected Senate), and it outlawed government censorship of the media, prohibiting "censorship by a competent official of news or articles before their publication in a newspaper, printed matter or radio or television broadcasting."[30] Cinema, however, was not afforded constitutional protection, and the film industry sought to rectify this oversight, lobbying (unsuccessfully) for a change in the law.

The constitution was abrogated after a coup in 2006, and rewritten by the military. Following another coup, in 2014, the military drafted another new charter. With each revision, the constitution became less democratic (replacing the fully elected Senate with a 50:50 elected and appointed system, then scrapping all Senate elections), and cinema was not added to the list of protected industries.

## Studios vs. Independent Cinema

Thai New Wave directors Pen-ek Ratanaruang, Apichatpong Weerasethakul, and Wisit Sasanatieng are fêted at international film festivals, though their work has made less impact at the domestic box office, which is dominated by studio-funded genre movies. Wisit's films have attracted a cult following, though he has not been comfortable collaborating with major studios. In a promotional interview for *The Red Eagle* (2010), he said: "I'm tired of making a big studio film with so many conditions imposed on me.... Maybe this is the last film I will make with a studio. From now on, I'll have to find a new way, perhaps go more independent, since that's the only way to make the kind of movie I really want to make."[31]

In fact, Wisit did work within the studio system again, though his frank comments indicate the tensions that can occur between studios and directors. Kanittha Kwunyoo explained that she also felt studio pressure to remove potentially controversial material from her supernatural horror film, *Karma* (2015): "The investors wanted to lessen and cut some content that may lead to public misunderstanding or anger, such as the scene of the novice monk (Sun) kissing the girl (Fai).... We had many fights until the investors and the studio eventually allowed me to keep this scene."

Asked why *Syndromes and a Century* (2006) was cut, Apichatpong concluded: "Because I am nobody. I am not really with a studio." His earlier film *Blissfully Yours* (2002) was distributed by a major studio, Sahamongkol, giving him more leverage in negotiations with the censors. Although *Blissfully Yours* was officially censored, selected cinemas screened the uncut version with the tacit approval of the police. No such deal was possible for Pen-ek Ratanaruang, as his smaller studio, Five Star, lacked the bargaining power of Sahamongkul. Consequently, after Pen-ek's *Ploy* (2007) was censored, "the cinemas were crawling with police ... they were afraid that in one of the cinemas we might show the uncut version. So, there were police everywhere." Pen-ek has contrasted his and Apichatpong's experiences with censorship, arguing that an independent director has more freedom whereas a studio director faces financial pressure to cut their films: "Apichatpong can say, 'No, I won't do it, it's stupid.

And I won't show my film.' But the investment in my film came from people who need to make a profit."

Pen-ek made his documentary *Paradoxocracy* (2013) independently, and was therefore no longer obliged to comply with the censors' verdict: "This is the first time that I actually have the kind of power that Apichatpong has, that I don't have to show this film." After the censorship of *Syndromes and a Century*, Apichatpong's *Cemetery of Splendour* (2015) was not commercially released in Thailand, as the director insisted: "I refuse to submit it to the censor board."[32] He clarified his decision in a BBC interview: "We don't want to show it to Thai audiences because in the current situation we don't have genuine freedom. I don't want to be part of a system where the movie director has to exercise self-censorship."[33] Similarly, Thunska Pansittivorakul explained that, due to the banning of *This Area Is Under Quarantine* (2008), "I decided not to show any of my films in Thailand." Once bitten, twice shy. Rather than attempting to change the system, Thunska dissociated himself from it: "Others struggle against censorship, but I don't anymore. I choose not to fight. That doesn't mean that I've given up. It's that I chose to keep making films and to ignore the country's censorship system."[34]

One of the most enduring impacts of the Thai New Wave has been an explosion of independent film production and exhibition. Apichatpong, a cofounder of the Bangkok Experimental Film Festival, is this movement's figurehead, and he has served as a mentor and role model for a generation of independent filmmakers. ThaiIndie, a collective of independent directors founded by Thunska in 2004, also played a significant role. The annual Short Film and Video Festival, organized by Chalida Uabumrungjit, goes from strength to strength, and is Thailand's longest-running film festival.

Since 1997, many more Thai venues have begun showing independent films. After the censorship of Apichatpong's *Syndromes and a Century* in 2007, uncut screenings took place at the French embassy. The director held a covert screening of *Cemetery of Splendour* (2015) at a mobile cinema in Chiang Mai. Pen-ek Ratanaruang's *Ploy* (2007) was screened uncut at the Foreign Correspondents' Club of Thailand (FCCT) in 2008. Ing Kanjanavanit showed *Censor Must Die* (2013) at the Bangkok Art and Culture Centre (BACC) prior to its submission to the censors. She also showed her banned film *My Teacher Eats Biscuits* (1998) at the Goethe-Institut in Bangkok, and organized a private screening of *Shakespeare Must Die* at Kasem Bundit University in 2012.[35]

Thunska Panisttivorakul has held similarly low-key screenings in Bangkok, after being excluded from Thailand's glitzier film events. *Voodoo Girls* (2002), which includes frank dialogue from its female protagonists, was cut from the Bangkok International Film Festival in 2004, as he explained shortly afterwards: "They said it would build a bad image of Thai women."[36] The World Film Festival of Bangkok dropped *This Area Is Under Quarantine* (2008) from its schedule in 2009, after what he describes as tactical procrastination by the censors: "I thought it was like their strategy to try to not show my film."[37] Because he was "afraid of being arrested by the police," *Happy Berry* (2004) had only a limited showing at the independent House Rama cinema.[38] He screened his short films, including *Sigh* (2002), *Unseen Bangkok* (2004), *Endless Story* (2005), *Life Show* (2005), *Vous vous souviens de moi?* (2005), and *Middle-earth* (2007), at Gallery VER in 2008. *This Area Is Under Quarantine* premiered at Makhampom Studio, *Reincarnate* (2010) at House Rama, and *The Terrorists* (2011) at the BACC. For an invitation-only screening of *Homogeneous,*

*Empty Time* (2017) at Democrazy Studio, the venue was revealed only a day before the event, and attendees were requested not to post any details about it on social media.[39]

Such screenings, however surreptitious, carry an element of risk. Police raided one of the country's very first independent film festivals during a screening of the Singaporean drama *Bugis Street* (1995). They were under the mistaken belief that Ing Kanjanavanit was showing *My Teacher Eats Biscuits* (1998), as she explained: "The police raided the *Bugis Street* screening which opened the festival. They went inside the auditorium, lights came up, all blinked, and then they apologized and left."[40]

Apichatpong Weerasethakul now deliberately limits the visibility of his work in Thailand: "I'm scared of social media. I cut myself off from this kind of flow.... I was worried people will do Facebook, and all these things, and I will be in trouble." Thunska Pansittivorakul has experienced a similar anxiety: "I need to show my films to an audience, but who are they? So, I just show in some events that I'm quite sure will not make problems for me."[41] This was not paranoia. Yuthlert Sippapak deleted his Twitter accounts after legal threats from the government, and Thunska explains that even the prime minister was aware of his films and their controversial content:

> Apichatpong told me that, when he got the award at Cannes, and he went to dinner with Abhisit Vejjajiva, Abhisit said to Apichatpong, "Your film is very good. It's good for filmmakers to make the world know about Thailand. Don't make a movie like that filmmaker who makes them about politics and nakedness." But he forgot my name. But Apichatpong knew who he meant.[42]

As Thunska gained more recognition, he also attracted unwanted attention from the government, and found himself under covert surveillance. He describes an Orwellian situation in which civil servants misrepresented themselves in order to monitor his work: "I didn't know who they were, and sometimes I got scared because I was not sure: some people told me that they needed to watch because they needed to write a thesis, but sometimes it's not, sometimes it's from the government."

## Self-Distribution

Some directors have resorted to self-distributing their films as studios and cinemas have been unwilling to release them. Prabda Yoon, for example, took over the distribution of his film *Motel Mist* (2016) after the studio, cable television company TrueVisions, cancelled its release. Studio executives saw the film for the first time at its press screening and objected to its sexual themes. "They were not OK with the content, so they told us afterwards to stop the screenings," according to Prabda.[43] The company's logo was removed from the film's credits, though TrueVisions product placement, comprising numerous expository sequences filmed at its TNN television channel, were too integral to be deleted.

The studio's decision to drop *Motel Mist* made the film a *cause célèbre*, though it also caused confusion for the potential audience. In retrospect, Prabda feels that it was detrimental to the film's eventual release:

> I think what True did hurt the film and its potential to do better at
> the box office because the people who looked forward to seeing the

film were confused by the situation. When we decided to release the film independently we had already lost most of the momentum that the film had generated prior to True's decision. Many people to this day still think that the film was never released at all.[44]

A TrueVisions television broadcast of *Motel Mist* had also been planned, though this would have required extensive censorship. Content on Thai television is heavily restricted, sometimes to the point of absurdity, with images frequently blurred, a policy parodied in *SARS Wars: Bangkok Zombie Crisis* (2004) and Thunska Pansittivorakul's short film *Life Show* (2005). As Prabda explained: "On TV, you can't show cleavage. You can't show people pointing guns at each other. You can't show people drinking alcohol."[45] *Motel Mist* features all of these, and much more, including sex toys, bondage equipment, and porn DVDs, as the film is set in a 'love motel.' TrueVisions decided against releasing the film, either in cinemas or on television, though the censors passed it uncut (rated 18) and Prabda organized an independent theatrical release.

Yuthlert Sippapak's *Fatherland* (2013) was initially supported by the army, who gave the director access to military bases and equipment. (Like a kid in a candy store, he could literally point to the tanks and other matériel he wanted.) Funding for the production "came from men in uniform, but the director won't say who they are."[46] A prestige picture about terrorism in the majority Muslim south of Thailand, it was intended to promote reconciliation, though instead it revealed uncomfortable truths about the military's role. As Yuthlert explains: "The one word that's so sensitive is *het kan sa-ngop, ngop mai ma*: 'if no war, no money.' Money is power. And the person who created the war is the military. I said that, and I don't want to take that out. That's the truth. And they don't want the truth. I want the truth."

It soon became apparent to the military that this was not the propaganda vehicle they were expecting, and army chief Prayut Chan-o-cha had a long list of questions for Yuthlert. ("The questions were stupid," the director says.) When Yuthlert refused to change the film, his military backers cut their (THB 100 million) losses and dissociated themselves from the project: "I went to the army; I needed them to be a sponsor. I used everything, like warships, helicopters. But they asked me, 'If you show this movie, somebody burns the theater. Who's gonna [take] responsibility for that?'"

Yuthlert's repeated efforts to distribute *Fatherland* himself have been unsuccessful, and he announced on Facebook: "It's certain now that Thais will not be able to watch this film."[47] Even after he re-edited it in 2015 to remove the most sensitive content, the film remains unreleased. It has since undergone another re-edit, to focus on Rachida, the female Muslim protagonist, with a new title, *Rachida*, as Yuthlert felt that *Fatherland* was too propagandistic. The director is biding his time until a democratic government is elected: "I got a problem with the military government. So, I decided to freeze for a while, maybe ten years…. If you show here, that's kind of dangerous. If the military's still here. I'll find a way."

Like *Fatherland*, Yuthlert's horror film *Seven Boy Scouts* (2020) also remains in limbo. *Seven Boy Scouts* is a sharp political satire, and the director was vocal in his criticisms of Prayut's government, both on social media and at public demonstrations. Due to Yuthlert's political activism, the distributor of *Seven Boy Scouts*, Phranakornfilm, dissociated themselves from the film, and its release was cancelled.

Thai film exhibition is effectively a duopoly, with two chains (Major Cineplex and SF Cinema) dominating the market. This has increased the challenges faced by independent filmmakers and fledgling distribution companies: there have been reports, for example, of "a theater chain's threat to keep a small film from reaching its audience unless its small distributor bought ad space in a national newspaper."[48] During the release of *Paradoxocracy* (2013), Pen-ek Ratanaruang experienced a similar lack of cooperation, which he describes as "another form of censorship." Apex, owners of the Scala cinema in Bangkok, reneged on their initial commitment to show the film: "They said that the venue that they planned to give us to do this thing is not available…. And so, my producer [Pasakorn Pramoolwong] called them, and said, 'So, what is going on?' And they said they don't think they could show the film."

After the deal with Apex collapsed, Major Cineplex agreed to show the film, though they, too, had second thoughts once they became aware of its political content. Specifically, it was the presence of Thaksin Shinawatra, the divisive former prime minister, which gave them cold feet. Since his first election victory in 2001, Thai society has been polarized between Thaksin's supporters and opponents. Pen-ek describes the reaction of a Major Cineplex executive:

> On the day before it was released, he was going to pull the film out. They switched the decision—'Pull out'/'No'/'Yes'—about five times before the noon showing, because my producer told them that, if they pull the film out, they have to answer questions to the journalists…. So, they had to go ahead with the film, but no promotion whatever.

Major Cineplex did screen *Paradoxocracy*, though they sometimes denied it. At times during its theatrical release, the film was missing from the Major Cineplex online listings, with some customers being wrongly informed that screenings had sold out. As Pen-ek commented: "It was the first time in the history of the world, where a cinema put a film in their theaters but tried to not sell any tickets."[49]

The sensitivity surrounding *Paradoxocracy* also affected the almost simultaneous release of Nontawat Numbenchapol's documentary *Boundary* (2013). Major Cineplex, presumably already regretting their commitment to show Pen-ek's film, decided that two potentially controversial documentaries at the same time was one too many. They cancelled an earlier agreement to provide theatres for *Boundary*, as Nontawat explains: "I had a problem. After the press screening at Major Cineplex, the programmer called to say, 'We have to take it out. Major cannot screen this film anymore.' We were shocked."

Although Major Cineplex developed cold feet over *Boundary*, they also recognized that dropping the film would generate more negative publicity. They therefore persuaded Nontawat not to take his film to their competitor, SF Cinema, and instead required him to hire their theatres privately and sell tickets by himself from a trestle table in the lobby of each venue:

I thought I would stop the press screening that day, and change to SF the next week, but finally Major told me I cannot do that. If I stopped the press screening and changed to another distributor, the problem is that the media and everybody would ask why the press screening was stopped. Finally, I had to rent the theatres by myself.

After hiring theatres to show *Boundary*, Nontawat cofounded an independent screening room in Bangkok, Dam'n Cineclub, one of several exhibition venues established by filmmakers. Paul Spurrier founded the members-only Friese-Greene Club in Bangkok, screening explicit foreign films such as *Pink Flamingos* (1972) and *In the Realm of the Senses* (1976) that would otherwise be impossible to distribute in Thailand. After the shelving of *Fatherland* in 2013, Yuthlert Sippapak announced his intention to build a cinema to be called Phet Chiang Khan in Loei, though the project did not come to fruition.

Ing Kanjanavanit founded Cinema Oasis, an arthouse cinema in Bangkok, and its inaugural screening was the previously banned film *Tongpan* (1977). Cinema Oasis is the only commercial cinema willing and able to show Ing's documentary *Censor Must Die* (2013), as she explained before the building opened: "We built this place because we don't have a venue to show our movies and we don't want other filmmakers to suffer the same fate."[50] *Censor Must Die* was declared exempt from censorship as a film of news events, and Ing chose not to submit her next production, *Bangkok Joyride* (2017), to the censors on the same grounds: "I'm going to use this ruling to exempt my next film … from the censorship process. Then it's a matter of finding a cinema." She solved this problem by building Cinema Oasis and was thus able to show *Bangkok Joyride* on her own terms.

## Censorship by Another Name

*Boundary* (2013) was politically sensitive, as it documents conflicts between Thailand and Cambodia, though it also attracted extra attention from the censors because of its title. The Thai title translates as 'low sky, high land,' and 'sky' (*fah*) can refer to the king as a metaphor for his position at the apex of the social hierarchy. In fact, Nontawat Numbenchapol intended the title as a reference to a song of the same name, with lyrics echoing the theme of *Boundary*: that people who think differently can coexist.[51] After he clarified this, *Boundary*'s title was not changed, though an earlier film about relations between Thailand and Cambodia, *Sisophon* (1941), did require a new title. *Sisophon*, named after a Cambodian town, was retitled to avoid potential conflict between the two countries.

Other films have also been required to change their titles over the years. A 1974 exploitation film about male prostitution, for example, was cut and retitled after being banned; its coy new title translates as 'male…?'[52] In one instance, the retitling actually reversed the intended meaning. A 1928 film whose original title emphasized the strength of 'dark forces' in the criminal underworld was renamed to focus on their ultimate defeat.[53]

In other cases, titles were rendered less provocative to avoid casting aspersions on specific regions or professions. The kinetic thriller *Som and Bank: Bangkok for Sale* (2001), about a drug dealer and a prostitute, was given the generic title *One Take Only*, as the censors felt that the original portrayed Bangkok in a negative light. The film was also re-edited by its studio, Film Bangkok, and released after a two-year hiatus.[54] The Thai title of the cannibal horror film *Meat Grinder* (2009) originally translated as 'human meat noodles,' though it was changed to 'slice before eating' to avoid any detrimental impact on the meat industry. Another horror film, *Cadaver* (2007), also had its title changed. Its original title meant 'principal,' a respectful nickname given by Thai doctors to corpses donated for anatomical research. (The original title is featured, lightly crossed out, on the

DVD packaging.) The title of *The Macabre Case of Phrom Phiram* (2003), a police procedural based on a real-life rape and murder case, was changed after complaints from local residents. They felt that the original title, which translates as 'sinners of Phrom Phiram,' tarred them all with the same brush. The revised title, meaning 'night of sin in Phrom Phiram,' focused instead on the specific incident in question.

The title of the slapstick comedy *Woak Wak* (2004) originally translated as 'Oak-ak,' a pun on Oak, the nickname of Thaksin Shinawatra's son, Panthongtae.[55] In the replacement title, *Woak* is a slightly more disguised reference to Oak. (The stylized typeface used for the film's opening credits and poster makes the title intentionally ambiguous, as *Woak Wak* and 'Oak-ak' in Thai are graphically similar.) After *Karma* was banned in 2013, Kanittha Kwunyoo was also required to make a phonetic alteration to its title, as she explains: "It was part of the censors' verdict. If you wanted to get a new verdict, you would have to change the film's title."[56]

## Diplomatic Censorship

Historically, foreign films were subject to more stringent censorship than domestic productions, and Thai censors were "repeatedly willing to risk the ire of Western film companies for the sake of regulation."[57] According to Rebecca Townsend, this was due to a disparity between foreign and Thai standards of acceptability. She argues that many foreign films were regarded as excessively permissive by Thai censors, whereas Thai directors were familiar with local prohibitions and avoided transgressing them:

Foreign films were more likely to violate Thai notions of appropriateness and morality because they were not produced in the sociopolitical context that informed domestic productions. Knowledge of censorship practices resulted in widespread self-censorship in Thai filmmaking but also informed filmmakers' approaches to sensitive subjects when they were broached. While a foreign film might be banned, a Thai film depicting the same subject might pass by the censors due to the filmmaker's understanding of how it might appropriately be portrayed and contextualized.[58]

Indeed, there are numerous instances of foreign films being cut or banned in Thailand, both before and after the introduction of the rating system.[59] In the vast majority of cases, the censors' verdict is accepted by the distributor and the film is cut or its Thai release is cancelled. This also applies to Thailand's domestic film industry, with most distributors editing their films when cuts are required in order to secure a commercial release, though Thai directors also self-censor their work to minimize the risk of censorship.

Thus, when Thai films cross the line, and, more commonly, when foreign films offend local sensibilities, they are censored accordingly. However, when the censors' verdict is challenged by the distributor, Hollywood studios seemingly receive preferential treatment. Plans to censor the female topless nudity from *Schindler's List* (1993), for example, were dropped after director Steven Spielberg threatened to withdraw the film from Thai distribution. Thunska Pansittivorakul has condemned this apparent double standard, criticizing the censors for caving in to pressure from foreign distributors: "Sexual images like nudity in Thai films would be censored while it is ok in foreign films."[60] A decision to cut the final ten minutes from *The*

*Da Vinci Code* (2006) was also swiftly reversed following an appeal by its American studio. Such clemency had its limits, however. When Hollywood tackled the most sensitive subject of all, the Thai monarchy, it received no special dispensation, and *The King and I* (1956) and *Anna and the King* (1999) were both banned from Thai distribution.

Films with the potential to damage Thailand's relations with other countries are regarded as especially problematic. A screening of the documentary *When Mother's Away* (2018) at the Foreign Correspondents' Club of Thailand (FCCT) was cancelled after "a visit to the club by a police colonel from Special Branch," acting on a complaint from the Vietnamese embassy.[61] The Bangkok International Film Festival dropped *Persepolis* (2007) from its schedule after pressure from Iran: "We both came to mutual agreement that it would be beneficial to both countries if the film was not shown," admitted the festival's director tactfully.[62] Similarly, the Thailand International Film Destination Festival cancelled a screening of *Twilight Over Burma* (2015) as it "caused concern over damage to ties between Thailand and Myanmar."[63]

Chulayarnnon Siriphol's short film *Birth of Golden Snail* (2018) was withdrawn from the Thailand Biennale because its depiction of Japanese soldiers could "make a bad relationship between Thailand and Japan." The film shows a group of soldiers hiding gold bars in a Thai cave and tying a local schoolgirl to a tree when she notices them. However, the film's tone is comical, and the soldiers are not, in fact, portrayed entirely negatively: they offer the girl food and, when she escapes and is punished by her father, they ask him not to beat her.

The Preah Vihear temple, located on the border between Thailand and Cambodia, was the cause of a long-running territorial dispute between the two countries. It became a domestic political issue in Thailand when the government was accused of ceding territory to Cambodia by signing a joint communiqué agreeing to a World Heritage Site application in 2008. Nontawat Numbenchapol's *Boundary* (2013) presents both the Thai and Cambodian perspectives on the controversy, and the censors told him that the film could contribute to "the instability of Thai–Cambodia relations."[64] Such was the sensitivity of the situation that Nontawat even used an alias to avoid revealing his Thai nationality while filming in Cambodia: "I could not tell anyone in Cambodia that I'm Thai, because it would be hard to shoot. I had to tell everybody I'm Chinese-American.... My name was Thomas in Cambodia. Finally, when I wasn't Thai, it was so easy to shoot at Preah Vihear."

*Boundary* documents real-life military skirmishes on the Thai–Cambodia border, though even fictional incidents can provoke tensions. The makers of *No Escape* (2015), an action movie about a violent coup, were permitted to film in Thailand on the condition that the country was not identified in the film. As the film's scriptwriter revealed: "We worked very closely with the Thai government and there were a lot of things they wanted us to shy away from."[65] To that end, Thai signs were replaced with upside-down Khmer text, and local characters spoke Lao dialogue. The country staging the coup is not named in the film, though the principal characters pass by river through a Vietnamese border checkpoint. Geographically, this could only happen on the Mekong River in Cambodia, and Cambodian censors banned the film for its implied slight against their country.

The horror film *Ghost Game* (2006) also increased bilateral tensions between Thailand and Cambodia. *Ghost Game* is set in a building resembling Cambodia's Tuol Sleng Genocide Museum, complete with piles of skulls and photographs of victims, leading to accusations of gross insensitivity. The producers apologized at a press conference, and the film was slightly re-edited before its release, though several inflammatory sequences, notably the smashing of skulls to provoke the spirits of the deceased, remained intact.[66] Cambodia regarded *Ghost Game* as the exploitation of a national tragedy, and a review in *Thai Cinema* described it as "a reactionary reaffirmation of Thai nationalism and the politically expedient racism that underscores it."[67] An editorial in Thailand's *The Nation* went further, arguing that the film "brings shame upon Thai society."[68]

The controversy over *Ghost Game* also affected *Lucky Loser* (2006), a comedy that had been scheduled for release a few weeks later by its studio, GTH. *Lucky Loser* depicted the Laotian national football team as simpletons, prompting a complaint from the country's ambassador to Thailand. To avoid a repeat of the insensitivity surrounding *Ghost Game*, GTH initially shelved *Lucky Loser*, eventually releasing it a few months later only after references to Laos had been replaced by the fictional country 'Arvee.' In a melodramatic gesture of repentance, the studio burned all fifty-seven prints of the original version (hundreds of 35mm reels).[69]

Arguably, Thailand's most important bilateral relationship was with the United States, particularly during the Cold War. Prime minister Phibun Songkhram cited this as a pretext to ban the Hollywood musical *The King and I* in 1956: "Anything that may adversely affect Thai–US relations should not be permitted to take place."[70] The potential adverse effects were indirect. The film portrays Rama IV (King Mongkut) as a rather boorish figure, and it was felt that Thai audiences would express hostility towards America for what they perceived as Hollywood's misrepresentation of their monarch. An appeal by the film's US studio, 20th Century Fox, was unsuccessful and the ban was upheld in 1965.

When the studio remade *The King and I*, they were determined to demonstrate their cultural sensitivity, and intended to film the remake, *Anna and the King* (1999), in Thailand, for added authenticity. A team of seven Thai historians and aristocrats was hired to eliminate any potentially problematic material from the script, though it was rejected five times by the censorship board.

After voting to ban *Anna and the King*, one of the censors commented: "The film-makers have made King Mongkut look like a cowboy who rides on the back of an elephant as if he is in a cowboy movie."[71] The implication was that the film represented a quasi-colonialist disparaging of Thai culture, though the censors themselves revealed a rather xenophobic attitude in their comments about both *The King and I* and its remake. One of their complaints about the original film was that it depicted Rama IV using chopsticks rather than a more 'civilized' spoon, an objection that could be attributed to upper-class Thai resentment of Chinese immigrants. Their judgement on *Anna and the King* made an equally disdainful ethnic comparison, describing the eponymous Anna Leonowens as "an individual with doubtful origin and could even be half Indian."[72]

## The Free Thai Cinema Movement

The Film Act was repealed following a campaign by an organization known as the Free Thai Cinema Movement, founded in 2007 by the Thai Film Foundation and the Thai Film Director Association. Free Thai Cinema lobbied the government to revise the antiquated censorship system after cuts were required to utterly harmless sequences in Apichatpong Weerasethakul's *Syndromes and a Century* (2006). Public reaction against the censorship of Apichatpong's film, and the banning of Nontawat Numbenchapol's *Boundary* (2013) several years later, increased the campaign's momentum.

The censorship of *Syndromes and a Century* provoked defiant artistic responses from fellow filmmakers. Apichatpong's assistant director included the cut sequences in his short film *Diseases and a Hundred Year Period* (2008). That film also quotes the censors, who chastised Apichatpong as if he were a naughty schoolboy: "The director disgracefully humiliates his parents before a global audience." Two short films, *Ye... Dhamma...* (2007) and Chulayarnnon Siriphol's *Monk and Motorcycle Taxi Rider* (2013), both feature monks strumming on guitars, in a recreation of a *verboten* act from *Syndromes and a Century*. Thunska Pansittivorakul made *Middle-earth* (2007) in reaction to the censorship of his friend Apichatpong's work. The short film *I Will Rape You With This Scissors* [sic] (2008) is intentionally provocative and excessive, in deliberate contrast to the inoffensive content cut from Apichatpong's film.

Apichatpong has speculated that the censorship of *Syndromes and a Century* was intended as part of a bargaining process: "They maybe hoped that I could discuss with them about money, or whatever." When he declined to make the cuts, the censors refused to return the 35mm print he had submitted "on the grounds that the director might secretly show it."[73] This petty decision, and the inexplicable cuts required of the film, galvanized opposition to the Film Act.

Free Thai Cinema began its anti-censorship campaign in 2007 with a press conference and a series of seminars.[74] An online petition, signed by more than 6,000 people, argued that "Thai cinema has continued to be systematically straightjacketed" by the Film Act.[75]

Chalida Uabumrungjit lobbied the National Legislative Assembly, arguing that a rating system would represent "the freedom of artists to express themselves and the freedom of the audience to receive information."[76] A defiant op-ed article by Apichatpong served as the unofficial manifesto of the Free Cinema Movement. In it, he rejected the Ministry of Culture's proposals for reform in the strongest possible terms: "I refuse to be bullied and raped by the so-called 'protectors' appointed by the government."[77]

The Free Thai Cinema Movement was revived in 2013 following the censorship of Nontawat Numbenchapol's *Boundary*. When *Syndromes and a Century* was cut, Apichatpong had campaigned the old-fashioned way, via public meetings and mainstream media coverage. Apichatpong intentionally avoided publicizing his later films online, for fear of attracting unwanted attention, and Thunska Pansittivorakul purged his Facebook friends for the same reason. Following the *Boundary* ban, however, Free Thai Cinema became a Facebook meme. For Nontawat, Facebook provided the perfect opportunity to spread the word about the censors' verdict to his fellow millennials: "The reaction on social media helped me to get people's attention giving me the chance to speak out and share my experiences regarding the film."[78] As he explained, the response on social media was overwhelming: "I wrote on Facebook, and posted about the ban. And I was surprised, because in one night there's around 2,000 shares about it ... it flew around the world. And I think the censors were surprised about this, too."

Two days of critical coverage, both on social media and in the international press, put the censors unexpectedly in the spotlight. They contacted Nontawat to apologize for what they called a clerical error, rescinding the ban as swiftly as it had been imposed. (In 2015, however, a planned screening of the film was prevented by the military junta.)

## Counter-Productive Censorship

*Syndromes and a Century* was released in Thailand in 2008, with the censored scenes removed, though the release was part of the Free Thai Cinema campaign. Apichatpong replaced each cut with silent black film of equal duration, thus drawing attention to the censorship. The longest of these dark sequences lasted for seven minutes, making a powerful visual statement about the extent of the censorship imposed on the film. (*The Sweet Gang* employed the same tactic in 2005, for comic effect, and the short film *The Six Principles* did so in 2010.)[79] This version of *Syndromes and a Century* was shown at Paragon Cineplex in Bangkok, accompanied by a small exhibition on the history of film censorship. Like Surasak Pongson's *Thibaan: The Series 2.2* (2018), the censored footage was uploaded online so viewers could judge it for themselves.[80] As Apichatpong says: "It was a statement, not a real screening. And the theater was willing to do it."

Pen-ek Ratanaruang made a similar point by censoring the dialogue in *Paradoxocracy* (2013) in the most conspicuous way: "It becomes like an art piece. Because the film itself is participating in this, becoming a victim." *Paradoxocracy* consists of a series of interviews with historians, and Pen-ek was told to remove some of their comments about the death of King Rama VIII.[81] Rather than unobtrusively cutting the problematic material, he muted the soundtrack and placed a black line over the English subtitles, exposing the censorship process as Apichatpong had done with *Syndromes and a Century*: "I said, 'Can I cut just the sound?' They said, 'Sure.' I said,

'But, if I leave the picture, they'd be silent, with the mouth moving.' They said, 'Fine.' I said, 'This can't be. They don't understand what I'm saying.' Because it would make them look like fools."

Kongdej Jaturanrasmee's comedy *Sayew* (2003), the underground film *Red Movie* (2010), and Thunska Pansittivorakul's documentary *Homogeneous, Empty Time* (2017) muted their soundtracks in the same way. Cutting the sound made *Paradoxocracy* all the more powerful as, even without the dialogue, audiences readily understood what had been censored and why: "They knew *exactly* what it was about. It made the point even stronger. It didn't matter what these people said, but it made the point. People understand what they were talking about: it has to be our monarchy. And then they became even more curious."

Pen-ek was also required to censor the film's prologue, though again the censorship paradoxically strengthened the film. *Paradoxocracy* begins by reproducing the text of a 1932 manifesto railing against King Prajadhipok in terms that would be unthinkable today, due to cultural veneration of the monarchy as an institution, not to mention increasing *lèse-majesté* prosecutions. The manifesto, written by Pridi Banomyong, heralded a revolution that transformed Thailand from absolute monarchy to constitutional democracy, announcing that the king "must be under the law of the constitution for governing the country, and cannot do anything independently without the approval of the assembly of people's representatives."[82] A film about the revolution, commissioned by the government the following year, was shelved by the prime minister, who argued that it would be "excessively traumatic to the king and members of the royal family" and was therefore "inappropriate to be shown in theaters."[83]

*Paradoxocracy* originally opened with the revolutionary manifesto heard in voice-over, though the censors insisted that the sound be removed and replaced with written text. This intervention ironically increased the manifesto's impact, requiring the audience to actively engage by reading the text rather than passively listening to the narration. Pen-ek argues that "the censorship actually brought the film to another level." The censorship thus became counter-productive, drawing the audience's attention to the forbidden material and strengthening it. The director recalls his negotiations with the censors:

> They said, 'Come on, please, you can't have the voice.' So we took out the voice. But it becomes even stronger when you take out the voice. People are reading it themselves: 'My God! They talked about the king this way!' Because if somebody was reading, as my original idea was, you would just be sitting there listening…. Again, it just made it a stronger statement, by the censorship.

Pen-ek describes the censorship of *Ploy* (2007) in a similar way. He conceived of that film's sex scene as a physical counterpoint to a psychological game involving two other characters, with cross-cutting emphasizing the differences between the relationships of the two couples. However, the censorship obscured the subtext, and the scene appeared more straightforwardly pornographic: "You don't see what is going on, you just see the reaction of the girl, so the idea of the game was completely destroyed. And it became like straight fucking, which is, for me, even more damaging. If you want to uphold the 'good values' of Thai society."

The censorship of Pen-ek's *Headshot* (2011) also paradoxically strengthened the film. In an early scene, an assassin disguised as a monk removes the lid from his alms bowl to reveal a gun inside, though the gun was digitally removed from the Thai version. The censors deemed this juxtaposition of a weapon and an alms bowl unacceptable, though Pen-ek struggled to comprehend their rationale: "The gun in the bowl tells *everyone*, even idiots, that this is a fake monk. No real monk would own a gun. So, this is the reason you should leave it there." Without the gun, the character could be misread as a real monk rather than a gangster in disguise, which was precisely the interpretation that the censors had sought to avoid.

Pen-ek has likened censorship to "asking you to cut your baby's arm off, your baby's legs." His consolation, however, is that "every time they censor my film, the meaning of the film after it has been censored not only changes, but it becomes against what they really wanted. It makes the film a bit stronger." Similarly, the act of censorship draws disproportionate attention to the forbidden material, and each of the films banned in Thailand has become a *cause célèbre*, receiving vastly more publicity as a result of the ban.

The act of censorship has also driven filmmakers to greater levels of provocation. After the banning of *This Area Is Under Quarantine* (2008), Thunska Pansittivorakul vowed, "I will do something harder than before." He also argued that the ban was more of a blessing than a curse: "I think the ban will benefit me…. I don't care anymore about censorship. I'll give up my worries and fears and think positively. This is my opportunity to be free."[84] Other directors whose films have been censored are also "unwilling to compromise their content."[85] Censorship begets resistance and subversion. As Pen-ek observes succinctly, "every time they try to censor, they shoot themselves in the foot."

## The Film and Video Act

A new Film and Video Act ultimately superseded the Film Act in 2008. The Free Thai Cinema Movement's campaign for a rating system had proved successful, as age ratings were a central feature of the new Act. Films were henceforth classified either G (suitable for general audiences), P (promoted for their cultural or educational value), 13, 15, 18, or 20. The lower age restrictions are advisory, while the highest level requires proof of age before admittance.[86]

This was a rather Pyrrhic victory, however, as the final category in the rating system is "films which are prohibited to be disseminated in the Kingdom."[87] An essay in *Thai Cinema* concluded, more in hope than expectation, that the film industry "won't suffer from this new law."[88] Film critic Kong Rithdee, on the other hand, argued that the combination of ratings and bans was "the worst cocktail imaginable."[89] Apichatpong Weerasethakul, who was instrumental in the campaign for censorship reform, came to an equally pessimistic conclusion: "I feel that the movement to change the law might not be so productive, and the movies will still be banned as long as the people are brainwashed on a daily basis."[90]

The Act states that a ban would be imposed on any film that "undermines or is contrary to public order or good morals, or may affect the security and dignity of Thailand," a catch-all clause even more restrictive than the original Film Act.[91] The law's description of what constitutes a cinema is also intentionally broad. The Film and Video Act defines a cinema for the purposes of regulation as "a building or any part of a building used as a place to exhibit a film"[92] or "an outdoor area for a film exhibition."[93] This all-encompassing definition brought almost any screening venue, including the marginal spaces founded since the New Wave, within the Act's purview, potentially leading to state regulation of the country's burgeoning independent film scene. Hence Thunska Pansittivorakul's concern about the Act:

> Thailand got the new law about ratings. But for me, it's worse than before…. If you made a wedding video, by that law, you must send the wedding video to the censors. Or you made a VCD that you gave for free with a magazine, you must send that VCD to the censors. Actually, they cannot check all of them, but if someone goes to a wedding, and saw that something was not good in the wedding video, he can tell the government to check it. Because the rule covers that, also.

The censors' assessments of banned films have been similarly opaque. When Thunska's *This Area Is Under Quarantine* (2008) was banned, for example, he did not receive any explanation: "They didn't give any reason. They just said they cannot decide to show or not to show." The censors gave Nontawat Numbenchapol an equally sweeping rationale after banning *Boundary* (2013): "She said, 'It's very sensitive.' I asked her, 'Which part is sensitive? Can I do something about it?' She told me, 'You cannot edit, because it's the whole film.' " The explanation offered to Tanwarin Sukkhapisit after the banning of *Insects in the Backyard* (2010) was similarly vague: "They simply said that they thought every scene is immoral, and they didn't give us any more details." The censors' justification for the banning of *Shakespeare Must Die* (2012) followed the same pattern, according to producer Manit Sriwanichpoom: "I asked the committee which part of the film fits that verdict and how I should go back to fix it, but they cannot tell me which scene."[94]

The inconsistency of the censors' decisions is also a cause of criticism: "What frustrates directors and artists here is the unpredictable nature of the censorship board. There are no clear standards."[95] As Kannitha Kwunyoo explains: "There is no consistency, and we don't know what the rules are." Thus, while it was apparently necessary to change the title of Kanittha's *Karma* (2015) after the film's ban, this was not required of *Insects in the Backyard* or *Boundary*, whose bans were also rescinded. The censors have also made inexplicable exceptions to their own policies. For example, the law states that the 18 rating is purely advisory, yet cinemas screening Bhandevanov Devakula's 18-rated *Jan Dara: The Beginning* (2012) were required to check patrons' identity cards.

Ing Kanjanavanit's *Censor Must Die* (2013) is another example of the "lack of consistency on the part of the censors."[96] Her documentary was deemed exempt from the rating system, though the censors also threatened to sue any cinema that screened it as it contains fly-on-the-wall footage filmed inside the Ministry of Culture. As Ing says: "They ruled it as news footage and refused to rate it (which incidentally means no cinema would show it, effectively banning it)." The Film and Video Act does indeed state that "films of news events"[97] are exempt, though this clause remains ambiguous as it was not applied to *Boundary*, which is also a current affairs documentary.

There are also procedural concerns about the Act, as its establishment of multiple censorship committees (rotating Film and Video Censorship Committees overseen by a National Film and Video Committee) echoes the bureaucratic complexities of the previous film law. Each committee includes members of the film industry, appointed by the Minister of Culture, though they are outnumbered by government representatives. The Film and Video Censorship Committee, responsible for issuing (and denying) ratings, has four members from the government and three from the private sector. The National Film and Video Committee, the body responsible for drafting film legislation, consists of sixteen ministerial representatives and "not more than eleven" non-governmental members.[98] (Note that the number of government members is fixed, while the film industry quota has no minimum requirement.)

Chulayarnnon Siriphol describes the ratings process as "like playing the lottery." He explains that, given the daily rotation of committee members, consistent verdicts are practically impossible: "The rating system sounds good, but the rating depends on the consideration of the Film [and Video Censorship] Committee. And the consideration of the Committee, in each group, is different, so it's very flexible."

The Act has also been invoked by government departments outside its jurisdiction. The Office of Contemporary Art and Culture cited the Act as justification when it banned Chulayarnnon's short film *Birth of Golden Snail* in 2018, though the relevant paragraph in the Act states:

> If the Film and Video Censorship Committee considers any film as having content which undermines or is contrary to public order or good morals, or may affect the security and dignity of Thailand, the Film and Video Censorship Committee shall have the power to order an applicant to edit or cut off the scene before granting approval, or may decide not to grant approval.[99]

Thus, the legal authorization to censor films rests with the Film and Video Censorship Committee (which had not viewed *Birth of Golden Snail*), rather than the Office of Contemporary Art and Culture, a technicality that was apparently overlooked or ignored. Similarly, the censors blamed their banning of *Boundary* (2013) on a bureaucratic error, and Nontawat says that the Act's multiple committees resulted in administrative confusion: "There are two rooms for the censors. My film was sent to the DVD room.... I asked them, 'My film is not for DVD now, but I want to screen in theatres.' And someone told me, 'This film is not for theatres, just for DVD.' The process is not professional."

## Thai Culture and 'Thainess'

The Ministry of Culture was a five-year-old institution when it took over responsibility for film censorship after the passing of the Film and Video Act. The Ministry had drafted the Act in consultation with representatives of the film industry, though the Ministry's agenda ultimately prevailed, and the film community abandoned the negotiations once it became clear that consensus could not be achieved. Apichatpong Weerasethakul described the process as "making a pact with the devil."[100] Kong Rithdee quotes an anonymous senior Ministry of Culture official involved in drafting the Act: "We cannot blindly accept everything practised by Western countries. We still have to protect society. Some Thai films, like Saeng Satawat [*Syndromes and a Century* (2006)], are very good, I'm sure, but Thai people may not yet be ready for it."[101]

Ladda Tangsupachai, also a senior Ministry of Culture official, made similar comments about *Syndromes and a Century* in an interview with *Time* magazine. Patronizingly, she claimed that the rating system was necessary due to a lack of sophistication among Thai audiences: "They're not intellectuals—that's why we need ratings."[102] In the same interview, she also dismissed Apichatpong's entire œuvre at a single stroke: "Nobody goes to see films by Apichatpong.... Thai people want to see comedy. We like a laugh."[103]

Such attitudes are satirized in 'Sunset,' Aditya Assarat's segment of the portmanteau film *Ten Years Thailand* (2018), in which a group of soldiers and police officers inspect a photography exhibition and remove some of the exhibits. One officer justifies such censorship by arguing that conceptual art could be misunderstood by uneducated Thai audiences, telling the artist: "You people studied abroad? But not everyone's like you. They're just ordinary people." The notion of soldiers discussing art interpretation and censoring an exhibition seems absurd, though the film is based on the military's removal of three photographs from a 2017 exhibition by Harit Srikhao.[104] Former prime minister Anand Panyarachun expressed very similar sentiments in support of the banning of *The King and I* (1956), claiming that, although he personally understood the film, it was beyond most of the population's comprehension: "You have to remember that I spent some time abroad.... But most Thais could not separate the musical parody from the history of their own country."[105]

Manit Sriwanichpoom has encountered equally condescending officials, recalling a film censor telling him that provincial Thai audiences "may not know the difference" between dramas and documentaries.[106] Justifying the banning of *Anna and the King* in 1999, Isorn Pocmontri, a Foreign Ministry advisor to the censorship board, told *The Washington Post* that "the Thai public may not be ready for the film."[107] Such attitudes are rooted in Thailand's hierarchical social structure, with the professional classes feeling—and having no qualms about expressing—a sense of intellectual superiority over blue-collar workers. In a vox pop interview, for example, a dentist also supported the *Anna and the King* ban: "Educated people would understand this is a Hollywood production; uneducated people might not."[108] Apichatpong Weerasethakul calls such views "an insult to the intelligence of the people and an allusion that most Thais are morons."[109] Ladda Tangsupachai's derisive comments on his work were widely reported, though the director was hardly surprised by her attitude: "In a seminar before that, she already stated that Thai people only have an average grade six education, so people are not ready for a certain kind of movies. So when this came, it's not so shocking, but just maddening."

Prayut Chan-o-cha also espoused the paternalistic notion that Thais are somehow 'not ready,' as a justification for his coup in 2014: "We understand that we are living in a democratic world, but is Thailand ready? Are Thai people ready?"[110] As May Adadol Ingawanij has argued, such authoritarian rhetoric has long been associated with the Thai state:

> The trope of the people being 'not yet ready' has long been part of the elite's defensive barrier against radical change. During the last days of royal absolutism in the late 1920s, the monarch attempted to fend off the constitutionalists' demand for change with the claim that the people were not yet ready for democracy. What is historically consistent about such claims is that they create a fiction of a people dependent on elite leadership amidst a context of the crisis of the latter's authority and furious discontent from below.[111]

As May suggests, this attitude exemplifies the worst extremes of the nanny state: maintaining a social hierarchy by stifling dissent. To preserve the status quo, radical or potentially agitational films are suppressed. This results in an anodyne entertainment landscape and, as Kong Rithdee has argued, audiences are conditioned to retreat to the comfort of the familiar: "In the Thai mentality, the arts have a social function to entertain and embellish, not to question or challenge. People expect cinema to soothe, not subvert; to endear, not defy; to calm, not critique; and filmmakers who stray from the norm do so in the corner, ignored and forgotten by the majority of viewers."[112]

The impetus underpinning Thailand's top–down cultural policy originates in the artificial concept of 'Thainess' introduced by Phibun Songkhram's administration. In 1938, Phibun issued a series of twelve proclamations (legally codified by the Culture Act of 1942) dictating accepted codes of dress and behavior, aimed at instilling a sense of patriotism and civility among the Thai population. Thus, modern 'Thai culture' did not evolve organically; rather, it was imposed by the state. However, David Streckfuss notes that this is now largely forgotten: "Many of today's Thai believe that the 'invented traditions' of this period are authentic Thai customs."[113] Phibun also utilized film as a propaganda tool, initiating and supervising the releases of two nationalistic melodramas.[114] Both films, funded by the military, feature jingoistic narratives in which the Thai army goes to war and emerges victorious. Phibun's central ideologue, Wichit Wathakan, was retained by Sarit Thanarat during the Cold War, and the 'Thainess' culturization project continued.

Marxist theorist Antonio Gramsci's term for this state-imposed ideology is 'cultural hegemony.' For Ing Kanjanavanit, it is "cultural indoctrination … laden with the stench of propaganda." 'Thainess' continues to dominate the cultural agenda, with Phibun's ideological project revived by the Ministry of Culture and Prayut Chan-o-cha's junta. Like Phibun, Prayut issued his own list of a dozen 'Core Values,' one of which was a deeply ironic instruction to learn "the true essence of democratic ideals," and initiated plans for a series of propaganda films about Thailand's military history.[115] As Michael Kelly Connors has shown, the Ministry of Culture also perpetuated Phibun's brand of 'Thainess,' as its first permanent secretary, Chakrarot Chitrabongs, advocated "the continuation of a hierarchical system of Thai manners that draws on feudalistic etiquette" in his essays on Thai culture.[116]

Ing has described the Ministry of Culture as a "Frankenstein's Monster" and, for good measure, she refers to the Ministry's censors as "a bunch of trembling morons with the power of life and death over our films." The Ministry's ultraconservative ideology is neatly encapsulated in Ing's documentary *Censor Must Die* (2013), a unique exposé of the censorship process that follows Manit Sriwanichpooom, producer of *Shakespeare Must Die* (2012), as he appeals against that film's ban. In one sequence, Manit waits for an appointment at the Ministry while an instructional video demonstrating traditional Thai posture is played on a loop in the foyer. The scene is comical as the quaintly anachronistic video stresses "Thai people's uniquely exquisite characteristics," though it also demonstrates the Ministry's outdated attitudes and didactic *raison d'être*.

## The Three Pillars

Devotion to nation, religion, and king is a central tenet of 'Thainess,' and any questioning of these three pillars provokes accusations of ingratitude or disloyalty. Although the film censorship rules have changed over the past century, underlying each revision was a commitment to the upholding of these three traditional pillars of Thai society. The tripartite motto 'nation, religion, king' was popularized during the reign of King Vajiravudh and revived by Thanin Kraivichien's government after the 6 October 1976 massacre: "Thanin's concept of social development demanded that Thai films strictly conform to the ideology of 'nation, religion, king.' One of the first actions of the Thanin regime was therefore to tighten the enforcement of the conservative film censorship."[117]

Apichatpong Weerasethakul argues that the sacrosanctity of these three institutions continues to dominate the debate around Thai film censorship today: "It's a theatrical society, a façade, all for the nation, religion, and king." He has previously expressed this in stronger terms: "Fear of offending the three revered institutions—the Nation, Buddhism and the Monarchy—has crippled our minds."[118] In Apichatpong's *Tropical Malady* (2004), the three pillars are symbolized by the country's tricolor flag. The film "pushes the limits of Thai censorship" with a shot in which the two protagonists lick each other's hands while a Thai flag flies in the background.[119] Apichatpong's temerity in questioning the three pillars may explain why he was singled out by the censors:

> Political turmoil and military coups are common, yet harmony and smooth relations are highly valued and citizens are expected to play by the rules to maintain harmony. Apichatpong does not play by the rules, either with the structure and nature of his films, nor with the way he goes about ensuring that he can work without compromising his artistic endeavours.[120]

In *Homogeneous, Empty Time* (2017), Thunska Pansittivorakul explores the construction of Thailand's national identity and the nationalist fervor stoked by state propaganda venerating the three pillars. He shows how such values are absorbed and passed from generation to generation, a result of media announcements that, according to Ing Kanjanavanit, "sicken the airwaves with constant saccharine exhortations to the people to love Nation, Religion, King."[121] The film shows how military propaganda, disseminated via radio, television, and billboards, inculcates an irrational fear of any notional threat to the three pillars.

'Protecting' these pillars has been cited as justification for the demonization of political opponents, from the unfounded *lèse-majesté* accusations used as a pretext for the 6 October 1976 massacre, to the 'yellowshirt' leaders who claimed in 2008 that, without their illegal protests, "the monarchy might collapse."[122] *Homogeneous, Empty Time*'s interviewees, some with tears in their eyes, vow to protect the three pillars with their lives. Army cadets, for example, pledge their commitment to defend Thailand against its enemies, though they are unable to specify who those enemies might be. A Village Scout leader, wearing a bright yellow shirt, boasts of his brief encounter with Rama IX: "I peeled a coconut for the King.... And the King ate my coconut! A round of applause for me, please!" The assembled Village Scouts all pledge to defend the monarchy. Cut to footage of Village Scouts and other ultranationalists attacking the students on 6 October 1976. The film thus reveals the ultimate consequences of state-sanctioned nationalist rhetoric.[123]

## Khon Dee

In addition to the three pillars of nation, religion, and monarchy, other "ideologies that have been used in controlling film content" include abstractions such as morality and national unity.[124] 'Causing division in society' is a common justification for Thai censorship, a de facto admission that differences of opinion are unacceptable. Nontawat Numbenchapol's *Boundary* (2013) is a case in point: "One reason they banned me is that my attitude doesn't match with the censors' attitude." The censors told Kanittha Kwunyoo that *Karma* (2015) "violated moral and cultural norms." In other words, the film was not sufficiently 'Thai,' as it did not follow state-proscribed notions of cultural conformity. Similarly, a Ministry of Culture official explained that *Insects in the Backyard* (2010) was banned because "it is deeply immoral" and told its director, Tanwarin Sukkhapisit, that she "should have made the film in a 'good' way."[125]

This emphasis on moral goodness is strikingly consistent with the justification given by 'yellowshirt' protesters for their proposed suspension of parliament. The demonstrators called for a government of appointed *khon dee* [good people] defined, in their view, as members of the establishment, implying that the general public could not be trusted to elect sufficiently 'good' politicians. Film censorship preserves the status of *khon dee*, ensuring that they are portrayed as paragons of virtue, which may account for the cuts to Apichatpong Weerasethakul's *Syndromes and a Century* (2006). Doctors drinking alcohol in moderation and monks gently playing music were censored from his film because, where the representation of *khon dee* is concerned, anything less than ideal is unacceptable.

The degree of transgression is not the point; the perfect façade must be maintained.

Ing Kanjanavanit's *Shakespeare Must Die* is perhaps the clearest illustration of the censors' ideological motivations. The film reimagines Macbeth as a power-crazed leader inspired by Thaksin Shinawatra, and it received public funding when his opponents, the Democrats, were in power. By the time production was complete, in 2012, Thaksin's sister Yingluck had been elected prime minister. At that point, the state was somewhat less disposed to Ing's political satire, and the Ministry of Culture banned the film it had funded. Similarly, Yuthlert Sippapak's *Fatherland* (2013) was commissioned during Yingluck's relatively progressive administration, though it was rejected by the military in the buildup to the 2014 coup.

## Promotion or Propaganda?

The Ministry of Culture's ideology is revealed not only by what it censors but also by what it endorses. The Film and Video Act's classifications include the P rating, reserved for "films which promote learning and should be promoted to be watched."[126] P is for 'promotion,' though it could also stand for 'propaganda,' as the category has the potential "to frame public opinions, to install dominant ideology."[127] The films receiving state promotion reinforce what historian Thongchai Winichakul has called a 'royalist-nationalist' history: the glorification of Thailand's monarchy, and the celebration of victories against nations historically regarded as enemies.

Thunska Pansittivorakul has criticized the production and impact of such films: "The most embarrassing rating is 'P' for promotion. It aims to advertise movies that spread misleading information to audiences."[128] Chatrichalerm Yukol directed the most prestigious of these royalist-nationalist period dramas. After the 2014 coup, the junta distributed free tickets to a film from Chatrichalerm's series about King Naresuan as part of a public relations campaign.[129] His *Legend of King Naresuan* series was controversial for its generous state funding and its mythologizing of royalist history, its most elaborate set piece portraying Naresuan's victory over the Burmese Prince Mingyi Swa in 1593. This iconic duel, with both men astride charging elephants, has been part of the Thai school curriculum for decades, and was even rendered in animated form, in *Khan Kluay* (2006). In the cartoon, the heroic title character, a Thai elephant, goes into battle with Naresuan against a monstrous Burmese elephant with demonic red eyes. The film's nationalistic, jingoistic message is unmistakable.

The elephant duel is the ne plus ultra of royalist-nationalist history. Its historical accuracy is more contentious, however. B. J. Terwiel contrasts Thai and Burmese accounts of the battle, concluding that their differing narratives are irreconcilable: "It is doubtful whether anyone will unravel the details of the battle in a decisive way. Suffice to say that *The Royal Chronicles* version, which has had a monopoly in Thai history writing, is only one version among many."[130]

Chapter 2

# *Nang R*: Sex and Sexuality on Screen

*"Are Thai films ready for sex and explicit titillation?"*[131]

## Thai Erotic Cinema

Cinematic depictions of sex and nudity have led to periodic moral panics, as permissive content is perceived as undermining traditional Thai cultural values. The first such incident came in 1932, the year of the first coup, with the release of Thailand's first sound film, *Going Astray*. The film featured the country's first on-screen kiss, which the press denounced as obscene, leading to a protracted defamation lawsuit.[132]

The reaction to *Going Astray* established a pattern that persists to the present day. Risqué films, especially those portraying 'unacceptable' behavior (as defined by the social conventions of each era), are regarded as indecent and subject to censorship. Such films, which became ever more explicit in the decades since *Going Astray*, are known in Thai as *nang R* [R-rated films], a reference to the American R (restricted) rating. Thus, prior to Thailand's official rating system, provocative films were given their own colloquial Thai R rating.

*Going Astray* is also a prototypical example of the Madonna/whore dichotomy that stereotyped female characters and typecast actresses for the next forty years: the virtuous *nang-ek* and promiscuous *dao-yua* character archetypes.[133] In *Going Astray*, the male protagonist (*phra-ek*) is seduced by a Bangkok prostitute (the *dao-yua*), though he is eventually reconciled with his dutiful wife (the *nang-ek*).

The binary distinction between *nang-ek* and *dao-yua* persisted for decades, though it became increasingly blurred in the 'New Wave' films of the 1970s, most notably Chatrichalerm Yukol's *Angel* (1974). That film's angelic heroine (the *nang-ek*) is forced to work in a brothel (a realm previously associated only with *dao-yua* characters), though this transgression ultimately leads to her independence and empowerment. Female characters could henceforth be as multidimensional as their male counterparts: "The *nang-ek* no longer needed to be lady-like and virginal. She could be tough, nasty and sexy—characteristics that were previously reserved for the *daoyua*."[134]

At the same time, previous restrictions on sex and sexuality were somewhat relaxed, with lesbian and gay characters being represented for the first time. In 1976, for example, the censors permitted Thai cinema's first lesbian kiss.[135] This newfound tolerance had its limits, however. Sex on screen was scrutinized by the censors not only in visual terms; morality was also a consideration. A film ran the risk of censorship if it presented promiscuous sex as inconsequential or acceptable, though the censors were more lenient towards movies with traditional moral messages.

Promiscuity was a key selling point in a successful 1972 sexploitation movie, though the film evaded censorship as its eponymous adulterer ultimately confesses her transgression: "I'm evil! I'm a very bad person! I have a lover! This whore is dirty! I should die!"[136]

Rebecca Townsend argues that this melodramatic confession redeemed the character—and the film—in the eyes of the censors: "While *The Adulterer* may have approached issues that were typically contentious for Thai censors, it did so by operating within the moral universe of modern Thai bourgeois values."[137]

In the 1980s, with the availability of VHS, the softcore erotica genre increased in popularity. Distributors routinely supplied retailers with two versions of erotic videos: censored and uncensored, the latter to be sold under the counter. This system of samizdat distribution was largely curtailed in 1987 with the imposition of stricter video censorship legislation (including custodial sentences for distributing pornography), and films released on VCD were heavily censored. 'Second-class' cinemas, struggling to compete with shopping mall multiplexes, provided an alternative outlet for erotic films such as *Just a Friend 2* (1991) and *Girls Girls Girls* (1992).[138]

Chatrichalerm Yukol has claimed that his crime thriller *Powder Road* (1991), with its topless go-go dancers, broke boundaries in Thai cinema as "the first film to show a nipple."[139] In fact, nudity was commonplace in softcore erotic movies long before *Powder Road*, and a topless woman even appears on *Just a Friend 2*'s poster. While *Powder Road* was not the first Thai film to show a nipple, it did represent the limits of nudity in mainstream Thai cinema prior to the rating system. Sex and nudity were strictly regulated. Multiple cuts were made to *Judgement* (2004), despite appeals by the studio, and protracted negotiations with the censors delayed the release of Nonzee Nimibutr's period drama *Jan Dara* (2001). When he made *Ploy* (2007), Pen-ek Ratanaruang stayed within the boundaries of the permissible, though the film was censored regardless: "I knew that you cannot show pubic hair, you cannot see genitals, I knew all that when I was filming it. But it was censored because it was kind of *dirty.*"

Once the rating system had been introduced, new standards were established. Female topless nudity became acceptable in films rated 18. Even frontal nudity was permitted, though this was initially rated 20. Bhandevanov Devakula's *Jan Dara: The Beginning* (2012), a steamier prequel to Nonzee's *Jan Dara*, took advantage of this newfound liberalism, and duly received an 18 rating. In a backhanded compliment, Kong Rithdee called this "a generous decision from the censors known for their superhuman sensitivity to naked flesh and political allusions."[140] (An even more explicit version, released on DVD, was rated 20.) The censors may have relaxed their rules, though this did not affect the superhuman sensitivity of politicians and wider society. Senator Sumol Sutawiriyawat spoke out against *Jan Dara: The Beginning*, calling for compulsory age verification at cinemas screening the film. The horse had already bolted, as the film had been on release for a fortnight, though the Ministry of Culture closed the stable door anyway. In a reactionary and legally questionable decision, the Ministry required cinema patrons to show their identification cards at subsequent screenings of *Jan Dara: The Beginning*, even though the 18 rating is purely advisory and ID checks are obligatory only for the 20 rating.

Despite the Ministry's dubious ruling on *Jan Dara: The Beginning*, the rating system did give filmmakers more freedom. The new limits were soon tested by two sexploitation films, *Brown Sugar* (2010) and *Sin Sisters 2* (2010), both of which were passed uncut. *Brown Sugar*, rated 18, includes an extended female masturbation sequence, though the character in question remains fully clothed throughout. In a later scene, a wisp of her pubic hair is briefly shown being shaved by a tattooist.[141] The 20 rating applied to *Sin Sisters 2* was a reflection of its generally salacious tone rather than any specific transgression.

Bhandevanov Devakula's films, although more lavish and literary than *Brown Sugar* and *Sin Sisters*, were no less exploitative. Bhandevanov cornered the market in high-class erotic dramas. In addition to *Jana Dara: The Beginning*, he also directed the equally steamy *Eternity* (2010) and *Mae Bia* (2015), and his international version of *The Scar* (2014) included male frontal nudity.[142] These films contain controversial softcore sex scenes, though they were also criticized for glamorizing adulterous relationships, adding a moral dimension to the controversies.

Anocha Suwichakornpong's critically acclaimed debut, *Mundane History* (2009), one of Thai cinema's most profound works, was the first Thai film to receive the dreaded 20 rating. The film can be read as a metaphor for Thai society under military rule, though it was visible nudity rather than political subtext that resulted in its restrictive 20 rating: when a paralyzed young man tries to masturbate while taking a bath, his flaccid penis is shown.

Almost a decade after *Mundane History*, a similar scene in Pen-ek's *Samui Song* (2017) resulted in an 18 rating. In *Samui Song*, a character's impotence is also revealed when he attempts to masturbate. As in *Mundane History*, his flaccid penis is visible, and the film's lower rating demonstrates that restrictions on nudity were relaxed in the years since the passing of the Film and Video Act. The censors recognized that "the masturbation scene was there to give depth to that character" and therefore felt that the frontal nudity was justified, a consideration of context and characterization that indicates an increasingly nuanced approach to censorship.[143]

This comparatively enlightened attitude occasionally resulted in surprisingly lenient judgments by the censors, as was the case with Wisit Sasanatieng's 'Catopia,' part of the portmanteau film *Ten Years Thailand* (2018). In one sequence, a naked woman with a cat's head is attacked by a baying mob. The film also has a subversive political subtext, though it was not subject to censorship; on the contrary, it was rated 13. The nude woman is not eroticized, though the 13 rating is still a remarkable anomaly given that full frontal nudity had previously been cut or restricted to the 18 category.

## Sacred and Profane

Mitigating factors, such as the character development in *Samui Song* from 2017, have occasionally led to less censorious attitudes towards nudity, though there are also aggravating factors with the opposite effect. In particular, sex and violence have been censored more stringently whenever they were juxtaposed with 'sensitive' subjects such as religion or politics.

The French comedy *Pattaya* (2016), for example, includes a masturbation scene that does not contain explicit nudity, though it attracted controversy because it was filmed at a Thai Buddhist temple, leading to its withdrawal from the Thailand Film Destination Festival. Similarly, a sequence in which a couple kiss at a temple was cut from *Soi Cowboy* (2008). Footage of assassins shooting into a mosque was removed from *The Vanquisher* (2009), as it too closely echoed a massacre at the Krue Se Mosque in Pattani. (In that incident, on 28 April 2004, the military used automatic weapons to kill thirty-two insurgents, only one of whom was armed.)

The combination of violence and religion also explains the censorship of Pen-ek Ratanaruang's *Headshot* (2011); he was required to digitally erase a gun from a monk's alms bowl. The director argued that the monk was a gangster in disguise and the gun alerted the audience to this, though the censors told him: "A gun and the alms cannot be together. The bowl is too sacred, and a gun is too evil." Likewise, a shot of a Red Cross sign falling from a hospital roof and killing a woman was cut from the slasher film *Sick Nurses* (2007) as the censors felt that this symbol of protection should not be associated with death.

Thunska Pansittivorakul's films are often sexually explicit and they are also highly politicized. This fusion of hardcore sex and political critique is an explosive combination. Indeed, he regards the representation of sex as a political act in itself: "It's my political expression. To just show it, without saying anything more, already means something. The authorities ban films for the stupidest reasons, so here it is."[144] In his banned documentary *This Area Is Under Quarantine* (2008), he choreographs a sexual encounter between two young gay men, one of whom is Buddhist and the other Muslim. Eroticized shots of the men are juxtaposed with news footage of the 2004 massacre at Tak Bai.

This "exposure of male bodies in tandem with the radical critique of various political contexts" recurs in Thunska's documentary *Homogeneous, Empty Time* (2017), which includes photographs of naked army cadets piled on top of each other in abusive and humiliating hazing rituals.[145] Coincidentally, a month before that film's first screening, a cadet died during a training exercise and his internal organs were removed to prevent his family from arranging an autopsy. This shocking case was not an isolated incident, as one of the film's interviewees confirms: "There is often news of soldiers getting beaten to death during training." Thunska's *Santikhiri Sonata* (2019) refers to the dead cadet, "whose insides, heart, and brain were all taken out of his body," and to a young human rights activist who was killed at a military checkpoint: "Eyewitnesses say he was unarmed, and was beaten before being shot."[146]

*The Terrorists* (2011) features Thunska's most provocative sequence: a naked man is shown masturbating while captions describe the 6 October 1976 massacre at Thammasat University. The film then cuts directly from the masturbation to archive footage of the Thammasat victims' desecrated corpses, accompanied by a sorrowful song.[147] Outwardly, the man's orgasm and the military massacre have nothing in common, except for their shock value. However, for the director, one is a metaphor for the other: "That massacre is like masturbation. Some people did it to make it better. They need to feel good and happy, but it's really cruel." His intention, therefore, is not to exploit or eroticize violence but to condemn what he views as the military government's quasi-sexual impulse to massacre its opponents. Needless to say, he did not submit *The Terrorists* to the censors.

## Thai Queer Cinema

*The Last Song* (1985), *Anguished Love* (1987), and *I Am a Man* (1987) constituted "the first wave of Thai queer cinema" in the 1980s.[148] In 1991, these three films were programed for the International Gay and Lesbian Film Festival in Amsterdam, though their screenings were prevented as the prints were "detained at the airport in Bangkok, prohibited from exiting the country."[149] The international success of *The Iron Ladies* (2001) and *Beautiful Boxer* (2003) instigated a second wave in the 2000s.[150] These films were groundbreaking for featuring gay men in leading roles, though their characters were largely restricted to *kathoey* [ladyboys], portrayed in the first wave as tragic outcasts and in the second wave as triumphant underdogs. *Kathoey* also appear in Thai popular culture, such as comedy films and *lakhon* [soap opera], though they are invariably sissified characters intended to provide comic relief. The Ministry of Culture has endeavored to reduce such representations, not because they are homophobic and transphobic stereotypes but because they apparently promote "sexually deviant" behavior.[151] These outdated characterizations, and the state's equally antiquated attitude, have been challenged by more realistic cinematic depictions of gay sexuality, particularly from the independent film sector.

The central figure in Tanwarin Sukkhapisit's *Insects in the Backyard* (2010) is also a *kathoey*, though Tanwarin reclaims the identity from its mainstream comic clichés. The character, played by the director herself, is the matriarch of a dysfunctional family, and her two teenaged children are drawn into prostitution. *Insects in the Backyard* has a camp sensibility, though Tanwarin also has a political agenda. She is depicting characters who, while clearly exaggerated, nonetheless represent culturally marginalized and socially ostracized members of the LGBT community. It is this focus on such unconventional characters (the insects of the title) that made the film so controversial.

Tanwarin appealed against the ban imposed on *Insects in the Backyard* "so that the law could be improved in order to promote and support Thai films, as opposed to using the law to deprive Thai people of their rights and freedoms," though the National Film Board rejected her appeal.[152] On Christmas Day 2015, five years after the ban, the Administrative Court overturned the censors' judgment that the film was inherently immoral and permitted its release with a single three-second cut.

*Bangkok Love Story* (2007), a melodramatic thriller with a set-piece softcore sex scene filmed on a rooftop, was an attempt to normalize on-screen gay relationships for a mainstream Thai audience. Like *Beautiful Boxer* (2003), *Bangkok Love Story* is also notable for its emphasis on muscularity, as opposed to the camp, asexual (therefore nonthreatening) characters that dominated previous queer films. *Bangkok Love Story*'s release was delayed after the police voiced concerns over its portrayal of a gay police informant, and cuts were made. Its widely distributed poster depicted one character slipping his hand suggestively under the waistline of the other's jeans. The high visibility of this publicity shot symbolized the increasing acceptability of homoerotic imagery in mainstream Thai media.

*Bangkok Love Story*'s poster (and DVD cover) can be contrasted with an earlier publicity campaign promoting a film about male prostitutes. In 1974, a billboard near Don Mueang airport featured two nude men with graphics covering their genitals. This sensationalist campaign backfired, as the billboard's visibility to tourists at the airport "was perceived to impact negatively on the international image and reputation of Thailand," and the film was banned.[153]

There is also a market for queer films on video as a sell-through release is easier and more cost-effective than securing wide theatrical distribution for films with gay themes. *Rainbow Boys: The Movie* (2005), for example, transcended its video origins by portraying gay characters as guys-next-door rather than stereotypes. *Rainbow Boys* has no nudity or graphic content—its gay sex scene fades discreetly to black—though it was cut by five minutes on VCD. A gay drama made by Tanwarin Sukkhapisit for the video market in 2003 was shelved altogether.[154] A decade later, however, following the introduction of the rating system, times had changed. The straight-to-DVD *Father and Son* (2015), a gay drama with science fiction elements (like Thunska Pansittivorakul's *Supernatural*, made the previous year for the American DVD market), includes several softcore sex scenes and even a shot of an erection, albeit lasting only four frames.

## The Last Taboos

Unsimulated sex in Thai cinema has not yet been passed by the censors and filmmakers are aware that, if such material were submitted, it would inevitably be cut even at the highest age rating. A woman stroking an erect penis was one of the shots censored from Apichatpong Weerasethakul's *Blissfully Yours* (2002), and a three-second clip from an American gay porn video was cut from Tanwarin Sukkhapisit's *Insects in the Backyard* (2010). *Motel Mist* (2016) also includes a pornographic DVD playing in the background, though soft focus discreetly obscures most of the explicit detail.

Thunska Pansittivorakul's films (none of which has been approved by the censors) often blur the boundaries between autobiography, documentary, and fiction, though sex has been a consistent thread throughout his work. There is semi-abstract, hardcore imagery in the final moments of *Homogeneous, Empty Time* (2017), and the erect penis is a recurring motif in his films. Glimpsed in sex scenes at the start of *Supernatural* (2014) and at the end of *This Area Is Under Quarantine* (2008), an erection later became a metaphor for military repression in *The Terrorists* (2011) and a symbol of defiance in *Middle-earth* (2007). *Santikhiri Sonata* (2019) includes a montage of clips from online adult videos, progressing from 'solo' scenes to hardcore material, accompanied by an acoustic folk song. The lyrics at first seem incongruous, though they end with the words "overflowing kindness" as a porn star reaches his climax.[155]

Thunska combines this phallic imagery with a participatory filmmaking style. A recurring trope involves his hand reaching from behind the camera to touch the groins of the men he is filming. This gesture originated in *Happy Berry* (2004), with the director reaching out in a playful attempt to pull down a nude model's shorts. His short film *Unseen Bangkok* (2004) features an interview with a male prostitute whose erection occupies the foreground of the frame, and Thunska touches it admiringly. A shot in *Reincarnate* (2010) is framed in a similar way, foregrounding an erect penis, which he masturbates to produce the first money shot in a Thai film. The autobiographical documentary *Avalon* (2020) features his most extreme form of directorial participation, as it consists largely of hardcore sex tapes he filmed with his former partner. The film includes a rooftop encounter that recalls *Bangkok Love Story* (2007), and a *ménage à trois*, though it ultimately documents the disintegration of the relationship.

Although male frontal nudity became permissible after the rating system, as depicted in the *Mundane History* (2009) and *Samui Song* (2017) masturbation scenes, it remains uncommon in mainstream Thai cinema. *The Scar* (2014) includes frontal nudity in a sex scene, though this was present only in the film's international version. Shots of an obese nude man taking a shower in *Soi Cowboy* (2008) were reduced for its Thai release, as the film's producer explained at a Thai Film Archive screening: "They said six seconds was too much, so we cut it down to two seconds."[156] The split-second erection in *Father and Son* (2015), rated 20, thus represents the current limits of nudity in commercial Thai cinema.

Chapter 3

# The Untouchables: Film and Politics

*"Thai politics is just like the Fast and Furious action film series.*
*The fight is getting faster and fiercer."*[157]

## Military, Monarchy, and Metaphors

Since the 1932 coup first established parliamentary democracy
in Thailand, the terms of office held by elected governments have
been outnumbered by extended periods of military rule. There
have been a dozen coups d'état, and pro-democracy protesters have
been massacred by the military on four occasions: in October 1973,
October 1976, May 1992, and from April to May 2010. The victims
of each of these massacres are listed in the documentary *Democracy
After Death* (2016) and the short film *Hush, Tonight the Dead Are
Dreaming Loudly* (2019).

By creating a culture of militarism, the armed forces have
legitimized their various coups and maintained a powerful influence
over successive civilian administrations. For example, *lakhon* [soap
opera] series broadcast on military-owned television channels
are utilized for propaganda purposes: "Lakhons have long been
employed by juntas to instill within viewers a sense of nationalism

and positive feelings towards the military."[158] The short film *Official Trailer* (2018) subverts this by intercutting footage of the 6 October 1976 massacre with clips from the popular *lakhon* series *Love Destiny* (2018). Similarly, for her video *The Treachery of the Moon* (2012), artist Araya Rasdjarmrearnsook projected footage of the 'redshirt' crackdown onto her surroundings as she sat watching a *lakhon* on television.[159] Patporn Phoothong's documentary *Silenced Memories* (2014) challenges the military's "culture of impunity, the culture of acceptance of state violence, and the culture of silence" in its epilogue. The military's suppressions of dissent have led to a vicious cycle in which nascent democratic reforms are repeatedly overturned by an authoritarian establishment.

The 1932 coup also abolished Thailand's absolute monarchy, though the constitutional monarchy retains a unique symbolic significance. Thailand has a profoundly hierarchical society, with the monarch at its apex. Monarchs are revered to the point of religious veneration, and the *lèse-majesté* law suppresses any perceived criticism of the royal family. Thailand's longest reigning monarch, Rama IX, died in 2016, and Taiki Sakpisit's short film *The Age of Anxiety* (2013), with its rapid-fire editing and screeching soundtrack, captured the anxious atmosphere during his prolonged illness. The film's English title reflects the national mood in the twilight of his reign, though its Thai title has an additional resonance.[160]

Given their untouchable status, cultural representation of the military and the monarchy is fraught with sensitivities. The legal penalty and social stigma associated with *lèse-majesté* have led to widespread self-censorship. Moreover, social polarization and the restrictions of martial law have made politics an equally contentious cinematic topic. While censorship of sex has become less restrictive, politics remains a potential minefield for filmmakers, as Kong Rithdee has argued: "No matter how conservative Thai authority can seem when it comes to flesh-flashing movies, they can be even more reactionary and paranoid when politics is served up in films."[161]

Apichatpong Weerasethakul once asked: "Will we ever see a movie about Field Marshal P Pibulsongkram and his dictatorial rule?"[162] The question was pertinent, as Euthana Mukdasanit had begun preproduction of a film about him in 1988, though it was abandoned to avoid a defamation lawsuit.[163] Pasakorn Pramoolwong, codirecter of *Paradoxocracy* (2013), made a revisionist documentary about Phibun and Pridi Banomyong (*The Frienemies*) in 2017, though his investor pulled out during postproduction and the film was shelved.[164] Banjong Kosallawat's proposed biopic of another military dictator, Sarit Thanarat, was thwarted by the censors in 2002.[165] Veera Musigapong made a film satirizing a fellow politician in 1978, a thinly veiled parody of Samak Sundaravej's ministerial career, featuring a principal character with an almost identical name. However, the film was censored so heavily—eighteen cuts, including references to Samak's corruption and his role as an agitator prior to 6 October 1976—that Veera decided against releasing it.[166]

Such sensitivities are even extended to fictional military characters. In action films made in Thailand, corrupt generals are invariably coded as foreign rather than Thai, thus preventing the dramatization of Thai military corruption. For example, before *Belly of the Beast* (2003) could be filmed in Thailand, the censors vetted the script and insisted that a corrupt army general "had to be changed so he wasn't Thai."[167] Thus, to secure filming permission, screenwriters practice self-censorship by routinely assigning non-Thai nationalities to military antagonists. Producer Tom Waller cites the case of *Ninja 2*

(2013), "in which the bad guy General needed to be Burmese to avoid any problems," a preemptive alteration at the script stage made as a direct consequence of the previous changes required for *Belly of the Beast*.[168] As Waller explains: "Changing corrupt military General characters from Thai to Burmese? That's normal when submitting a foreign film for approval. They don't want negative characters to sully the 'image and reputation of the kingdom.'"[169]

To circumvent restrictions against royal, political, or military commentary, filmmakers have resorted to various metaphors and indirect allusions. Thunska Pansittivorakul explains, for example, that *Reincarnate* (2010) "tells something about politics and royalty. But I was still living in Thailand, so I could not say it directly, so I said it like a poem." *Reincarnate* begins with a prologue outlining the rules imposed by the Film and Video Act (referred to as "a confusing ministerial regulation"). The film then proceeds to intentionally flout these rules, both covertly (with its political subtext) and overtly (with hardcore imagery). The prologue also describes the political factions of the period (the 'redshirts,' 'yellowshirts,' and 'blueshirts'), and these are later symbolized by a game of Jenga played with red, yellow, and blue blocks.

Thunska also uses typographical and numerical codes, hidden in plain sight, that refer to sensitive subject matter. In *Santikhiri Sonata* (2019), the Roman numerals 'CXII' are a reference to *lèse-majesté*, which is article 112 of the penal code. In *Supernatural* (2014), social contact is restricted to an Internet chatroom, and one character has the password '09.06.1946.09.20' and the username '1721955,' both of which refer to Rama VIII. The king died on 9 June 1946 at 9:20am, and three of his servants were executed (as scapegoats) on 17 February 1955. '1721955' also appears in 'Remember' (2019), a music video directed by Thunska.[170] The title of the short film *246247596248914102516... And Then There Were None* (2017) uses a similar numerical code, referring to three historical events: *2462475* is 24 June 1932 (the date of the first coup, 2475 in the Buddhist Era), *962489* is 9 June 1946 (Rama VIII's death, 2489 BE), and *14102516* is the 14 October 1973 massacre (2516 BE).[171]

Thunska and Apichatpong Weerasethakul have both adopted sleep as a metaphor for life under military rule. In Thunska's short film *Middle-earth* (2007), made shortly after the 2006 coup, two nude men sleep in a minimalist white room. For the director, sleep represented the suspension of liberty: "That time is like a time that freedom was sleeping." In the film's final seconds, one of the men's penises slowly becomes erect, an indication that there is still hope for freedom: "In the last part, I tried to say that we, as a people, are still alive. But still in a dream." His short film *KI SS* (2011) tells the story of *Snow White* in a series of captions, ending with a photograph of the Democracy Monument, suggesting that Thai democracy lies as dormant as Snow White herself, waiting to be revived.

In 'Song of the City,' Apichatpong's segment of the dystopian, futuristic anthology film *Ten Years Thailand* (2018), a man attempts to sell a "Good Sleep Machine" that guarantees peaceful sleep. Throughout his sales pitch, a statue of the Cold War-era dictator Sarit Thanarat looms over him, indicating the perpetuation of the country's militaristic ideology. Sarit's ominous presence is also felt in Apichatpong's *Cemetery of Splendour* (2015), as his portrait hangs on a canteen wall. In that film, also made after the 2014 coup, soldiers suffer from a mysterious epidemic of sleeping sickness, and Apichatpong explained that sleep is both a metaphor for an oppressed society and a source of escapism for the oppressed: "They are trapped and choose to sleep as an escape. They seek a better place in their dreams. Since we are powerless, we are like sleeping puppets, controlled even in our dreams. This film reflects those feelings. About life under the current situation."[172]

Other directors have created microcosms of Thai society as a means of commenting on political issues. In the short film *Demockrazy* (2007), set in a high school, a student with a populist agenda wins an election for class president, though his authoritarian teacher disqualifies him. Symbolically, the film, which ends with the teacher erasing the word 'democracy' from the blackboard, was made shortly after the 2006 coup overthrew the populist government of Thaksin Shinawatra.[173] Thailand's political polarization is referenced in the short film *This House Have Ghost* [sic] (2011), with the country symbolized by a house with arguing residents, haunted by a red-clad ghost representing the victims of the 2010 'redshirt' massacre. Similarly, the condominium in Prabda Yoon's *Someone from Nowhere* (2017) is a metaphor for the country; the building is called 'Liberty Land' and 'Thai' means 'liberated.' In the comedy *Bus Lane* (2007), a bus is hijacked and the passengers bicker about who is to blame. Metaphorically, the bus driver represents the prime minister, the hijacker symbolizes the junta, and the arguing passengers evoke the rival 'redshirt' and 'yellowshirt' protest groups. Yingluck Shinawatra made a similar comparison after being deposed by a coup: "It's the same as if the people had handed me the car keys and said I must drive and lead the country. Then suddenly, someone points a gun at my head and tells me to get out of the car while I'm at the wheel driving the people forward."[174]

Anocha Suwichakornpong's *Mundane History* (2009) can also be read as a socio-political microcosm, though its scope is literally cosmic, with computer-generated images of a supernova. The film's principal character, Ake, who is paralyzed below the waist, resents his emotionally distant father. The son's paralysis is a metaphor for the restrictions imposed on Thai society under military rule, with his father representing the authorities. As Anocha explained: "The conflict between the father and son mirrors the conflict between those in power and the citizens of my country."[175] Anocha does not extend the patriarchal metaphor further, though it has wider significance, as Father's Day in Thailand is celebrated on the king's birthday.[176]

*Mundane History*'s repetitive structure—like that of Apichatpong Weerasethakul's *Syndromes and a Century* (2006) and Prabda Yoon's *Someone from Nowhere* (2017)—also contributes to its political subtext. For example, when Ake is asked if he would like the light to be switched off, he does not respond, and it is turned off anyway. This sequence is subsequently repeated, echoing the cyclical nature of Thailand's political history. The country has experienced a dozen military coups, and its constitution has been abrogated and rewritten twenty times. Anocha's *Krabi, 2562* (2019) features an equally oblique political commentary, with the distant sound of marching boots serving as "a reminder of the military junta controlling the Land of Smiles."[177]

However, this reliance on metaphor has its drawbacks, as indirect references may not be understood by the audience: "If the films are too opaque then the communicative power of cinema has not been utilized. The hidden idea, then, is impotent."[178] The short film *Friendship Ended with Mudasir Now Salman Is My Best Friend* (2018) acknowledges this dilemma, challenging the audience to decode its rapid-fire montage of allusions to the 6 October 1976 massacre.[179] Apichatpong has said that he regrets the necessity of relying on such cryptic references: "It's almost an excuse, like cheating, when you have to resort to other means to say another thing…. I censor myself, and when I censor, I feel shame."[180] He has also described how metaphors stifle creativity: "When you feel comfortable with metaphors I think that's wrong—it becomes like a formula so that you no longer need to think."[181]

When highlighting egregious state injustices, Thunska Pansittivorakul avoided ambiguity and allusion, resorting instead to direct criticism. In *Supernatural* (2014), he name-checks two military figures: "General Pallop Pinmanee and Major General Chamlong Srimuang joined the anti-Communist war in Laos and conducted assassinations."[182] *The Terrorists* (2011) begins with a prologue denouncing the state's crackdown on protesters in 2010: "Abhisit Vejjajiva's government shall be condemned." In *This Area Is Under Quarantine* (2008), a clip of Thaksin Shinawatra telling parliament that "the officials did their best" is juxtaposed with footage of soldiers beating protesters at Tak Bai. The film ends with a written dedication to the Tak Bai victims who died "under Prime Minister Thaksin Shinawatra's government."

Neti Wichiansaen's *Democracy after Death* (2016) is equally uncompromising in its condemnation of politicians and the military. Like Thunska's *The Terrorists*, Neti's documentary holds Abhisit personally culpable for the 'redshirt' massacre, accusing him of "Thailand's new record of the number of people shot by the military." In Neti's case, such direct criticisms carry less risk as he lives in self-imposed exile due to previous *lèse-majesté* charges. His film, therefore, examines divisive political issues—the 2006 coup and its repercussions—that were excluded from Pen-ek Ratanaruang's *Paradoxocracy* (2013). Despite this, however, Neti self-censored

*Democracy after Death* to some extent, pixelating photographs linking the monarchy to the 2006 coup and bleeping out a soldier's pledge of loyalty to the monarch ("I'm a soldier of His Majesty the King").[183] Chulayarnnon Siriphol's *100 Times Reproduction of Democracy* (2019), filmed after the 2014 coup, includes a similar declaration from a soldier, who tells a group of anti-coup protesters, "We serve the same king."

## Lèse-majesté

Thailand is one of the few countries that still enforces a *lèse-majesté* law, and the punishment is severe—a jail sentence of up to fifteen years per conviction. *Lèse-majesté* cases are tried in camera, and publication of the evidence under investigation is regarded as a repetition of the offence. Legally, *lèse-majesté* refers only to the three most senior members of the royal family (and the regent, if appointed), though in practice it has been applied increasingly broadly.

As Pen-ek Ratanaruang discovered when he made his political documentary *Paradoxocracy* in 2013, any reference to the monarchy, however neutral, factual, or historical, results in intense scrutiny: "I thought, as long as you don't attack the monarchy ... then you're fine. But, of course, the reality is not like that. You can't even *mention* it, you can't even *talk* about it." As a result, Pen-ek's rushes from *Paradoxocracy* will never see the light of day: "Half of the footage that we have, you can't show to people. You'll just have to bury it in the ground somewhere."

Apichatpong Weerasethakul has touched on *lèse-majesté*, which he describes, without mincing words, as "a disgusting law," in two films. His short film *Ashes* (2012) includes footage of a protest in support of Ampon Tangnoppakul, who was convicted of *lèse-majesté*. A handwritten diary entry in *Cemetery of Splendour* (2015) calls for Ampon's release from prison.[184] (A caption in Thunska Pansittivorakul's *Supernatural* (2014) reveals that Ampon died while serving his sentence.) Likewise, Nil Paksnavin's short film *Damaged Air* (2013) ends with the caption "Free Somyos Praeksakasemsuk" in reference to another *lèse-majesté* prisoner.[185] In *Homogeneous, Empty Time* (2017), Thunska discusses the vagaries of *lèse-majesté* with Weeranan Huadsri (credited under the pseudonym Methee Jitr-Asanee). At one point in their discussion, the soundtrack is muted and the English subtitles are self-censored.[186]

Mindful of the particular sensitivity surrounding references to the monarchy, Apichatpong and Thunska have declined to submit certain films to the Thai censors, preferring to restrict themselves to overseas distribution rather than face censorship or *lèse-majesté* charges in Thailand. Given the global nature of digital distribution and video sales, the directors have taken additional precautions in case these sensitive works became available in their home country. *Cemetery of Splendour* and *Supernatural*, for example, both avoid the use of royal iconography, as such content is potentially inflammatory in Thailand. The directors thus felt bound by Thai restrictions even though their films were intended for international markets.

In Thai cinemas, audiences are required to stand while the royal anthem is played before film screenings, though in *Cemetery of Splendour* a cinema audience is shown standing in silence. Apichatpong had originally intended to include the anthem, though he reconsidered after it was censored from an earlier film. As he did in *Syndromes and a Century* (2006), Apichatpong replaced the forbidden content with silence: "I actually wanted to show the royal anthem…. But I know it's impossible, because in the movie *Soi Cowboy* [2008], this was cut out. Censored. So, I said, 'It's impossible anyway.' So, just silence." For *Cemetery of Splendour*'s DVD and blu-ray releases, Apichatpong removed the shots of the audience standing, as he was concerned that they could be misinterpreted if the discs found their way to Thailand.

Thunska self-censored *Supernatural* in 2014 for the same reason.[187] The film depicts a dystopian, Orwellian future in which Thai society is dominated by a figure known as 'the Leader,' whose authoritarian presence is reflected by images of Greek gods. Thunska made *Supernatural* for the American DVD market, and he chose this mythological imagery as a symbolic substitute for Thai royal portraits in case the DVD was circulated in his home country: "Every house in Thailand has the king and queen's picture. But I cannot put the picture of the king and queen in the movie, so instead I put Greek gods. In the story, I tried to compare the king with a Greek god or Hindu god."

As Thunska explains, royal portraits are ubiquitous in Thailand, in both public and private spaces, though such imagery is routinely excluded from the country's cinematic self-representation. (The short film *This House Have Ghost* [*sic*] (2011), which includes a strategically placed Rama IX calendar, is an exception.)[188] Royal iconography is sometimes removed because its use is deemed exploitative. Thus, a sequence in *Soi Cowboy* showing a cinema audience standing for the royal anthem was cut in 2008, as its producer explained: "The censors felt that use of the royal anthem in the film was deemed commercial use of the monarchy and that was not allowed, so they ordered that scene be cut from the film."[189]

In other cases, censorship has been imposed to avoid associating the monarchy with potentially contentious subject matter. *No Escape* (2015), for example, is set during a coup, and its makers were therefore told to "never show the king or the colour yellow because that's the colour of the king."[190] Similarly, a New Year's Eve announcement praising Rama IX was removed from the soundtrack of Nontawat Numbenchapol's *Boundary* (2013), as the censors deemed it inappropriate in a political documentary. The cut appeared tokenistic, though it was a condition of the film's release, as Nontawat explained:

> The censors called me again: 'Okay, let's lift the ban.' But they asked me about one scene with sound about the king.... It's like an ambient sound, celebrating the king and celebrating the new year at Ratchaprasong. They wanted to mute this sound. It was okay, because it was just two seconds. But Apichatpong told me it's not good, not the right thing.[191]

In Nontawat's short film *Gaze and Hear* (2011), a fictional royal legend is narrated in a droning monotone. The film parodies royalist propaganda, though, as its title suggests, it was also designed as an exercise in sensory arousal. Its hypnotic voice-over and flashing lights induce a trance-like state of obedience, at which point the viewer becomes susceptible to manipulation by propaganda.

Enforcement of the *lèse-majesté* law is determined to a large extent by the political climate. Thus, for example, Apichatpong Weerasethakul felt able to wear a 'NO 112' tee-shirt at the World Film Festival in 2012, when Yingluck Shinawatra's civilian government was in office, and there were fewer restrictions on public discourse.[192]

Commenting four years later, when Prayut Chan-o-cha's junta was in power, Apichatpong noted that times had changed: "Before, when I could wear that tee-shirt, it was quite okay if you talked with logic and reason why this is not healthy. Now, it's worse, to not be able to talk in a civil manner."

*Lèse-majesté*'s political dimension is neatly encapsulated by the differing Thai responses to three Hollywood dramatizations of the friendship between Anna Leonowens and Rama IV. The first version, *Anna and the King of Siam* (1946), was not subject to censorship in Thailand, and indeed it received a gala premiere in Bangkok. At that time, during Phibun Songkhram's first term as prime minister, King Rama IX had not yet been crowned, and the government launched a cultural revolution that promoted ultranationalism and minimized the symbolism of the monarchy.

The second Hollywood dramatization of Leonowens and Rama IV, *The King and I*, was released ten years later, during Phibun's second term in office. What a difference a decade makes. The political situation had changed dramatically and *The King and I* was banned. At the height of the Cold War, Thailand had entered a strategic alliance with the US. Phibun's second term was unstable, with several attempted counter-coups against his leadership. Furthermore, the monarchy was becoming more prominent following Rama IX's coronation. The banning of *The King and I* was announced by Phibun himself, rather than the censorship board (leading the film's distributors to argue that the decision was unlawful). The ban was imposed not to uphold the *lèse-majesté* law, but rather for political expediency. Phibun sought to maintain bilateral relations between Thailand and the US (by preventing criticism of Hollywood from offended Thai filmgoers), and to cling to power (by making a token gesture of loyalty to appease his monarchist political rivals).

In 1999, *Anna and the King*, the third Leonowens and Rama IV drama, was also banned in Thailand. By this time, successive governments (beginning with that of Phibun's successor, Sarit Thanarat) had elevated the monarch to the status of national father figure. The monarchy was not merely respected, but worshipped, and *lèse-majesté* was strictly enforced to maintain the monarch's position as an unimpeachable symbol of unity. Thus, the censors issued a lengthy and detailed list of their objections to *Anna and the King* at the script stage, denying the production permission to film in Thailand. The script was initially rejected "on the grounds that certain scenes were factually inaccurate or culturally implausible or potentially insulting to the Royal family, the institution of Buddhism or Thai people in general."[193] The banning of the film itself was also rigorously enforced, with three vendors arrested for selling bootleg videos of it.

The underlying reason for the ban may be found in *Anna and the King*'s final moments. The film ends with Rama IV's young son, Chulalongkorn, observing in an awestruck voice-over that "Anna had shined such a light on Siam." This is followed by a written epilogue: "Thanks to the vision of his father, King Mongkut, and the teachings of Anna Leonowens, King Chulalongkorn not only maintained Siam's independence, but also abolished slavery." Chulalongkorn is Thailand's most venerated monarch, and the intimation that his reforms were, even in part, inspired by Leonowens directly undermines the state's royalist-nationalist narrative.

# 14 October 1973

In October 1973, after a decade of military rule led by prime minister Thanom Kittikachorn, a group of students began campaigning for a democratic constitution. A dozen campaigners were arrested, prompting a rally of 2,000 students from Thammasat University calling for their release. Within a week, the protest had increased to 500,000 people, who gathered at the Democracy Monument in Bangkok. Pen-ek Ratanaruang's documentary *Paradoxocracy* includes interviews with some of the protest organizers and newsreel footage of the demonstration. On 14 October 1973, King Rama IX indicated his support for the students and assured protest leader Seksan Prasertkul that their demands would be met. Despite this, tensions between the authorities and the protesters boiled over, and the army opened fire, killing seventy-seven people. The massacre was documented by two cameramen, whose footage appeared in *The Shadow of History* (2013).[194] The short film *Octoblur* (2013) intercuts their footage of 14 October with Thanom's 2004 funeral.

*The Moonhunter* (2001), a biopic about Seksan's role in the 14 October uprising and the Communist insurgency, opens with a prologue calling the incident an event "that many want to erase from history." This description could equally apply to subsequent acts of state-sponsored violence, such as the 1976 Thammasat massacre, the 1992 'Black May' protests, the 2004 Tak Bai killings, and the 2010 'redshirt' crackdown. The film is dedicated to "those who have fought for freedom and democracy in Thailand."

Though *The Moonhunter* avoided censorship, its trailer was cut. Scenes of riot police beating peaceful protesters were removed, as were images of the Thai flag. The trailer also featured a series of revolutionary slogans, one of which, "Get up and fight! Even with bare hands!" was deleted.[195] *The Moonhunter* was one of several historical films released in the early 2000s, though its portrayal of pro-democracy protesters and Communist guerrillas set it apart from the others in the cycle, which were nostalgic or nationalistic dramas. Its failure at the box office goes some way to explain the subsequent lack of commercial films with overt political themes.

The period romance *Sunset at Chaophraya 2* (1993) concludes with one of Thai cinema's most dramatic and uncompromising recreations of state brutality. Archive footage of students linking arms and waving flags on 13 October 1973 is followed by a restaging of the moment when the violence began—a crowd of students fleeing as riot police fire tear gas. Several students stumble and fall and are trampled underfoot in the rush to escape. Then, in a reenactment of the 14 October massacre itself, soldiers using automatic weapons fire on students from a helicopter. The director cuts from over-the-shoulder shots of the soldiers firing to hand-held reaction shots as the students are hit, in an extraordinary sequence that recalls Hollywood Vietnam War movies. When one student is shot, a blood squib splatters onto the camera lens.

Chatrichalerm Yukol filmed the 14 October protest as it happened. His actuality footage appeared in *Angel* (1974), released less than a year after the massacre: a student protest at Bangkok's Democracy Monument intercut with dramatized violence as a prostitute is beaten by a gang of pimps. The 14 October imagery in *Angel* appears only briefly—some shots last only a few frames—though Chatrichalerm's color 35mm footage is technically superior to the more familiar 16mm black-and-white newsreels.

Anocha Suwichakornpong's *By the Time It Gets Dark* (2016) references the aftermath of 14 October, with a flashback to a group of students debating the appointment of a new prime minister.[196] One student argues that the government is tainted by its military origins: "This government has no legitimacy. Don't forget how they came to power. On the back of a military coup!" Although the scene is set in 1973, the film was released in 2016, during another period of military rule, giving the dialogue a contemporary resonance.

The 14 October massacre was followed by a brief period of political stability. There was also a liberalization of state censorship, which "began to relax its rules, with the censors showing greater flexibility and a more open-minded attitude."[197] This enabled the 'new wave' of social-conscience films, such as *His Name Is Karn* (1973), to flourish in the 1970s. The permissiveness of the period was also evident from the release of films that challenged previous restrictions on sex and sexuality, with the representation of homosexuality becoming more acceptable in mainstream cinema.

*Tongpan* (1977), made after the events of 14 October, is emblematic of this newfound freedom of expression. The film is a realistic recreation of a 1975 seminar debating the construction of a dam on the Mekong River, and a dramatization of the life of the eponymous Tongpan, a farmer who attended the seminar with a group of students. It begins with a prologue that captures the euphoria of the victorious student movement following 14 October: "A military junta fled into exile, and the students from the city went into the countryside to tell the farmers." This period of political and artistic freedom was short-lived, however. In 1976, the military reasserted its authority in brutal fashion, with a massacre of students in Bangkok. *Tongpan*'s epilogue describes the attack, and the film's release was cancelled in the newly repressive atmosphere: "In October 1976, shortly after the shooting of this film, a violent coup d'etat of a magnitude never before seen in Thailand brought to an end Thailand's three-year experiment with democracy. An extensive purge followed the coup. Many of the participants in TONGPAN were jailed or sought by police."

## 6 October 1976

The massacre of students at Thammasat University on 6 October 1976 came almost exactly three years after the 14 October 1973 killings. Forty-six people died at Thammasat, and their corpses were desecrated by a baying mob. The incident began with a small group of students protesting against Thanom Kittikachorn's return from exile. On 25 September 1976, the police hanged two of the anti-Thanom activists (Choomporn Thummai and Vichai Kasripongsa) from a gate in Nakhon Pathom, and on 4 October 1976 a group of Thammasat students performed a reenactment of the hanging.

The right-wing newspaper *Dao Siam* reported the mock hanging on its front page on 6 October 1976, with a photograph of one of the students posing as a hanging victim. The image had allegedly been retouched, accentuating the man's resemblance to Crown Prince Vajiralongkorn, and the headline accused the students of hanging the prince in effigy.[198] The result was a devastating example of the power of propaganda, with the incendiary front-page condemnation of the students precipitating the massacre at Thammasat.

The short film *Friendship Ended with Mudasir Now Salman Is My Best Friend* (2018) makes indirect reference to 6 October using animated clips, with the *Powerpuff Girls* cartoon characters replaced by pictures of director Nawapol Thamrongrattanarit, the Red Bull logo, and the Scout emblem. These refer respectively to Nawaphon, the Red Gaurs, and the Village Scouts, the three paramilitary groups that joined the police and army in storming the university. As a cryptic clue to its political subtext, the film also includes a split-second image of the nondescript gate from which the two anti-Thanom activists were hanged.

The mock hanging, and the media's misrepresentation of it, remain taboo subjects. Pen-ek Ratanaruang's documentary *Paradoxocracy* (2013) describes the press coverage only in general terms, without specific reference to *Dao Siam* or the prince, indicating the episode's continued sensitivity. *Different Views, Death Sentence* (2011), a documentary commemorating the massacre, claims euphemistically that *Dao Siam* accused the students of expressing "severe ill-will to the Crown Prince." Even Thunska Pansittivorakul's otherwise uncompromising *The Terrorists* (2011) refers only indirectly to "the hanging of an important person in effigy."

*The Terrorists* examines the demonization of protesters in 1976 and 2010, when the government used scaremongering rhetoric as a pretext for military crackdowns. In both cases, the state defended the massacres as preemptive measures against supposed violent insurgencies. In 1976, a monk (Kittivuddho Bhikku) encouraged attacks on the students, whom he unashamedly dehumanized. *The Terrorists* quotes him justifying the killing of Communists: "It's the same as killing a fish to cook and offer it to the monks." Thunska's film develops this extraordinary pronouncement into an extended visual metaphor, with sequences filmed on a fishing trawler and at an aquarium. The short film *Don't Forget Me* (2003) also quotes the monk's "terrible words" and the drama *Time in a Bottle* (1991) portrays the resulting social vilification of the students: a doctor refuses to treat a massacre victim, leaving her to bleed to death.

Thunska made *The Terrorists* in the aftermath of the 2010 military crackdown, and the documentary is a passionate response to the cycle of recurring state oppression. It juxtaposes archive footage of the 1976 massacre with explicit male masturbation, suggesting that the military obtains sexual gratification from violence. In response to the events of 2010, the film includes a provocative caption asking the rhetorical question, "Who do you think has the power to order the soldiers to shoot?"

Several short documentaries have emphasized the human tragedy of the 6 October massacre. For her films *Silenced Memories* (2014) and *Respectfully Yours* (2016), Patporn Phoothong interviewed elderly relatives of the dead students, presenting the victims as individuals rather than the battered corpses visible in news coverage. In the intervening four decades since 6 October, the victims' families had rarely spoken about the massacre, though the director encouraged them to "break through the silence after all these years."[199] For her subsequent documentary, *The Two Brothers* (2017), she interviewed relatives of the two men hanged for protesting against the return of Thanom Kittikachorn. Again, their case had been forgotten for forty years, as Patporn's codirector Teerawat Rujenatham explained: "The truth of Oct 6 is still stuck in a different world."[200] Exceptionally, *The Two Brothers* also shows the *Dao Siam* headline and photograph that sparked the massacre.

The short documentary *"Red" at Last* (2006) is told from the first-person perspective of one 6 October victim (Manus Siansing). The film begins and ends with a fictitious voice-over from the dead man, and a survivor of the attack narrates flickering archive footage of the incident. *Don't Forget Me* (2003) is a multilayered documentary featuring archive footage of 6 October and scathing political captions, accompanied by the plaintive title song and a narration appropriated from an ethnographic documentary on the nomadic Mlabri tribe.[201] The voice-over describes the tribe's elaborate ceremonies and rituals, its tone and content providing an intentionally ironic counterpoint to the massacre footage.

Aside from documentaries, the events of 6 October have also been represented in narrative films, most prominently *By the Time It Gets Dark* (2016). In Anocha Suwichakornpong's film, a young director (Ann, a surrogate for Anocha herself) is making a biopic about a 6 October survivor, who describes the attackers "dragging the dead bodies out to burn them." Although the film was not censored on its original release, a screening to commemorate the massacre was blocked by the military government in 2017.

As in Anocha's *Mundane History* (2009), Apichatpong Weerasethakul's *Syndromes and a Century* (2006), and Prabda Yoon's *Someone from Nowhere* (2017), scenes in *By the Time It Gets Dark* are replayed to suggest history repeating itself. Ann's first session with the massacre survivor is later restaged, with the two women played by different actresses. Anocha self-reflexively questions the motivations of a director in tackling such a politically loaded event, as Ann confesses to her interviewee: "Your life is meaningful. A life worth living. Whereas me, I appropriate someone's life and turn it into a film." She also challenges the ethics of such appropriation, as another character advises Ann to let the film's subject write the script herself: "You should give it to her. She's a writer. And it's about her life, so it's her story." The film therefore acknowledges the inherent limitations involved in representing historical events in works of fiction.

*By the Time It Gets Dark* recreates a familiar photograph from 6 October, of a police officer aiming his gun while nonchalantly smoking a cigarette, though it begins by subverting the audience's expectations.[202] Students are shown lying on the ground, watched over by armed soldiers, though what initially appears to be a flashback to 6 October is, in fact, taking place on a movie soundstage. The sense of verisimilitude is further confounded when an off-screen voice (Ann, the director) instructs the soldiers to kick the students and point guns at them.

Other films use similar distancing devices when referencing 6 October. The Carabao biopic *Young Bao* (2013) and the horror movie *Colic* (2006) both recreate newspaper headlines about the event, though *Colic* is one of the more unusual interpretations of the massacre. In it, a general from 1976 (Arun Dvadasin) is reincarnated as a newborn baby, and the restless spirits of his victims torment the infant and his parents. The film suggests that, in the absence of legal accountability, karma is unavoidable. News of the event is conveyed via radio in *The Moonhunter* (2001). A short film by Manussak Dokmai (2010) includes photographs of the massacre shown on a digital camera's LCD screen.[203] In *Time in a Bottle* (1991), the incident is announced via a radio broadcast. The Malaysian film *River of Exploding Durians* (2014) shows 6 October newsreel footage via a projector, and features a brief play about the massacre by Malaysian students. The film's message is that Malaysians are permitted to study the historical controversies of other countries rather than their own, though this also applies in Thailand, as 6 October is omitted from the Thai national curriculum.

This practice of distancing the viewer also applies to films depicting other politically sensitive events. The short film *Re-presentation* (2007) shows the junta announcing the 2006 coup on television, radio, and via a *Bangkok Post* banner headline. In *Sunset at Chaophraya 2* (1993), news about 14 October 1973 is conveyed via newspapers, television, and radio. Kongdej Jaturanrasmee's *Sayew* (2003) begins with a radio news bulletin describing the buildup to 1992's 'Black May.' In Pimpaka Towira's road movie *The Island Funeral* (2015), radio news reports of the 2010 'redshirt' demonstrations contribute to an increasing sense of foreboding. In Kongdej's *Tang Wong* (2013), television news reports convey updates on the 'redshirt' protests. *October Sonata* (2009) features newspaper headlines about 14 October 1973. These representations of historical events, filtered through the news media, reflect how most Thais experienced the events themselves—as passive media consumers rather than participants or eyewitnesses.

On the other hand, directors who depict 6 October without such distancing techniques run the risk of censorship. Films that capture the full horror of the massacre, either through realistic reconstruction or archive footage, have been cut or banned. When Ing Kanjanavanit appealed against the banning of *Shakespeare Must Die* (2012), the Appeals Court upheld the ban in 2017 on the grounds that her recreation of 6 October could cause division in society.[204] The film includes a reenactment of an incident in which a man hit a hanging corpse with a folding chair, as depicted in a news photograph taken by Neal Ulevich that symbolizes the extreme violence and prejudice of the event. As Ing explained: "I want people to remember: this happened before. Do we really want this to happen again?"[205]

In 2012, shortly after the *Shakespeare Must Die* ban, a committee met to consider Ing's appeal against the decision. The meeting was attended by the culture minister herself, and its collective verdict, to uphold the ban, was reached via a confidential written ballot. One participant, attending on behalf of a ministerial department head, was required to vote against overturning the ban: "I had to vote no, because it was an instruction from my director. But if I could have voted freely, I would have voted yes."[206]

The censors advised Ing to replace the sequence with a new ending, in which concerned citizens discuss the nature of violence. Instead, five years after the ban, she appealed to the Supreme Court. As her producer Manit Sriwanichpoom says in *Censor Must Die* (2013), the massacre remains a forbidden subject for Thai cinema: "October 6 returns to haunt us, to be used as a tool. To justify the ban."

The short film *Friendship Ended with Mudasir Now Salman Is My Best Friend* (2018) also references the notorious Neal Ulevich photograph, with an animated clip from *The Simpsons* in which Bart hits Homer with a chair.[207] The hanging body from the photograph appears in animated form in the music video 'Democrazy' (2019).[208] It is represented by a mannequin in the music video 'Which Is My Country' (2018) by Rap Against Dictatorship. 'To Whom It May Concern' (2019), a music video by the same group, features folding chairs and a noose in another reference to the photograph. It also shows a soldier shooting a student. The music video 'The Devil of Time' (2019) includes footage of 6 October and the subsequent 'Black May' massacre.

The horror film *Haunted Universities* (2009) also recreates the violence of 6 October, and was censored as a result. In the segment 'The Elevator,' ghosts of student victims are gunned down by soldiers, one shot in the chest, and a second shot in the back as he tries to escape. Another horror movie, *Meat Grinder* (2009), includes archive footage of bodies being burned on 6 October, though this was deleted

THE UNTOUCHABLES: FILM AND POLITICS

in its entirety for the film's domestic release. (*Meat Grinder*'s title was also changed, among numerous other revisions.)[209]

In contrast, other films have avoided censorship by toning down the horror of the event. The comedy *Blue Sky of Love* (2009) begins with a police officer's flashback to 6 October, showing the student protests though not the violent retribution. *Young Bao* (2013) merely shows students lying on the ground, with soldiers watching over them, a scene also recreated at the start of *By the Time It Gets Dark* (2016). Chatrichalerm Yukol's *Somsri* (1985) includes a contemporary sequence in which riot police beat protesters, followed by a match cut to a 6 October flashback of a woman being beaten, though this is seen in black-and-white and lasts only a few seconds. A film by Bhandevanov Devakula (1986) also includes a black-and-white flashback. Although non-diegetic gunshots are heard repeatedly on the soundtrack, the violence depicted is limited to hand-to-hand combat.[210] The short film *Pirab* (2017) begins with a 6 October flashback in sound only, leaving the violence to the viewer's imagination. Thus, sanitized representations of the massacre, devoid of blood or death, are deemed acceptable, whereas real or realistic imagery is censored.

## Guilty Landscapes

Thanin Kraivichien, who was appointed prime minister after the 6 October massacre, overturned the liberal reforms of the previous regime. His intensified political censorship included literal book-burnings, which are dramatized in *October Sonata* (2009). He also revived the guerrilla war against Communist insurgents that had begun earlier in the decade. In Chatrichalerm's *Grounded God* (1975), a soldier refuses an order to kill Communists when he realizes that they are loyal patriots, not the terrorists of propagandist misrepresentation. The 6 October survivor in *By the Time It Gets Dark* (2016) describes "the methods with which the government clamped down on what they called "the terrorists." They'd be thrown out of helicopters or set on fire in oil barrels." (The title of Thunska Pansittivorakul's *The Terrorists* (2011) refers to this term's demonization of both Communists and 'redshirt' protesters.) Suspected Communists were indeed burned alive in red oil barrels, and Thunska alludes to these 'red barrel killings' in *Santikhiri Sonata* (2019) with a caption describing the elimination of subversives by "pushing them into a 'CXII Red Suitcase.'"

*Santikhiri Sonata* was filmed in Chiang Rai province, in the villages of Mae Salong and Hin Taek, whose names were changed by the government to draw a line under their sinister legacies. Mae Salong was renamed Santikhiri [hill of peace], and Hin Taek became Thoet Thai [honor Thailand], though they were previously sites of anti-Communist violence. The film highlights this violent heritage ("A lot of people were killed, including villagers") demonstrating that, despite their new names, they remain silent witnesses to their traumatic past. They are, to use Dutch artist Armando's term, 'guilty landscapes.'

Apichatpong Weerasethakul made several films in and around the village of Nabua, a similarly 'guilty landscape' with an equally loaded history to that of Santikhiri, as its inhabitants were among the first victims of the anti-Communist purge. In his short film *A Letter to Uncle Boonmee* (2009), a narrator recalls the area's past: "Soldiers once occupied this place. They killed and tortured the villagers and forced them to flee to the jungle." Thus, as Dana Linssen puts it, Apichatpong is projecting the past onto the present: "In Weerasethakul's films …

the landscape not only embodies trauma and becomes a witness, but also acts as a time machine."[211]

Apichatpong's *Uncle Boonmee Who Can Recall His Past Lives* (2010) was also filmed in the vicinity, and that film's most iconic image, a man-ape with glowing red eyes, also has a political subtext. The creature is Boonmee's young son, who became an outcast in the jungle, as did many Communists from Nabua and elsewhere. (The short film *Pirab* (2017) dramatizes a student's anguished decision to join the Communist insurgency, allowing the audience to empathize with the young man.) When the eponymous Boonmee confesses that he killed Communists, his sister reassures him that he did so "for the nation," a justification given by many who unquestioningly support the military regime. In fact, Apichatpong says that even his own family members are "totally submissive, no questions asked: disruption of the flow and unity is really a big deal."

On the surface, Chulayarnnon Siriphol's short film *Planking* (2012) is merely a series of comic tableaux, in which a prankster lies incongruously on the ground, oblivious to the bystanders around him. The film has further layers of meaning, however, relating not only to 6 October but also to Thai national identity itself. Each scene takes place at 8am or 6pm, when it is customary to stand while the national anthem is played. Planking rather than standing is therefore an irreverent example of the "disruption of the flow and unity" that Apichatpong described.

*Planking* also evokes specific episodes from Thai history, by appropriating politically charged 'guilty landscapes.' For example, one sequence was filmed at the Thammasat University football pitch, where hundreds of students were forced to lie during the 6 October massacre, as restaged in *By the Time It Gets Dark* (2016) and *Young Bao* (2013). The planking man in Chulayarnnon's film, adopting an identical pose on the same ground, provides a jarring reminder of the area's violent past. As the director explained, reenacting the event in the present day also alludes to the military's continuing interventions in Thai politics: "I think it's a good place to make a connection relating to history and the current situation." Chulayarnnon expresses political commentary indirectly through absurdist satire, and there are pragmatic reasons for his avoidance of explicit political statements:

> By using satire and sarcasm, many of my works focus on questioning the power of conservatives which try to control people through education, history, and propaganda.... We cannot talk about political conflict directly. It's too dangerous. Satire and sarcasm are tools to criticize these sensitive political conflicts in a subtle way instead of serious criticism. Moreover, satire and sarcasm can go through censorship easily.[212]

In 'Planetarium,' Chulayarnnon's segment of the dystopian *Ten Years Thailand* (2018), citizens under constant electronic surveillance demonstrate loyalty by standing to respect their leader. However, a group of rebels show their resistance by lying down; again, planking became a visible expression of nonconformity. In 'Catopia,' Wisit Sasanatieng's *Ten Years Thailand* segment, almost everyone has (CGI) cat's heads, and the few remaining humans are hunted down and killed, echoing the lynch mob mentality of the 6 October massacre and the subsequent anti-Communist purges.

Prabda Yoon's short film *Transmissions of Unwanted Pasts* (2019) anticipates an equally dystopian future, in which images of military massacres and other sensitive events broadcast via satellite are deleted by the military to erase such events from the collective public memory. The images are not shown, though the character who identified them lists the years in which they took place: "2014, 2010, 2008, 1992, 1976, 1973, 1932…." (These refer respectively to the 2014 coup, the 2010 'redshirt' crackdown, the 2008 police violence against 'yellowshirt' protesters, 'Black May' 1992, 6 October 1976, 14 October 1973, and the 1932 abolition of absolute monarchy.) She excitedly suggests that researchers could use the satellite data to study this secret history: "They might discover many new things, things that they were previously unaware of, or things that were never documented." Her boss has other ideas, however, and three soldiers destroy the transmissions.

Like Chulayarnnon Siriphol's satirical short films, *Transmissions of Unwanted Pasts* was made in response to the state education system, which Prabda describes as "pretty much propaganda, because they don't tell you the things they don't want you to know or to remember. So, there is that censorship always in Thai culture and society."[213] Artist Vasan Sitthiket commented on this process with *Delete Our History, Now!* (2008), a video in which he digitally erased photographs of the 6 October massacre, just as they are deleted from national historiography.[214]

## 'Black May' 1992

Whereas the 1973 and 1976 protests were organized by students, the 'Black May' 1992 demonstrations against Suchinda Kraprayoon consisted primarily of middle-class Bangkokians. Suchinda launched a coup in 1991, though after elections were held in 1992, parliament appointed him prime minister.[215] Approximately 200,000 protesters, led by Chamlong Srimuang, gathered at Sanam Luang on 17 May 1992. The following day, Chamlong was arrested and the violence escalated. On 20 May 1992, Rama IX summoned Suchinda and Chamlong to a televised meeting, at which he insisted on an end to the crisis. After this direct and public intervention, Suchinda agreed to an amnesty for Chamlong and the other protesters, though by that time fifty-two people had already been killed in clashes with the military. A drama about 'Black May' was filmed shortly after the event; its original title, which described the army as 'cold-blooded animals,' was changed to the less emotive 'Black May,' though ultimately its release was blocked altogether.[216]

Pen-ek Ratanaruang's political documentary *Paradoxocracy* (2013) omits the 'Black May' protests entirely, as its chronological narrative jumps forward twenty years from 6 October 1976 to the rise of Thaksin Shinawatra. However, the violence of 'Black May' was documented on VHS tapes distributed in the weeks after the events.[217] *Paradoxocracy* also glosses over the Tak Bai incident, the 'yellowshirt' versus 'redshirt' demonstrations, and the 2006 coup. Pen-ek argues that such issues are less significant in the long term— "when we look back into the journey of democracy, this thing will be like dust"—though a more pragmatic explanation is that such omissions are a safeguard against potential defamation lawsuits from surviving participants.

Kongdej Jaturanrasmee's comedy *Sayew* (2003) was self-censored to remove the names of the key players involved in 'Black May.' The film begins with a radio news bulletin announcing the buildup to the massacre, though Kongdej muted the soundtrack and edited the subtitles, a tactic subsequently used by Pen-ek for *Paradoxocracy* and Thunska Pansittivorakul for *Homogeneous, Empty Time* (2017). Thus, when the news anchor names Suchinda Kraprayoon, the audio is momentarily cut and the subtitles are replaced by asterisks.[218] Regardless of this elision, Thai audiences were well aware of Suchinda and the other participants, making the self-censorship an effective comic moment. Similarly, audiences reacted with laughter when Pen-ek muted the sound in *Paradoxocracy*: "They started laughing. And people knew right away what the deleted sound was about."

The short film *Bat in May* (1992) was an immediate response to 'Black May', and compares the chaos of the massacre with a colony of bats hunting for prey. A more recent and reflective short film, Taiki Sakpisit's *A Ripe Volcano* (2011), includes scenes shot at the Royal Hotel in Bangkok, which became a makeshift field hospital during 'Black May' and was stormed by the army. The dialogue-free film evokes the violence of the event through indirect signifiers, such as a fire engine (several of which were set ablaze during 'Black May'), creating an uncanny sense of foreboding. The short film *Re-presentation* (2007) includes news footage filmed inside the Royal Hotel during 'Black May' itself. (It also intercuts archive clips of 14 and 6 October with present-day footage of the Democracy Monument and Thammasat University.) The Royal Hotel has an equally macabre connection to the 6 October 1976 massacre, as *Homogeneous, Empty Time* (2017) reveals: "They hid the bodies of dead students in this hotel." With their static, contemplative shots of the hotel, *A Ripe Volcano* and *Homogeneous, Empty Time* acknowledge its politically charged atmosphere, just as Thunska's *Santikhiri Sonata* (2019), Chulayarnnon Siriphol's *Planking* (2012), and Apichatpong Weerasethakul's *A Letter to Uncle Boonmee* (2009) draw on the notorious local histories of Santikhiri, Bangkok, and Nabua respectively.

## Tak Bai

More than a thousand Muslim protesters were detained at Tak Bai on 25 October 2004, packed into pickup trucks, and driven to Pattani. During the five-hour journey, seventy-eight of the detainees died of suffocation.[219] Thaksin Shinawatra, prime minister at the time, announced a ban on video footage of the Tak Bai incident, though the journal *Same Sky* released a Tak Bai VCD.[220] Viewing this footage was such a revelation to Thunska that he included extracts from it in *This Area Is Under Quarantine* (2008). It was this material that led to the film's ban, as he explained at the time: "It's not because of nudity or depiction of the male organ but because of political issues. The ban is like we're stepping backward. We can't present the facts about things happening in our own country."[221]

Similar recordings of political violence have been distributed since the 1990s. VHS tapes of the 6 October massacre were released in 1996 to commemorate the twentieth anniversary of the event.[222] In the weeks following 'Black May,' vendors sold massacre videos that "serve as a collective memory of the tragic events."[223] Footage of the 14 October massacre was released on VHS in 1993 to commemorate its twentieth anniversary (*October 14 Thai Student Uprising 1973*).[224] 'Redshirt' groups produced various VCDs and DVDs documenting anti-'redshirt' violence in 2008 and 2010.[225]

*This Area Is Under Quarantine*, which is dedicated to the Tak Bai victims, begins with shots of a young Muslim man, and the camera lingers on his body. This teasingly erotic sequence is accompanied by a romantic song on the soundtrack, and the same song is played over footage of Tak Bai, which features the naked torsos of the male victims.[226] Thus, the film not only juxtaposes homoerotic imagery with political violence, it also draws a parallel between them, linking them aurally (through the recurring pop song) and visually (with the shared motif of the male body).

## Ta Sawang

Viewing the Tak Bai VCD was Thunska Pansittivorakul's political awakening, inspiring his commitment to documenting further examples of state violence: "I didn't know anything about politics.... I didn't question about the soldiers. But I started to learn about politics." Other directors also experienced a political enlightenment, a phenomenon known in Thai as *ta sawang*, in the post-Thaksin era.[227] Apichatpong Weerasethakul, for example, admitted that when *Syndromes and a Century* (2006) was censored, "I was old enough to understand things, but I didn't. I was a royalist. I was politically naïve." Similarly, Pen-ek Ratanaruang, speaking in 2014, described how a newfound political engagement led to *Paradoxocracy* (2013): "For somebody like me, who five years ago had no interest in politics at all—I was happily making my love stories here—to become very interested in politics." Yuthlert Sippapak, also a genre director, felt the same way a few years later: "I never gave a shit about politics. But right now, it's too much." Chulayarnnon Siriphol also became politically engaged following the 'redshirt' protests: "I questioned why they came to Bangkok, because most of the 'redshirt' people were from the countryside. And from that point, I turned to be interested in the political situation." Nontawat Numbenchapol's experience was much the same, and he was inspired to make *Boundary* (2013) after the 'redshirt' crackdown: "I was a teenager, a young man not interested in politics so much. But, at that time, it happened in the middle of Bangkok, and everything stopped and I couldn't go anywhere. I wanted to know what happened. I started to read lots of articles about that."

This political engagement led to the production of politically charged films, though some directors also became involved in direct political activism and party politics. Tanwarin Sukkhapisit was elected to parliament in 2019 as a Future Forward Party candidate, becoming Thailand's first transgender MP. Yuthlert also campaigned for Future Forward, and founded the No More General (NMG) campaign to protest against the 2014 coup and its aftermath. (Yuthlert's online activism led to legal threats against him, after he criticised the Constitutional Court and the military government on Twitter.)[228] Ing Kanjanavanit and Vasan Sitthiket both spoke at anti-government rallies in the buildup to the 2014 coup. Vasan, a painter and video artist, has a long history of political engagement, stemming from his reaction to the 14 October 1973 massacre. In 2004, he even launched his own political party, the Artist Party, and stood as a candidate in the general election the following year.[229]

## 'Yellowshirts'

Thaksin Shinawatra won landslide election victories in 2001 and 2005, and transformed Thailand's political landscape, though his populist agenda was perceived as a threat to established power structures.[230] He was also accused of corruption, after relaxing the corporate ownership law days before selling his own communications company (Shin Corp.) in 2006. Reaction to the sale was swift: Sondhi Limthongkul and Chamlong Srimuang formed the People's Alliance for Democracy (PAD) and organized anti-Thaksin protests attended by thousands of middle-class Bangkokians. (The PAD movement advocated replacing an elected prime minister with an appointed one, in contrast to Chamlong's pro-democracy 'Black May' protests.) The demonstrators all wore yellow shirts, symbolizing their loyalty to the king and, by extension, implying Thaksin's disloyalty. (In the short film *Re-presentation* (2007), all color is desaturated except the yellow of the shirts worn by PAD supporters.)

Although his popularity decreased during his second term, and the PAD openly campaigned for his removal, direct criticism of Thaksin was rare in films made during his premiership. The comedy *Woak Wak* (2004) satirized Thaksin's son Panthongtae, though the film was cut after a police investigation, and its title was changed, to downplay the reference to Panthongtae.[231] Thunska Pansittivorakul's *This Area Is Under Quarantine* (2008) condemns Thaksin's handling of the Tak Bai incident, though the film was made two years after he left office. Ing Kanjanavanit's documentary *Citizen Juling* (2008) is hyperbolic in its criticism of Thaksin, as an interviewee says: "We talk of Hitler … But villagers, all citizens nowadays fear PM Thaksin 10 times more." However, like Thunska's film, it was released two years after his premiership. In part four of Ing's documentary *Bangkok Joyride* (2019) a protester says that Thaksin is "worse than Hitler." The animated short film *Tossaliam* (2006) also compares him to the German dictator.[232]

Ing's *Shakespeare Must Die* (2012) is a contemporary interpretation of *Macbeth*, with its title character, renamed Mekhdeth, inspired by Thaksin. The comparison is noted self-referentially when a policeman asks: "Your actor looks like our Dear Leader. Is this intentional?" Scenes of protesters demonstrating against Mekhdeth recall the anti-Thaksin PAD movement: the protesters shout *ok pai!* [get out!], and *Thaksin ok pai!* was the PAD's rallying cry. The film's protesters condemn their leader's sanctioning of extrajudicial killings, a reference to Thaksin's 2003 anti-methamphetamine campaign. Ultimately, the protesters are infiltrated by assassins listed in the credits as 'men in black,' a term also used to describe the armed agitators at 'redshirt' rallies. *Shakespeare Must Die* received state funding when Thaksin was out of government, though by the time it was completed Yingluck Shinawatra was in office and the film was banned.

Ing's *Bangkok Joyride* documented real-life anti-Thaksin protesters, though there are also several pro-Thaksin documentaries. *Democracy after Death* (2016) is biased in his favor, and is unusual in endorsing not only the 'redshirt' campaign but also the former prime minister himself. The film notes sympathetically that Thaksin "was forced to leave and has had to remain outside Thailand" though it neglects to mention the reason for his self-imposed exile: a conviction for corruption. Documentaries distributed by 'redshirt' organizations are equally partisan. A VCD about the 2010 massacre, for instance, summarily dismisses credible rumors of 'men in black' as "outlandish tales … concocted and circulated, to discredit Red Shirt demonstrators."[233]

Thaksin filed punitive libel lawsuits against his media critics, which may explain filmmakers' reluctance to criticize him while he was prime minister. Pimpaka Towira's documentary *The Truth Be Told* (2007) highlights one such defamation case, against Supinya Klangnarong, a journalist who investigated Thaksin's business dealings. The director, interviewing Supinya and her family, describes her as "a brave woman who dares to fight Thaksin." The film also serves as a record of the PAD demonstrations, and it ends the day after the 2006 coup. Supinya was cleared of defamation, though in a voice-over she reflects that she and the protesters are pawns in a larger game: "There's always someone waiting to exploit the people's fight.... We want the power to be with the people, but when we protest, the power falls into someone else's hand. And they use that power to continue the cycle of corruption."

Years later, when Pen-ek Ratanaruang included Thaksin in his documentary *Paradoxocracy* (2013), its distributor asked him rhetorically: "How can you put a film with Thaksin in the cinema?" Sulak Sivaraksa makes a similar point in the film itself, saying: "Your movie shouldn't waste too much time on Thaksin." This line received applause at screenings in Bangkok. Coverage of Thaksin no longer posed a legal challenge, though after prolonged political unrest metropolitan audiences had developed Thaksin fatigue.

## 2006 Coup d'état

Thaksin dissolved parliament in 2006, and an election was held, though it was boycotted by the opposition and later invalidated. Meanwhile, PAD protesters lay the groundwork for a coup, which was launched by General Sonthi Boonyaratglin on 19 September 2006. (Exactly the same chain of events reoccurred in 2014, when Thaksin's sister, Yingluck, was prime minister.)

Less than a year after the coup, the Short Film and Video Festival provided a timely opportunity for filmmakers to comment on the junta. The festival's founder, Chalida Uabumrungjit, directed *Silence in D Minor* (2006), which challenges those who acquiesced to the coup. Anocha Suwichakornpong's *3-0* (2006) features footage of a peaceful anti-coup demonstration and a boy receiving physiotherapy.

Like *Mundane History* (2009), the film uses physical disability as a metaphor for political paralysis.[234] Prap Boonpan's *Letter from the Silence* (2006) includes a letter written by a taxi driver (Nuamthong Praiwan) who crashed his cab into a tank to protest against the junta (an act of martyrdom that also inspired the documentary *Democracy after Death* ten years later). *Bangkok Tanks* (2007) juxtaposes the transcript of a superficial online chat with dramatic CNN footage of the coup. Similarly, *In the Night of the Revolution* (2007), in which students attend a drunken party on the night of the coup, is another commentary on misplaced priorities. *19.09.2549* (2008), whose title refers to the date of the coup (2006 being 2549 BE), questions whether the junta's pledges to eradicate political corruption were fulfilled. Tanwarin Sukkhapisit's short film *I'm Fine* (2008) shows the director sitting in a metal cage near Bangkok's Democracy Monument, oblivious to her captivity, in a commentary on Thai society's tolerance of authoritarianism.[235]

There are also humorous metaphors for the coup, with the junta personified by a teacher in *Demockrazy* (2007), a bus passenger in *Bus Lane* (2007) and a toy duck in *The Duck Empire Strike Back* [*sic*] (2006). *The Love Culprit* (2006) draws a comical analogy between repetitive karaoke lyrics, *lakhon* remakes, and the cycle of coups. Pen-ek Ratanaruang makes the same point, comparing coups to cinematic remakes: "We've had twenty-one coups d'état. As many versions as *Nang Nak*! The coup d'état is exactly the same: they keep remaking it in different versions."

Thaksin's Thai Rak Thai party was dissolved by the Constitutional Court in 2007, though a proxy funded by him, the People's Power Party (PPP), won a general election later that year. The prospects of a PPP government and Thaksin's eventual return are the subjects of a heated political conversation in the short film *National Anthem* (2008). The PAD returned to the streets of Bangkok in 2008, occupying Government House to campaign against Thaksin's continued political influence. Prime minister and PPP leader Samak Sundaravej was disqualified by the Constitutional Court, and the PPP replaced him with Thaksin's brother-in-law, Somchai Wongsawat. The PAD escalated its campaign, briefly blockading parliament, though they were dispersed by riot police using tear gas. They also occupied Bangkok's Suvarnabhumi international airport. In an apparent attempt to placate the PAD, the Constitutional Court disqualified prime minister Somchai and dissolved the PPP.

The docudrama *Agrarian Utopia* (2009) is bookended by footage of fiery political events in Bangkok. In an early scene, two farmers attend a PPP rally, though one loses interest as Samak begins his speech. As the film ends, the farmers return to the city, where 'yellowshirt' and 'redshirt' rallies are taking place. Visually, the two sequences differ from the film's otherwise bucolic evocation of rural life, though the contrast also highlights social disparities, such as the gap between poor farmers in the traditional agricultural sector and middle-class urbanites in Bangkok, where national development is centralized. The short documentary *Lice in the Wonderland* (2014) also contrasts rural farmers with Bangkok's political rallies, in this case, footage of protesters demonstrating against Yingluck Shinawatra. The film begins with a farmer searching for crabs, in a reference to Yingluck's nickname Poo [crab]. The interviewees are evenly split (both pro- and anti-Yingluck), though shots of crabs scuttling in a bucket and a caption describing Thaksin as "a fugitive accused of corruption" indicate the filmmaker's political position.

Anocha Suwichakornpong's *Mundane History* (2009) includes double-exposed footage of a 'yellowshirt' demonstration in Bangkok. A PAD banner proclaims that the campaign is entering its final stage, while a voice-over suggests that it (and much else besides) is fizzling out, like the remnants of a dying star: "After it explodes, the star goes dark and leaves behind a trail of gas and dust where it once shone bright."

The country was politically polarized both before and after the coup, with Thaksin's supporters defending his democratic mandate and the PAD protesting against his corrupt self-interest. This volatile atmosphere was captured in the short films of Prap Boonpan, such as *The White Short Film* (2009), in which the PAD's campaign is discussed. Prap's most powerful film, *The Bangkok Bourgeois Party* (2007), is an indictment of the PAD's extremist rhetoric: middle-class Bangkokians wearing yellow shirts murder a man merely because he disagrees with their ideology. Less than a year later, Prap's dystopian satire became a reality, when Narongsak Krobtaisong was "beaten to death by members of the PAD" in 2008, as documented in *Democracy after Death* (2016). Another short film, *The Pob's House* (2011), also depicts the ultimate consequences of social polarization: villagers beat a grandmother to death, believing her to be an evil spirit. Their attack recalls the 6 October 1976 massacre, though the film was also a reaction to the 2010 'redshirt' crackdown. As the director explains in the film's epilogue, extreme prejudice is endemic: "Structural violence and cultural violence are buried in people's minds."

In contrast to the dystopia of *The Bangkok Bourgeois Party* and *The Pob's House*, Chulayarnnon Siriphol's short film *Karaoke: Think Kindly* (2009) offers a vision of social and political harmony, with 'redshirts' and 'yellowshirts' hugging each other. The film was named after a Buddhist song, which is played with onscreen karaoke lyrics, and after the song finishes it is played again, this time accompanied by images of 'redshirt' protests. The message, that reconciliation can be achieved despite the conflict, is sincere though idealistic. Similarly, *Red Movie* (2010) ends with John Lennon's 'Imagine' and optimistic captions calling for unity and democracy.[236] More realistically, in the short film *The Taxi Meter* (2014), a 'redshirt'-supporting taxi driver and his anti-Thaksin passenger engage in a civil debate and agree to disagree.

*Karaoke: Think Kindly* concludes with a photograph of the Democracy Monument under construction, showing the unfinished structure surrounded by scaffolding. As Chulayarnnon says, the implication is that Thai democracy itself is incomplete: "Today there are many incidents that make us question: do we really have democracy? So, I think that image can represent our situation at this time." Another short film, *Re-presentation* (2007), ends in a similar way, with an artist unsuccessfully attempting to draw the Democracy Monument. As in *Karaoke: Think Kindly*, the implication is that democracy remains elusive, though *Re-presentation* goes further still. The artist tears up his sketch, revealing a drawing of a Rama V statue on the page beneath, a reference to the established hierarchies underlying Thai democracy. Hockhacker's music video 'Citizen' (2020) ends with the Democracy Monument on fire, symbolizing Thailand's political crisis. Similarly, in *Homogeneous, Empty Time* (2017) Thunska Pansittivorakul shows the Democracy Monument upside down, a metaphor for the topsy-turvy state of Thai politics.

## 'Redshirts'

After the PPP's dissolution in 2008, Abhisit Vejjajiva's Democrat Party assumed office in coalition with other opposition parties, in a deal negotiated by the military. Naturally, this transfer of power without an election provoked demonstrations by Thaksin's supporters who formed the United Front for Democracy against Dictatorship (UDD) and wore red shirts to differentiate themselves from the PAD. During the Songkran festivities in 2009, the UDD protests turned violent, with an attack on prime minister Abhisit's motorcade.[237] This event was recreated in Wisit Sasanatieng's film *The Red Eagle* (2010) released the following year, a cinematic restaging of a specific political incident comparable to the reenactments of photographs from 6 October 1976 in *By the Time It Gets Dark* (2016) and *Shakespeare Must Die* (2012).

*The Red Eagle* is also notable as a rare commercial film with a prime minister as a central character, and for his unsympathetic characterization as a politician who abandons his principles once he assumes office. The fictional prime minister campaigns on an anti-nuclear platform, though once elected he reneges on a pledge to halt construction of a nuclear power plant. Wisit insists: "I didn't set out to criticise any particular Prime Minister.... I only want to mock those who began as good guys fighting for the poor, then, like Darth Vader, they become villains once they have power."[238] That sounds awfully like a description of Thaksin Shinawatra. (A *lakhon* directed by Yuthlert Sippapak, broadcast in 2012, also featured an unscrupulous politician modelled on Thaksin. The character uses black magic to obtain a satellite concession, a thinly veiled reference to Thaksin's Shin Corp. satellite. The final three episodes of the twelve-part series were not televised.)[239]

A fictional prime minister also appears in the disaster movie *13–04–2022 Tsunami* (2009), though in this case the PM is an absurdly idealized figure.[240] He selflessly declares his willingness to sacrifice his career for the greater good: "The lives and safety of my people are more valuable than my assumed position…. I'm willing to lose everything in exchange for the lives of my people." He even becomes an action hero, declaring "I must be with my people when they need me most" before rescuing a busload of drowning children, while a news reporter praises "our Prime Minister's fearless courage."

UDD demonstrations feature in Kongdej Jaturanrasmee's *Tang Wong* (2013) via periodic television news reports, though otherwise their cinematic appearances are limited to short films, which are subject to less commercial or regulatory pressure. In *This Way* (2010), for instance, pedestrians are inconvenienced by the roadblocks around the protest camps, a commentary on the tendency of some residents to focus on the obstruction caused by the protesters in the shopping district rather than the underlying causes of the protests. In another observation of political apathy, the short film *The Six Principles* (2010) features vox pop interviews with people who are unaware of the 1932 coup, followed by scenes shot at UDD rallies, implying that the coup-makers' aims have not yet been achieved.

In 2010, the UDD drew thousands of protesters to Bangkok. On 10 April 2010, the army opened fire on UDD protesters at Makkhawan Bridge and Khao San Road. UDD protest camps at Lumpini Park and Ratchaprasong were surrounded by military forces on 14 May 2010, leading to prolonged street battles throughout the city. The short film *Shooting Stars* (2010) is an abstract representation of the conflict, featuring the sounds of falling bullet casings. Another short film, *Tear of Child* [*sic*] (2014), also represents the incident aurally. In it, a child watches television, and the picture shows only white noise, though the sounds of the crackdown can be heard. Thunska Pansittivorakul filmed some of the clashes for his documentary *The Terrorists* (2011) and he witnessed people being shot: "When I think about what I did at that time, at Soi Rangnam, I scare myself, because that area was really dangerous. When I was shooting that clip at Soi Rangnam, I didn't know who they were, but they were shooting guns at the people.... But at that time, I needed to keep shooting. I must keep shooting."

On 19 May 2010, the army launched an assault, with armored personnel carriers, on the UDD demonstration at Lumpini Park. Soldiers then advanced on the main Ratchaprasong rally site, in what the documentary *Democracy after Death* (2016) calls "the most brutal political massacre in Thai history." Six wounded protesters were shot by military snipers while they sheltered at the Pathum Wanaram temple, as documented in the short film *I Remember* (2011). After the protest leaders surrendered, arsonists destroyed several nearby buildings, including the Siam cinema and the Zen department store. The ruined cinema is shown in the short film *Awareness* (2014), and the burning store appears in the short film *Ghost of Centralworld* (2012) and Ing Kanjanavanit's *Shakespeare Must Die* (2012).

Captions in Nontawat Numbenchapol's documentary *Boundary* (2013) describe the aftermath of the crackdown, including the number of victims: "Almost 100 people were killed."[241] This statistic, which the censors claimed was unproven and contentious, was one of the reasons for the film's initial ban. (Eighty-seven people died, making 'almost 100' a reasonable approximation.)[242] The powerful short film *Rajprasong* (2012) ends with a black screen and eighty-seven gunshots—one for each victim.

Several of the victims' stories were told in short films that "embody the loss of life through tribute and memorialization."[243] In *Galanusathi* (2010), for instance, a monk learns that his brother was killed during the 2010 crackdown, and he is left to deal with his grief alone. In *We Will Forget It Again* (2010), a victim of the crackdown returns as a ghost, a trickle of blood running down her face, to be reunited with her surviving daughters. The short film *Hush, Tonight the Dead Are Dreaming Loudly* (2019) also features the ghost of a crackdown victim, who cannot come to terms with his death. (In both cases, these are sentimental dramas with corporeal ghosts, rather than horror films with ethereal spirits.) *Women in Democracy* (2009) features the widow of a UDD protester, with scrolling text describing celebrity gossip and political history. Like *The Two Brothers* (2017), *Respectfully Yours* (2016), and *"Red" at Last* (2006) these films personalize the conflict, highlighting the tragic individual impacts of a national crisis.

Chulayarnnon Siriphol's documentary *A Brief History of Memory* (2010) also focuses on a single victim—Yuthakarn Joichoichos, a teenager who was shot by UDD protesters at Bangkok's Nang Loeng market in 2009.[244] Yuthakarn's mother, Supatra Chotikamol, describes her grief in a voice-over, accompanied by black-and-white images of the local community. As in *Karaoke: Think Kindly* (2009), Chulayarnnon conscientiously included both sides of the political divide: "I didn't want to show the victims of only one side, because it seems that the Nang Loeng community are against the 'redshirts'.... I also included the 'redshirt' victims from Ratchaprasong, to talk about the victims of politics."

Thus, in the interests of balance, *A Brief History of Memory* concludes with footage of a vigil for 'redshirt' victims. However, the film's moving narration serves as a reminder that the 'redshirts' themselves instigated violence at Nang Loeng. Also in 2010, Chulayarnnon directed the satirical *Thai Contemporary Politics Quiz*, a parody of university examinations with multiple-choice questions. As in the political crisis itself, Chulayarnnon's politics quiz has no easy answers: "Maybe some audiences are looking for the correct answer from me, but I said: 'It depends on you, your perspective and your belief in political ideology.'"

## 'Shutdown Bangkok'

Yingluck Shinawatra, Thaksin's sister, won a general election in 2011. Protests against her began the following year, when her government proposed a reconciliation bill that was widely regarded as an attempt to rehabilitate Thaksin's reputation. A demonstration against the bill plays a minor role in Ing Kanjanavanit's documentary *Censor Must Die* (2013), as the director's appointment with a senator is delayed due to PAD protesters surrounding parliament. Concerns about the bill intensified when an amnesty for political crimes—a pretext to quash Thaksin's corruption conviction—was approved by parliament. In November 2013, opposition politician Suthep Thaugsuban formed the People's Democratic Reform Committee (PDRC) to protest against it. Yingluck withdrew the amnesty bill, though the PDRC's demonstrations against her continued. Suthep escalated the demonstrations in January 2014 with a 'Shutdown Bangkok' campaign, following the playbook of the PAD. In fact, the events of 2014 were a carbon copy of the 2006 crisis: the dissolution of parliament, a general election boycotted by the Democrat Party and later invalidated, anti-Thaksin protesters causing disruption to provoke a military intervention, followed by a coup d'état.

Ing's documentary *Bangkok Joyride* provides an exhaustive record of the PDRC protests. Filmed entirely on her iPhone, it was released in five feature-length chapters between 2017 and 2020, each covering an increasingly narrower time period.[245] Ing did not submit the film to the censors, as they had ruled that her previous documentary, *Censor Must Die* (2013), was exempt from classification. Although *Bangkok Joyride* contains only raw footage of the protesters and clips from television news reports, it is not a neutral account of the events it documents. Ing can occasionally be heard from behind the camera, wishing the protesters luck. For example, in part four she tells a demonstrator, "We fight the exact same battle," and in parts three and four she appears on the protest stage, critiquing international media coverage of the demonstrations.

*Democracy after Death* (2016), which emphasizes the anti-democratic nature of the PDRC's campaign, provides a counterpoint to *Bangkok Joyride*. The documentary revisits the 2014 general election, which was disrupted by a combination of PDRC sabotage and a lethargic Election Commission (or, as *Democracy after Death* describes it, the "anti-election commission"). Likewise, the short documentary *This Film Has Been Invalid* [sic] (2014) comments on the dysfunctional election process. It was filmed at a polling station that remained closed during the 2014 election, disenfranchising the local electorate. The film ends by recognizing the ultimate futility of the election: "This country is still ruled by military dictatorship."

Chulayarnnon Siriphol filmed PDRC protests for *100 Times Reproduction of Democracy* (2019), a commentary on the repetitive nature of Thai protests and coups. His short film *Myth of Modernity* (2014) also offers a critical commentary on the PDRC, by superimposing a floating neon pyramid over the protest rallies. This pyramid, a recurring motif in Chulayarnnon's films, is a distinctly modern religious icon, lacking the ornate decoration traditionally associated with such objects. The suggestion is that polarized Thai politics, like religious iconography, is losing its nuance and complexity. The film equates the PDRC's mass rallies with the worship of this sacred pyramid, presenting them as communal reveries rather than political events.

Another of Chulayarnnon's short films, *Here Comes the Democrat Party* (2014), features news footage of PDRC protesters singing upbeat songs, emphasizing the festive (rather than political) atmosphere of the rallies and, as in *Myth of Modernity*, presenting them as collective emotional experiences rather than ideological gatherings. It also comments on the hypocrisy of Democrat Party MPs, who appeared at PDRC rallies despite distancing themselves from the movement's undemocratic agenda. As the director explained, "the Democrat Party said they were not a part of the PDRC, but we saw that many politicians were part of the PDRC. So, it's kind of sarcastic, to make fun of the protests and question the politicians." The short film *Shut Sound* (2014) also links the protests with music, featuring footage of PDRC rallies accompanied by the tune from a Thai love song.[246]

Other films have also used musical soundtracks as commentaries on political events. The short films *Don't Forget Me* (2003) and Chulayarnnon's *Karaoke: Think Kindly* (2009) both use contemplative songs to emphasize the respective gravity of the 6 October 1976 massacre and the 'yellowshirt'/'redshirt' protests. *Young Bao* (2013) underscores its recreation of 6 October with a socially conscious ballad.[247] A documentary on the 'Black May' massacre uses music more subversively: footage of soldiers beating protesters is accompanied by an ironic Carabao song praising the government.[248] Thunska Pansittivorakul also uses music as a counterpoint to political violence. In *The Terrorists* (2011) and *This Area Is Under Quarantine* (2008), romantic songs accompany footage of the 6 October and Tak Bai massacres, respectively. In *Santikhiri Sonata* (2019), one of Rama IX's compositions is repurposed as an ode to a human rights activist shot by the military.[249]

## 2014 Coup d'état

General Prayut Chan-o-cha launched a coup on 22 May 2014, and was later appointed prime minister.[250] The coup was anticipated by *Auntie Has Never Had a Passport*, a short film released in 2014; and by Ing Kanjanavanit's *Shakespeare Must Die*, made two years earlier. *Auntie Has Never Had a Passport*, a comedy about the ramifications of the PDRC's protests, accurately predicted a "supersonic coup d'état that would drag us way back." *Shakespeare Must Die* foretold the junta's propaganda tactics with uncanny precision. In the film, children sing "Dear Leader brings happy-ocracy!" and in 2014, Prayut released the propaganda song 'Returning Happiness to the Thai Kingdom.'

The title of the short film *I Wish the Whole Country Would Sink Under Water* (2014), filmed on the day of the coup, expresses a widespread sense of hopelessness regarding the country's political regression. The title of another short film, *Bangkok Dystopia* (2017), also encapsulates the pessimistic post-coup climate, and the film captures the paranoid atmosphere in Bangkok, a capital city in which soldiers patrol the streets. In Chulayarnnon Siriphol's short film *Blinding* (2014), a man hides his identity while intentionally violating the junta's curfew order. Like Chulayarnnon's *Planking* (2012), this is cinema as subversive performance art. The short film *Night Watch* (2014) highlights the extent of the military's media control. Channel hopping by a television viewer reveals almost every station broadcasting the same junta announcement. In the short film *Democrazy.mov* (2019), a cellphone signal is jammed by a 44 GHz frequency, in reference to article 44 of the interim constitution, which granted absolute power to the junta. (Like the short film *Demockrazy* (2007), the documentary *Paradoxocracy* (2013), and the 2004 Bangkok Experimental Film Festival's strapline 'Bangkok Democrazy,' the film's title puns on the undemocratic nature of Thai 'democracy.')

In Yuthlert Sippapak's horror film *Seven Boy Scouts* (2020), the seven scouts share their nicknames with Thai politicians—Tu (Prayut Chan-o-cha), Pom (Prawit Wongsuwan), Thep (Suthep Thaugsuban), Mark (Abhisit Vejjajiva), Nu (Wissanu Krea-ngam), Tae (Mongkolkit Suksintharanon), and Noo (Anutin Charnvirakul)—and a girl scout shares her nickname, Poo, with Yingluck Shinawatra. The boy scout characters, representing the seven deadly sins, all die as a consequence of their transgressions. Yuthlert's intention was to make a political point within a commercial genre movie: "It's a political satire. Finding a way to fight back in a film in the mainstream. I put the names of the politicians, seven boys.... Try to let the audience imagine: when the bad boy becomes prime minister, what's gonna happen. But I kill them all."

When the studio pulled the plug on *Seven Boy Scouts*, Yuthlert responded with an even more direct and topical political statement: in *The Last Dictator* (2020), a Thai director becomes infected with the COVID-19 coronavirus and pledges that, before he dies, he will kill Prayut. The fictional director is, of course, a proxy for Yuthlert himself, who campaigned against Prayut's government.

Whereas Thunska Pansittivorakul directed *This Area Is Under Quarantine* (2008) several years after Tak Bai, the military massacre it condemned, his documentary *Homogeneous, Empty Time* (2017) was released while the 2014 coup was still in force, making it a timely and powerful excoriation of military rule. Its ideological message is conveyed from the very first frame, with an opening drone shot that pulls back from a giant poster of Rama IX while a broken pledge from the junta's song 'Returning Happiness to the Thai Kingdom' ("We will keep our promise and won't let you wait for too long") repeats on the soundtrack like a stuck record. Chulayarnnon Siriphol's video installation *Give Us a Little More Time* (2020) takes its name from the song's chorus, and includes a sample on its soundtrack.[251] The short film *Ghost Rabbit and the Casket Sales* (2015) appropriated the same song, showing a DJ sampling snippets from it with a cassette recorder.

Prabda Yoon's *Someone from Nowhere* (2017), a sustained metaphor for the coup, was also released during military rule. The film is set almost entirely in a condominium unit, and it begins with the female occupant's morning routine: swimming, greeting various neighbors, and taking a shower. She then discovers an injured man outside her front door, and telephones the condominium staff and the police for help. Meanwhile, the man claims to be the unit's rightful owner, demanding: "The only thing I want is to have this place back." She insists that he is lying, and replies: "I won't let you people get away with this atrocity." However, her deeds of ownership are blank pages, and the assistance she called for never arrives. The analogy to the 2014 coup is clear: like Yingluck Shinawatra, the woman is intimidated by a powerful interloper (the man, representing the military); she has no legal defense (her deeds were erased, just as the constitution was abrogated); and she receives no external support (Thailand's judicial system did not intervene to prevent the coup).

The film's political subtext becomes increasingly direct, culminating with the national anthem playing as the man and woman stab each other. It also highlights the cyclical nature of the military's interventions and the country's constant tensions between civilian and military rule. The man places the woman's unconscious body outside and assumes occupancy of the condo, going through the same morning routine as the woman. He then discovers her outside the door, whereupon she claims to be the rightful owner and he insists that she is mistaken. By implication, the two protagonists have relived the same debate, with alternating roles, many times over. Their apparent amnesia echoes the national tendency to gloss over repeated acts of political violence, as the title of the short film *We Will Forget It Again* (2010) also implies.

*Someone from Nowhere*'s title ostensibly refers to the injured man, as the woman occupies the condominium when the film begins and the audience's sympathies therefore initially lie with her. However, there are suggestions that the woman is the interloper: the neighbors do not acknowledge her during her morning routine, for example, while they readily converse with the man. One neighbor tells him that there has been no good news for eighty years, suggesting that the condo's residents harken back to the pre-democratic era before the 1932 coup, and therefore that they accept him (the symbol of authoritarianism) rather than her (representing a disruption of the traditional status quo).

In 2018, with the junta still in power four years after the coup, Rap Against Dictatorship released their single 'Which Is My Country,' a song condemning political corruption, military impunity, and state violence. Whereas anti-coup films and artworks disguise their messages with coded metaphors, 'Which Is My Country' is uncompromising in its criticism of the junta. The lyrics include a litany of political scandals, and the rappers make no concessions to Thailand's culture of conformity, deference, and emotional restraint. This anthemic song succinctly and directly encapsulated the frustration of anti-coup protesters whose dissent was otherwise suppressed. Chulayarnnon Siriphol's *100 Times Reproduction of Democracy* (2019) includes a live performance of the song, juxtaposed with Children's Day footage of toddlers posing with tanks and military weapons, demonstrating the inculcation of militarism at an early age.

Comparable artistic expressions of anger towards the state, in Thunska Pansittivorakul's documentaries, for example, did not cross over to mainstream audiences. 'Which Is My Country,' on the other hand, benefitted from its popular modes of expression (rap) and distribution (online streaming): the song's YouTube video went viral, being viewed more than ten million times in its first week of release. The video, dedicated to "all victims from all state crimes," ends with a battered mannequin hanging from a tree, representing the corpse in Neal Ulevich's photograph of the 6 October 1976 massacre.

Following the coup, political censorship and surveillance increased dramatically. Soldiers were stationed in the lobby of the Paragon Cineplex cinema during the Bangkok premiere of the Hollywood film *The Hunger Games* (2014), as student activists had reappropriated the film's three-finger salute as an anti-junta gesture.[252] A few weeks after the coup, a planned screening of *Nineteen Eighty-Four* (1984) was cancelled "after police intimidated organisers with suggestions that it violated the law."[253] A showing of Anocha Suwichakornpong's *By the Time It Gets Dark* (2016) was prevented by the junta in 2017; and a 2015 university screening of Nontawat Numbenchapol's documentary *Boundary* (2013) was cancelled following an order from the military, giving Nontawat's film the unique distinction of being banned twice.[254]

Chapter 4

# Saffron Cinema: Monks in the Movies

*"Undignified portrayals of Buddhists in films have been*
*somewhat policed by Thai censors."*[255]

## From Reverence to Ridicule

Religion is one of the three traditional pillars of Thai society, alongside the monarchy and the nation itself, and respect for religion has been a prerequisite for film distribution in Thailand since the silent era. In fact, the first film to be banned from Thai screens was prohibited on religious grounds. *The Light of Asia*, a dramatization of the life of the Buddha, was banned in 1925, and was finally screened in Thailand more than eighty years later.[256] Thai filmmakers have conventionally portrayed Buddhist monks as sources of moral and spiritual strength, and Kong Rithdee summarizes this reverential tradition: "In the movies from the 1960s and '70s, monks were always depicted as the ultimate moral force. They're the pillars in the village community, they mediate, end violence and find resolutions, and of course they purge demons and restore order."[257]

This long-standing characterization—that of the wise and benevolent monk—was partly a reflection of the high esteem in which monks were held by society at a time before the monkhood had become tarnished by sex and corruption scandals.[258] However, it was also a result of strict censorship: "Directors couldn't portray monks in a bad light because of censorship—that has always been the case. In the past, even scenes of a monk running away from ghosts wouldn't pass the cut."[259]

Given such stringent restrictions, the banning of Ing Kanjanavanit's provocative *My Teacher Eats Biscuits* in 1998 was hardly surprising. A religious satire in which a cult worships a dog, the film features a monk who advocates sex with male corpses. Nevertheless, the tone is clearly parodic, and the director maintains that the authorities overreacted: "It was a witch hunt, and there was no reason. It was like *Alice in Wonderland*. It was completely insane."[260] *My Teacher Eats Biscuits* is very rarely screened, either in Thailand or elsewhere, and has been called "a film so controversial that it has been 'disappeared' from history."[261] The short film *Molding Clay* (2018) also includes a highly provocative sequence, of a monk receiving oral sex from a rent boy, though it was screened under the censors' radar at the Thai Film Archive.[262]

The lack of negative representations of monks in mainstream cinema reinforced the public's respect for the monkhood. Thus, society was all the more scandalized when monks were accused of sexual and financial impropriety. One such case dominated the headlines in 1990 when a monk, Nikorn Dhammavadi, accused a woman of blackmailing him. It soon transpired that she was his mistress, and indeed she gave birth to his son. Nikorn was eventually convicted of perjury, and the twists and turns of the legal case against him kept the story in the public eye for several years.

A film released in 1991 encapsulates Thai cinema's transition from traditional reverence of monks to unsparing depictions of their shortcomings.[263] The film begins in conventional mode, celebrating the life of a respected monk, Luang Ta. However, the gentle humor of the first half is replaced by a thinly veiled dramatization of the Nikorn lovechild scandal. Chokchai Wongsilp, the actor playing the amorous monk, was cast due to his physical resemblance to Nikorn. The film was criticized for bringing Buddhism into disrepute and censored before its release, though more reputational damage was caused by the sordid real-life case than by the movie.

After this and subsequent scandals, the monkhood was no longer regarded as unimpeachable. Changes in public attitudes towards the institution were reflected by the emergence of a noticeable cinematic trend: slapstick comedies featuring monks. Increasingly, monk characters provided comic relief, in a manner previously regarded as undignified. These irreverent movies occasionally attracted controversy, though they were popular at the box office.

The cycle of monk comedies first achieved mainstream commercial success with the release of *The Holy Man* (2005). Its fish-out-of-water plot, in which a seemingly inappropriate figure enters the monkhood, set the template for an entire franchise: two *Holy Man* sequels, and two *Joking Jazz* spinoffs. These and other films in a similar vein, such as *The Golden Riders* (2006) and *Sathu* (2009), derive their comedy from their incongruous protagonists: well-meaning though unlikely monks behave outlandishly, and calamity ensues.

However, beyond their farcical humor, these films reinforce traditional Buddhist values, albeit in an unorthodox manner. Their monk characters ultimately unite communities, solve problems, and earn respect, just like the more conventional monks in films made decades earlier. As one reviewer commented, for example: "Despite its raucous gags … *The Holy Man* offers a serious meditation upon the merits of faith."[264] These comedies are accessible, contemporary, and entertaining vehicles for Buddhist teachings, in contrast to traditional, didactic films about the lives of monks.

## The Buddhist Lobby

Despite their moral messages, the notion of slapstick comedies featuring monks was an unconventional concept in an overwhelmingly Buddhist country, and the films were criticized for undermining the monkhood. Buddhist groups campaigned, with partial success, against films that they regard as blasphemous and demeaning towards monks.

The Council of the Buddhist Organisations of Thailand wrote to the censors insisting that *See How They Run* (2006), another monk comedy, should be cut. The Council was particularly concerned about a scene in which a monk encourages villagers to run away from a ghost, and then joins them in fleeing. Arguing that a monk "should be calm and help people, not run away himself," the Council posed a fundamental question: "If filmmakers mock our religion, who will respect the Buddhist monk?"[265] Who indeed, though any decline in respect should surely be attributed to the scandalous behavior reported in the press rather than the relatively benign antics of comedy characters. "The way some monks behave in real life is far worse than anything I present on film," observed the director of the *Joking Jazz* movies.[266]

Despite the controversy, *See How They Run* was released uncut, marking a relaxation in the rules governing how monks are depicted. The film's most contentious image, that of an apparently scared monk running from a ghost, was a genre convention that had been routinely censored from previous movies. Boundaries still remained, however. A shot of a tray falling onto a monk's head was cut from the comedy *Kapi* (2010) as it was deemed humiliating to the monk.

Campaigns against films perceived as sacrilegious are not limited to comedies. The action movie *Angulimala* (2003) was criticized for its glamorization of the eponymous Angulimala, a disciple of the Buddha who was ordained after killing 999 people. (His redemption occurs only in the final reel, though his killing spree dominates the first ninety minutes.) A parliamentary committee asked the censors to modify the film and a prominent monk called for it to be banned.[267] The film was only released after cuts and reshoots and it was not a commercial success.

*In the Shadow of Naga* (2008) also attracted complaints from the Council of Buddhist Organisations and the Buddhism Relations Association as it features gangsters who disguise themselves as monks. They hide out at a temple, though they take their weapons with them, and repeatedly threaten the genuine monks and abbot at gunpoint. Fearing a ban, the studio (Sahamongkul) shelved the film for three years, as the director explained: "We assumed that we were asking for trouble if we submitted it to the censors."[268] When it was eventually submitted, in 2010, after the rating system had come into effect, it was unexpectedly passed uncut, though warning captions were added as a condition of its release. The director of this monks-with-guns thriller noted that, before the ratings system, it would almost certainly have been censored: "I realise that without the rating system my film might not have been permitted to be shown at all. This is a good development."[269]

Pen-ek Ratanaruang was not so fortunate. In his thriller *Headshot* (2011), a gangster also disguises himself as a monk and hides a gun in an alms bowl, though the gun was digitally removed by the censors. *In the Shadow of Naga*'s monks are explicitly identified as criminals in disguise, though the monk in *Headshot* appears in the pre-credits sequence, before the character's background is clearly established. As the director recalls: "I tried to reason with the censors. First of all, I tried to say that this is a fake monk." Nevertheless, the censors insisted that audiences could mistake the assassin for a real monk, telling Pen-ek: "A lot of stupid people go to cinemas, and they think a monk can kill people." While the monks with guns in *Headshot* and *In the Shadow of Naga* are gangsters in disguise, the horror film *Inhuman Kiss* (2019) features a bona fide monk character who does indeed kill someone: in a climactic slow-motion action sequence, he shoots a man possessed by a *krahang* spirit.

The clear delineation of characters as imposters rather than real monks is one reason for the censors' leniency towards films such as *In the Shadow of Naga*. Another mitigating factor involves the presence of a moral message, as the director of the Sangha Supreme Council explained: "If a film has a moral lesson, we won't object to it … we look at the whole film and see if it means to spread a good message or not."[270] This consideration of the entire film, rather than judging individual sequences out of context, is an enlightened approach, though expecting every film to be a morality play is somewhat reductivist. Such attitudes may explain the surprisingly uncontroversial release of the detective drama *Mindfulness and Murder* (2011), in which monks become suspects in a sexualized murder case. The film was rated 15 uncensored, perhaps redeemed by the Buddha quotations in its prologue and epilogue, framing the narrative as a moral lesson.

The robes worn by monk characters can also determine the level of censorship required. Inappropriate behavior by or towards monks is generally tolerated by the censors provided that the monks in question are not wearing the saffron robes of the Thai monkhood. Pen-ek Ratanaruang's thriller *Samui Song* (2017) features rape and murder committed by a cult-like group of monks, though they wear generic gray robes rather than Buddhist saffron. Thus, as the director explains: "They didn't resemble" Thai monks, and the film was not censored.[271] In the American comedy *The Hangover Part 2* (2011), set and filmed in Bangkok, a water bottle is placed under a monk's trousers, simulating an erection. Again, the scene was permitted as the monk was wearing layman's clothing. The 'Planetarium' segment of *Ten Years Thailand* (2018) features a monk in an incongruous crash helmet, and the producers cautiously filmed two versions of his costume: one with saffron and an alternative with a white robe. As director Chulayarnnon Siriphol explains: "They were scared of censorship against the monk's uniform." The character first appeared in Chulayarnnon's short film *Monk and Motorcycle Taxi Rider* (2013), which climaxes with the monk, without removing his helmet or even raising the tinted visor, engaging in a surreal homoerotic embrace.

## Double Standards

It has become increasingly acceptable to depict monks in comic situations, and films featuring fake monks or moral messages have been judged less harshly by the censors. Such leniency has its limits, though they are not clearly defined, leading to inconsistencies in censorship policy. As Kanittha Kwunyoo argues: "It seems that, regarding monks in films, there are different rules for comedies and dramas." Indeed, the censorship of monks in films remains an arbitrary process: "Some movies can make fun of monks but others can't. It's all about what the board feels; they follow their own attitudes rather than a set of standards."[272] For each case of unexpected clemency—*See How They Run* (2006), *In the Shadow of Naga* (2008), and *Mindfulness and Murder* (2011)— there is a contrasting instance of equally inexplicable censorship: *Syndromes and a Century* (2006), *Karma* (2015), and *Thibaan: The Series 2.2* (2018).

Apichatpong Weerasethakul's *Syndromes and a Century* became notorious for the particularly innocuous content that was censored from it. When Apichatpong submitted the film in 2007, cuts were required to four scenes: a monk playing a guitar, monks playing with a remote-controlled UFO toy, doctors drinking whiskey in a hospital basement, and a doctor kissing his girlfriend. Recreational activities are forbidden for monks, as they may be distractions from meditation, and drinking alcohol or kissing on hospital premises is clearly not exemplary behavior for doctors. Yet these are minor transgressions. The only potentially risqué moment comes after the kiss, when a suggestive bulge is visible in the doctor's trousers, though the film contains no vulgarity or debauchery whatsoever.

When Apichatpong appealed against the cuts in March 2008, the censors not only upheld their initial verdict but also objected to two further shots, depicting statues of Prince Mahidol Adulyadej and Princess Srinagarindra, that had not previously been flagged as problematic. (The director had predicted this outcome a year earlier, speculating that the appeal committee "might find even more to object to.")[273] Apichatpong responded by launching the Free

Thai Cinema Movement, and the apparent vendetta against his film galvanized public support in favor of a rating system. His next film, *Uncle Boonmee Who Can Recall His Past Lives* (2010), shows a monk leaving his temple, taking a shower, and visiting a karaoke bar—a signal that Apichatpong remained undeterred.

While the doctors in *Syndromes and a Century* were forbidden from drinking whiskey and kissing, the censors did not bat an eyelid at the extreme violence perpetrated by doctors and nurses in the horror film *Sick Nurses* (2007), submitted shortly afterwards. *Sick Nurses* is also a revealing indicator of Thai censorship priorities in the period before the rating system: it features graphic gore, though it is careful to avoid any nudity. (One of its female characters takes a shower while still wearing hot pants and a crop top, for example.)

A decade after the introduction of the rating system, Surasak Pongson's comedy *Thibaan: The Series 2.2* (2018) demonstrated that censorship standards remained unpredictable. The film ends with the death of a monk's ex-girlfriend, and his emotional breakdown at her funeral marks the climax of an extended narrative arc spanning the entire *Thibaan* trilogy. As Surasak explains, the monk's reaction reveals his vulnerability: "To create the most emotional scene, it needs to focus on his humanity, regardless of his role as a monk." At the funeral, the monk sobs as he approaches the coffin, knocks the side of the casket in sorrow, and is pulled away and consoled. These moments (three shots, lasting approximately a minute in total) were censored from *Thibaan*, as such emotional distress was deemed unbecoming for a monk.[274] Again, however, the rationale was inconsistent, as the stoicism imposed on *Thibaan* was not required for previous movie monks. Long before *Thibaan*'s release, there were numerous precedents for Thai films depicting "monks not only breaking their precepts, but displaying a wide range of, what might seem, inappropriately public and explicit emotions."[275] (Several music videos, including ones by Room39, MJTD, and Yiaz, also show monks crying over the deaths of their former partners.)[276]

The uncensored funeral footage was posted online by the Thai Film Director Association, though Surasak diplomatically implies that the upload was unauthorized: "What they did with the video was up to them, it wasn't our decision. They could do whatever they wanted with it, and I was okay with that." Regardless, it quickly went viral, being viewed 600,000 times on the first day alone, generating even more social media exposure than the censorship of Nontawat Numbenchapol's *Boundary* (2013).[277]

Although this online interest did not prevent the censoring of *Thibaan: The Series 2.2*, it did perhaps benefit *Ten Years Thailand* (2018), which was classified a few weeks later. Despite its political content and its helmeted, saffron-clad monk, *Ten Years Thailand* was passed uncut, pleasantly surprising its producers, who had submitted it somewhat trepidatiously. Chulayarnnon Siriphol speculates that online criticism of *Thibaan*'s censorship may have prompted the censors' leniency towards *Ten Years Thailand*: "Maybe because *Thibaan: The Series* got cut. Maybe the Film [and Video Censorship] Committee didn't want to have trouble again in a short period." If so, this was unusual, as controversial films tend to have detrimental impacts on subsequent releases: *Lucky Loser* (2006), for example, was censored following the scandal surrounding *Ghost Game* (2006); and *Boundary* (2013) was dropped by its distributor after their half-hearted release of Pen-ek Ratanaruang's *Paradoxocracy* (2013).

Like that of *Thibaan: The Series 2.2*, the ban imposed on *Karma* (2015) lasted only a matter of days. In both cases, the censors' verdicts went uncontested, and the films were duly edited by their studios and released a few days later. Whereas independent directors have embarked upon lengthy appeals against censorship (Ing Kanjanavanit and Tanwarin Sukkhapisit), or withheld their films from distribution (Apichatpong Weerasethakul and Thunska Pansittivorakul), directors working in the studio system must balance principles and profit. For studio films, complying with censorship is a commercial decision, as Pen-ek Ratanaruang explains: "I'm not in a position like Apichatpong. He's free from commercial bounds. He can say, 'Fuck you! I don't have to release the film.' But in my case, the producers and the investors are all the time on my back, and I *have* to release the film."

Similarly, Kanittha Kwunyoo reveals that, after *Karma* was banned, appealing against the decision was not on the cards: "I was called by the investors to discuss about cutting the scenes so that the film could be released, to minimize the damage." Time is money, and cooperating with the censors avoids disrupting the studio's release schedule. Surasak Pongson describes his dilemma after cuts were required for *Thibaan: The Series 2.2*:

> If we didn't cut it, there would be a financial impact. As it's also a business decision, I had to evaluate the situation. If we didn't cut it, and appealed, the whole process would take six months. By that time, we would lose everything, because if the later release date was in blockbuster season, our income would be affected. Even postponing for a few days, we would lose millions of baht.

*Karma*'s trailer caused instant controversy as it shows a young monk touching a girl's cheek in a romantic gesture. This was followed by a dramatic flash effect, to emphasize its apparently shocking nature. The trailer also featured a close-up of the monk's hand on the girl's back, an incidental moment included purely for its transgressive value. (Monks are forbidden from touching women, even platonically.) The trailer was certainly provocative, though Kanittha, perhaps naïvely, maintains that this was unintended: "I never thought that the movie could cause controversy or problems in society." Intentionally or otherwise, the film became a *cause célèbre*, and Kanittha even received death threats from some outraged monks.[278] (Chulayarnnon Siriphol also received a death threat, after a Muslim activist saw his short film *Birth of Golden Snail* in 2018.)

The romantic gesture in *Karma*'s trailer was merely a foretaste: in the film itself, the monk actually kisses the girl. This sequence was a point of contention when Kanittha submitted the script to the studio, though she resisted pressure to drop it: "As director and writer, I didn't want to do that. I thought it wasn't exploitative but necessary to the story." After winning this first battle, Kanittha found the censors less accommodating than the studio: "The censorship board told us that the film disrespected Buddhism…. They felt that it would be hard to cut those scenes, so the film was banned."

The National Office of Buddhism not only objected to the monk kissing the girl, but to all physical contact between them. Other transgressions, such as monks drinking alcohol and touching the head of a Buddha statue, were also deemed unacceptable. Significantly, the National Office of Buddhism is more influential than other Buddhist pressure groups, as it has a representative on the Film and Video Censorship Committee. Thus, despite an anti-censorship petition signed by 60,000 people, the censors required more than two minutes of cuts from *Karma*. Two years later, the monk touching the girl's cheek was reinstated for an extended director's cut, *Pret Arbut* (2017), though their kiss remained *verboten*.[279]

While controversy most often arises from the misrepresentation of monks, their absence became a point of contention when the television broadcast of the national anthem was updated. The anthem is played twice daily, accompanied by a patriotic video montage, which was replaced with a new version in May 2019. Buddhist monks were not included in the replacement, prompting a complaint by a Buddhist pressure group. A month later, the Office of the Prime Minister amended the video by adding footage of monks receiving alms.[280]

## Non-Buddhist Religious Censorship

Buddhist issues dominate the debate around censorship and religion as Thailand is a predominantly Buddhist country. However, Thai film censors have also adjudicated on controversies surrounding the representation of other religions. In 2006, for example, a coalition of Christian groups called for the final reel of *The Da Vinci Code* to be cut from its Thai release.[281] (The film ends with the revelation that living descendants have continued Christ's bloodline.) This demand was initially approved by the censors, though the film's Hollywood studio (Columbia) refused to release a truncated version and the censors capitulated.

Muslims constitute a significant demographic in Thailand's southern provinces, and Chulayarnnon Siriphol's short film *Birth of Golden Snail* (2018) was accused of offending Islamic sensibilities in the region. Intended as a site-specific installation, to be projected onto a cave wall at the Thailand Biennale exhibition in 2018, the film blends local history and mythology. In a dream sequence, snails appear on a schoolgirl's body. One shot shows the creatures on her breasts, though strategically placed gastropods and shallow focus ensure that there is no explicit nudity. The sequence is comical (with a "Pregnant!" intertitle) and surreal (as a snail shell suddenly appears via a jump cut).[282]

Nevertheless, after a preview screening, the Office of Contemporary Art and Culture claimed that its portrayal of a pregnant schoolgirl set a bad example, and that the shot of her breasts was indecent. They were particularly concerned because Krabi, the exhibition venue, has a one-third Muslim population, and they told the director: "It shouldn't be screened in the Muslim community." Those concerns were apparently well founded, as Chulayarnnon received a death threat from a local Muslim community leader: "He had a chance to see my film, and he posted on Facebook: 'Do not look down on the cave, otherwise you will die!' "[283] The Office of Contemporary Art and Culture asked the director to cut the film, though he declined to do so, as he explained: "The committee asked me to reedit and cut some scenes out from the film because they were afraid of negative feedback from local people in Krabi. I understood the comments from the committee but I refused to censor my film."[284]

On the eve of the Biennale, Chulayarnnon was informed in writing that *Birth of Golden Snail* violated the "peace, morality, national security and dignity of Thailand."[285] His proposed compromises—to give the audience copies of the script in lieu of screening the film, or to show a montage of brief extracts—were rejected. Negotiations with the Office of Contemporary Art and Culture progressed at such a snail's pace that no agreement had been reached by the close of the four-month exhibition. The golden snail finally emerged from its shell a year later, at the Thai Film Archive.

Figure 1:
*Syndromes And A Century* (2006), directed by Apichatpong Weerasethakul.
(Photograph courtesy of Apichatpong Weerasethakul.)

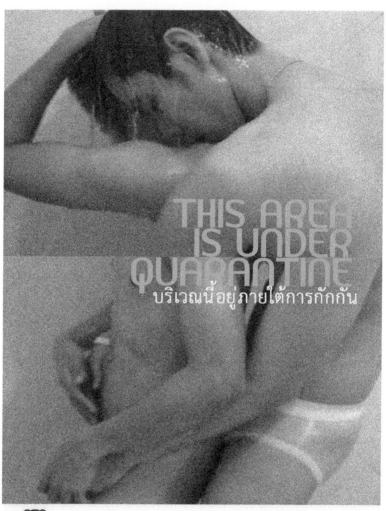

Figure 2:
*This Area Is Under Quarantine* (2008), directed by Thunska Pansittivorakul.
(Photograph courtesy of Thunska Pansittivorakul.)

Boundary

Figure 3:
*Boundary* (2013), directed by Nontawat Numbenchapol.
(Photograph courtesy of Nontawat Numbenchapol.)

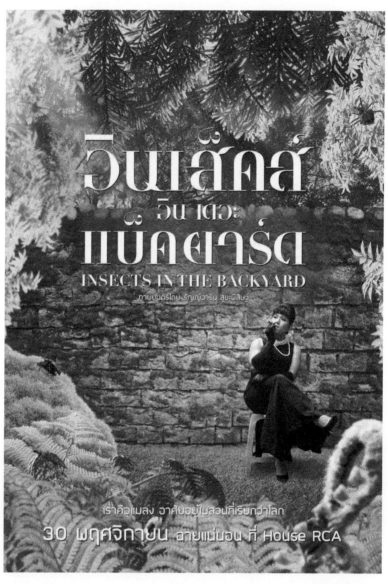

Figure 4:
*Insects in the Backyard* (2010), directed by Tanwarin Sukkhapisit.
Poster designed by Witcha Suyara. (Photograph courtesy of Witcha Suyara.)

Figure 5:
*Thibaan: The Series 2.2* (2018), directed by Surasak Pongson.
(Photograph courtesy of Serng Production.)

Figure 6:
*Birth of Golden Snail* (2018), directed by Chulayarnnon Siriphol.
(Photograph courtesy of Chulayarnnon Siriphol.)

Figure 7:
*Shakespeare Must Die* (2012), directed by Ing Kanjanavanit.
(Photograph courtesy of Cinema Oasis.)

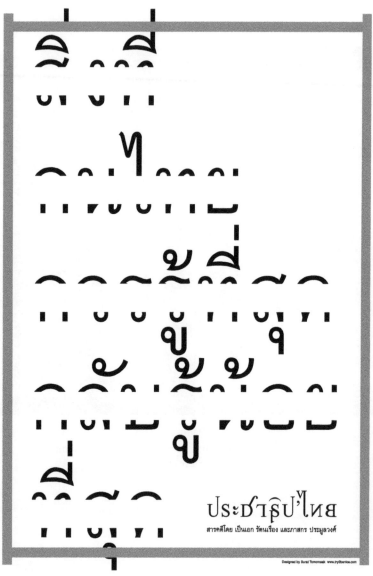

Figure 8:
*Paradoxocracy* (2013), directed by Pen-ek Ratanaruang and Pasakorn Pramoolwong.
Poster designed by Surat Tomornsak. (Photograph courtesy of Surat Tomornsak.)

Part Two

# Interviews with Directors

# APICHATPONG WEERASETHAKUL

*"Maybe they wanted some money under the table."*

**Shall we start with *Blissfully Yours* and the shots that were cut from that film? Whose decision was it to cut those scenes?**

It was a mutual decision, because I totally understood at that time that it's not a film for kids, and we didn't have a rating system. I wanted to have the film released, so I talked with Sahamongkol. I don't know why they bought the film [*laughs*]. Maybe because the film went to Cannes. But I told them, "Cut it." To be able to show it. At that time, I didn't think much about censorship. And they actually showed the full version in some theaters.

**Oh really?**

Yeah. Randomly. Secretly.

**So, who organized that and allowed that to happen?**

Sahamongkol. So, I think this might be—I don't know, but maybe—that is the deal with the police.

Pen-ek [Ratanaruang] said that when *Ploy* was released it was cut, and when they had the premiere of the cut version, police were at the cinemas checking the print to make sure it was cut.

I think Sahamongkol has a bigger power [*laughs*]. During that time, 2002, I was old enough to understand things, but I didn't. I was a royalist. I was politically naïve. I think at that time, there was no Thaksin [Shinawatra].

**That was his first term?**

Not yet creating such a huge conflict.

**So, you were happy for them to cut it at that time.**

Even now. I wouldn't, but if there's no rating system.

**You would?**

For that film, yes. Because it makes sense, for sex and violence. But what happened with *Syndromes* [*and a Century*] doesn't make sense.

**So, there was no problem when the uncut version was shown in some cinemas?**

No, I was secretly happy.

**On your website, you put a notice to say: don't buy the Thai DVD of *Blissfully Yours*.**

Yeah [*laughs*].[286]

PART II : INTERVIEWS WITH DIRECTORS

**And since then, your films have not been released on DVD in Thailand.**

*Tropical Malady* was. *Syndromes*, no, because I'd learned my lesson, and tried to have more control over the DVD release, to be able to limit the theaters or to design the package or whatever. It's still a wish to make a package of the films that I own. But many of the films were actually shown on TV, on cable.

**So, you're hoping to have a boxset eventually? In Thailand?**

In Thailand specifically, because I own the rights. *Blissfully Yours*, actually the rights are about to finish this year, and I talked with Grammy for *Tropical Malady*. They actually own it forever, but they're okay to have a percentage.

**Going on to *Syndromes and a Century*, I was surprised when that film was singled out for censorship because, as you said, it made no sense, what they wanted to cut. Do you know why they needed the cuts?**

Because I am nobody [*laughs*]. I am not really with a studio. Maybe they wanted some money under the table, I don't know [*laughs*]. In the beginning. Because there were two rounds. The first round, they cut, I think, four scenes.

**And then you appealed, and they cut two more. Is that right?**

Yes. So, in the beginning, it was not such a big deal for them, because they maybe hoped that I could discuss with them about money, or whatever.

But you were not prepared to do that, so then they got tough, maybe?

Right. But, I think, from *Tropical Malady*, there's this issue of releasing the film, and marketing, that I don't like. And also the studio was not interested in the film, anyway, because there's no selling point: there's no tiger, there's no sex, so it's very personal.[287] And really I had no financial risks, because it was paid for by a friend's company [Anna Charles Films], and distributed abroad, so I'm okay. So, it's just a personal pursuit to show it.

What was it about the marketing and distribution that you were not happy with?

Just little things: posters, number of theaters, location of theaters; the films are not really available out of Bangkok.

What about the Culture Ministry official, Ladda [Tangsupachai], and her comment that nobody goes to see Apichatpong's films? She was talking to *Time* magazine, so she knew it would get wide coverage.

Of course, I was mad [*laughs*].

Of course.

I tried to find a way to sue her. After I came to my senses, late, I called whatshisname [Simon Montlake]: "Do I have a case? Do you have a recording of her?" But it was too late.

It wasn't shocking, because in a seminar before that, she already stated that Thai people only have an average grade six education, so people are not ready for a certain kind of movies. So, when this came, it's not so shocking, but just maddening.

**Prayut [Chan-o-cha] said people are not ready for democracy. It's the same thing.**

Yes, the mentality of these *kharatchakan* [civil servants].

**In Ing's documentary, *Censor Must Die*, they go to the Ministry of Culture and a video showing the traditional Thai way of sitting is playing in the reception of the Ministry. It seems a very conservative institution, very traditional.**

Yes, but you've been here many years [*laughs*]. It's very normal. It's a theatrical society, a façade, all for the nation, religion, and king. When I was young, everybody was totally brought up on that: your personal identity is always to serve these three institutions. So, growing up and looking now at what happens, it's totally understandable why people are so passive. Even if people have whatever kind of education.

With the Chinese mentality of not losing face. The media has become very representative of this kind of face, so it's all about theater, and the media is the first to be hit, or to be controlled by the military. All these things in the same mold. And people automatically think like that, too, in the media. So Ladda's comment is not so shocking.

**More shocking is that the military owns television channels.**

For us, it's normal. My family, and friends who studied in Chicago, are totally submissive, no questions asked: disruption of the flow and unity is really a big deal. Like my Mum says, "Why bother?" [*laughs*]. And she is in the generation of Sarit [Thanarat], all these people who were very powerful. She just enjoys her way of life. It's almost rude or wrong to question.

Even worse, maybe, is when people say that nothing can change, and they become apathetic. And nothing changes. It becomes a self-fulfilling prophecy.

At the same time, they have religion and the monarchy to justify this kind of climate.

**Well, I was going to ask you about 112. You've worn an anti-112 tee-shirt before.**

Yeah. It's amazing that we cannot now [*laughs*]. It's a disgusting law. Again, the mentality of people: "Why do you need to go against this law? Because it protects the king from slander." But people in their right mind wouldn't agree with this kind of punishment.

I think, before, when I could wear that tee-shirt, it was quite okay if you talked with logic and reason why this is not healthy. Now, it's worse, to not be able to talk in a civil manner. I don't know what I can say [*laughs*].

**How did the censored version of *Syndromes and a Century* in Thailand happen?**

Someone suggested, "Why don't you take this opportunity to try to educate the public?" It also shows that times are changing, because the cinema also started to pay attention.

**They had a small exhibition in the lobby.**

Yeah. During *Blissfully Yours* or *Tropical Malady*, there would be no theaters. But now, with SF Cinema, they start to try to tap into the middle-class, teenage, hipster market.

**But you would not release that version on DVD?**

The cut version? Why? It's just to see in the dark, in the theater, to see this black.

**You wouldn't get the same effect on DVD?**

I would, if there's someone who could invest [*laughs*]. At that time, it was a statement, not a real screening. And the theater was willing to do it. But releasing a DVD is financially impossible.

**Pen-ek was saying that he had many problems with the theaters showing *Paradoxocracy*, discouraging people to see it.**

I think Thailand is shifting so quickly. At that time, the political situation was quite strained. I think *Syndromes* was not the same climate.

**When you showed the cut version, you distributed postcards with links to the cut scenes. Was that your idea?**

No, it was Chalida [Uabumrungjit]. The Thai Film Foundation really advised us how to make it work: the exhibition area, and all this.

**When did you start thinking about the Free Thai Cinema Movement?**

My main interest was to hear from others. Because I was independent, and I wanted to hear: is this about independents only, or studios? Of course, we heard from many studio filmmakers of many ridiculous things that they had to go through. And also to share and make myself feel better [*laughs*]. "You've gone through worse." It's very interesting: these things are objected to, and these things are okay. Showing how the police work, and what they want to control. We learnt a lot, and I was so happy that people joined from the studios.

**Was the aim to introduce the rating system? That was the main goal?**
Yes, to change the Film Act of 1930.

**And it was changed in the same year. Was that because of your campaign?**
I think so. Mainly Chalida and the Film Foundation, because they have big connections. Chalida and Dome [Sukwong] have access to the NLA, which I had no idea about [*laughs*], so I learnt a lot about how to approach it: go to the right people. Thai style [*laughs*].

**One more question about *Syndromes*. Who organized the screenings at the Alliance Française?**
Did we screen it?

**Sure, you were there to introduce it. It played on two nights.**
I think that was showing from a DVD

**Yes, but it was the only chance to see the uncut version at that time. Did you approach them, or did they approach you?**
I think I approached them. At that time, I was in Bangkok; I moved here eight years ago.[288] At that time, I was really close to the cultural attachés of Alliance Française, each successive person. Just in a friendly chat, I asked to show it.

**Is that something you would consider for other films, now or in the future?**

Yeah, actually we talked about the new film there. I started to get more concerned about quality now, and they said they have a DCP coming, so: perfect.[289] And also the Thai Film Archive.[290] But I hesitate because at that time, *Syndromes and a Century*, people came out because it was fun, Thai style.

Now, with the release of 'love in Khon Kaen' [*Cemetery of Splendour*], I'm scared of social media. I cut myself off from this kind of flow.

**I noticed that you'd stopped using Facebook.**

I really want to work on my own, and I don't care about this shit country [*laughs*]. I was worried people will do Facebook, and all these things, and I will be in trouble. Because we are not in a democracy. Of course, I could do it during *Syndromes*. And I could wear that tee-shirt. But now, it's serious. It's true, it's a reality that you can be detained by these thugs. Of course, I'm scared. They have done this. It doesn't make sense to mess with this mafia.

I'd better work on my own, and I don't care if I show it in this climate. But I want to share with Dome, with other friends, so there's a kind of hesitation. I want to show it, but I don't want people to post about it. Because it's more personal. I'm not a hero. I don't want to waste my time at camp [*laughs*].

**Absolutely. 'Attitude adjustment' for seven days.**

Yeah [*laughs*].

**So, the rating system was introduced. Do you feel that it was successful?**

Better, to a certain degree. But still, you've seen how they judge many recent films. So, it's one step. But I think the best is to do like the American model: to have the film federation do it ourselves.

**Even films in the highest category, 20, would be relatively mild by American standards. And there are still bans, of course.**

But, again, it's not shocking, because of what is going on. The military still control the media.

**So, what would be the perfect situation?**

Military out. Because I think film is really tied with other things. It's going to be hard to have total freedom, because in our DNA we have this saving face thing, and the media is still the mask. We have prostitution and all these things going on, but we cannot do it in the media. With the military out, I could wear tee-shirts, I could do seminars. I think that's the way.

**Do you ever censor yourself, when you're writing scripts or in editing?**

Of course, yes. But I was happy doing that, until the last film. I was happy because I think it's more interesting. And when you see a lot of work from the past, other people's work, they're talking about something so direct that I think it's not a movie, it's not cinema. Cinema is something else. As long as I have to censor my own self when I talk in public, my cinema will be like that. So, it reflects that. So, I'm happy to censor, because that's me.

But for the last film, there's a certain point that, with the military, it's getting *more*. And you're not really happy to censor yourself in public, too. And the film suffers, like I suffer, myself. To the point that working in a subversive way has become an excuse to be weak. And I don't like that. Again, with this climate, that's why this happens.

**Is there any financial pressure to censor yourself?**

No, not at all.

**Because the financing is from outside Thailand?**

Yes.

**Is there anything specifically that made you decide not to release *Cemetery of Splendour* in this country? Was it because of the political situation?**

Yes, the political situation. And I think that whatever I do, I will be targeted. Either a ghost movie, or whatever [*laughs*]. It's a paranoid time. They're willing to do a witch hunt, so I become paranoid of them in my own way, and I don't want to risk it. As long as I manage to finish this film as I want, and show it, but not here.

**Thunska [Pansittivorakul] decided not to release *any* future films in Thailand.**

That's what he said?

**That's his plan. He's not interested in any Thai releases in the future.**

Because it makes you tired and discouraged from making more films. I think filmmakers need to get in touch. So much of film has been politicized, it's not its own artistic creation. So, it becomes very discouraging. Not healthy, if you think as a professional.

**Do you think that will change? Is it possible?**
I think so, because it comes in a loop, the military.

**Yes, the cycle.**
They'll still be there, in the background, but at least there are certain players coming.

**In *Cemetery of Splendour*, in the cinema scene, the audience stands up and there is just silence.**
Yes, before the royal anthem.

**But I got the DVD from France, and it's not there. Was it changed?**
Yes. Because it's a format that's been the most pirated. And it's true that, after it was released, it's already available here, everywhere, and people just share it. I mean, for me, it can be interpreted in many ways. It can be whatever [*laughs*]. But it's too sensitive now.

I actually wanted to show the royal anthem, because it's documentary-like. It's what we do. But I know it's impossible, because in the movie *Soi Cowboy*, this was cut out. Censored. So, I said, "It's impossible anyway." So, just silence.

**In *Boundary*, Nontawat [Numbenchapol] had to cut something similar, at the new year countdown.**
Yes, but that's silly. I think he shouldn't have cut that out. He should fight. I mean, not at this time, but at that time.

**How did you decide to edit the DVD version?**

We had a big discussion among the producers, and they learned a lot [*laughs*] about 112 and all these things. "Oh, shit, okay." And at this time, it's these mad people running the country.

**What about the theatrical version in other countries?**

Theatrical, okay. Because, for me, I really care about the big screen experience.

**Is there any connection with the short film *The Anthem* from a few years ago?**

A bit, yes. At that time, or maybe afterwards, there was a case with people not standing up.[291] A sentiment among many people, asking the question: why do we have to stand up to show respect? It's not logical: why do we have to stand at 8 o'clock? But again, it's a really remote expression, not so direct.

**Would you be interested in making a direct political statement on film?**

No, not so interested. I would rather write. I do, in a way, but not really about myself or my friends, but someone who thinks differently. For example, some royalists or Ladda. I want to make a film about that. Why? Because I want to understand the North Korean effect, how it works on people, and I want to record that.

It's not about only film. I was reading yesterday that they went to interview teenagers and other people who'd just worked for a few years, about what they think about school uniforms. And all of them were positive. It's crazy.

**But this is an attitude that's created very young.**
Yes, very young, and very hard to change. I've read quite a number of books on North Korea. It was shocking, but when you compare to what happened here, it's understandable. The idea of the tribe, that you have to protect the nation.

**Exceptionalism: Thailand is so special that things like democracy should not apply.**
Yes [*laughs*]. But there's so many fucked up things every day. But the film is talking a lot about that, but you have to find it. *Nai nam me pla, nai na me khao* [we have fish in the river and rice in the field] is a big motto, and the film talks about that. Besides those things, there's nothing in this kingdom.

When censorship happens, it's mostly sex, religion, something that's in other media already, in books, that people try to express in cinema, and they realize, "Oops, we cannot do it." But for politics, there's very little, because people automatically don't create it.

If you talk to the Ministry of Culture, they have their own reasons: it's harmful to national security, and *samakkhi* [harmony]. And what can you say when they have this mentality? Again, it comes back to exceptionalism.

**And why should there be social unity? People are different: there should be diversity, not unity.**
The final card for them is: "Because we are Thai. It's Thailand, you don't understand." But you're right: we are different.

**When people say "You're not Thai, you don't understand" it's offensive.**
And insulting.

**And it seems like that's the only excuse they have.**

You could say many Thais don't understand either [*laughs*]. Prayut only cares about China. I wish there were more foreigners messing with our politics [*laughs*]. Before, of course, the Americans were really messing and manipulating our politics, and they created monsters. They created Sarit.[292] And it seems like now you're leaving us with these monsters of your doing. I think pressure from abroad is quite important.

I said many times about not shocking things, but Prayut is a bit shocking [*laughs*]. This monkey. Maybe this should be off the record….

(The interview took place at Apichatpong's home in Chiang Mai on 27 June 2016.)

# PEN-EK RATANARUANG

*"The cinemas were crawling with police."*

**What was your earliest experience with the Film and Video Censorship Committee?**

My second film that I made was called *6ixtynin9*, and that's interesting because with that film I think we went to Rotterdam. We premiered in Rotterdam, and since it was my second film, I was in competition. After Rotterdam, then we went to Berlin, so the film was shown at a few—not too many, but a few—festivals before it was shown in Thailand. And when we submitted it to the censor in Thailand, at that time, mind you, the censor board was not as it is now. The censorship board at the time was just police. That's it.

For the Thai version, they asked us to put a rolling credit at the end, after the film is finished. The last shot was with the girl, she threw the money away, she burned her fake passport, and she just drove off, and presumably, from the scenery it looks like she's going down south, going home, or wherever. And we were asked by the police to put the rolling credit saying that she was caught [*laughs*] and went to jail.

Usually, I don't see the censor people, usually just the producers. They bring the film to the censor, and they come back and tell you what they said. And you had to do it. There's no way, you cannot say, "No, I won't do it." Apichatpong [Weerasethakul] can say, "No, I won't do it, it's stupid. And I won't show my film." But the investment in my film came from people who need to make a profit. A big studio. So, they said, "Please put it on."

I thought the reason would be that you might corrupt the young minds of the country, as they always say, that you can kill people and get away with it. But that's not the reason at all [laughs]. The reason was that, if the girl could do this, the police look bad. They look stupid. That was the reason. But at least they were kind of honest. Because if I were them, I would make up another reason that sounds more reasonable, but they didn't. "No, we would look bad."

**In *Invisible Waves*, didn't they put an anti-smoking caption?**
Oh, yeah. They put that on. And every time you see a cigarette, they put an 'X' mark on. But to put an 'X' mark on the pack of cigarettes is not to say that you can't see the pack.

**It's the brand?**
Yeah. So that you don't know it's Marlboro, or Lucky Strike, or whatever. But how can you not know? If it's Lucky Strike, it's Lucky Strike [laughs]. In *Ploy*, there's a big red mark. But in the cinema, it's not. Cinema is okay, when you show it in cinemas. But on DVD and when they show it on television.

**For the *Ploy* DVD, the sex scene is uncut, but it was cut for the cinema. Why would they allow it on DVD but not in the cinema?**
The reason is simple. The reason is that when a film goes into the cinema, it's a big deal if some people go there and complain, and it

becomes news, in the papers, and they have to come out and defend the film: "Why did you let this pass?" But once on DVD, nobody cares, it's old news. There are more films in the cinema. So, in fact, it's not out of sincerity that they do all this, they just do it to protect themselves.

**For *Ploy*, did you recut the sex scene yourself or was it just cut by the censor?**

I was told to cut, and they tell you to cut things in your film, and they tell you exactly, from this frame to this frame. So, I had to go back to the editing. With my films, the rhythm of the film is very important, because my films don't have 'exciting' stories, so usually it's mood and it's the rhythm. If you take out ten frames, the rhythm is different in each scene. So, at least if I can't get the shots or the scenes the way I wanted because of censorship, at least I have to maintain the rhythm of the film. So, if we're asked to take out five seconds, then five seconds in film is a lot. It's so many hundred frames.[293] Or if you're asked to take out five minutes, I have to, at least, not lose that five minutes, so I have to replace it with another five minutes of something they would allow and pass. Which is something closer, tighter, or whatever.

**Did you reframe the same shot or use an alternate take?**

No, I used a completely different shot. But what's interesting about *Ploy*, if you compare the two versions: the uncut version—I knew that you cannot show pubic hair, you cannot see genitals, I knew all that when I was filming it. But it was censored because it was kind of *dirty*. It was deemed *dirty*. I don't think there was any film in Thailand—at least, any commercial film—before that film, where you see a guy take off her panties, and the film showed that.

But the idea was that it had to be *dirty*, because for me that film was about a game. In one room, you have a husband and wife who've been married for seven or eight years. And the game they play in that room is a verbal game. The wife just complains and complains. Both the husband and wife knew that their problem could be solved so easily by just touching each other. If they just hold each other, everything would become fine. But they decided not to, like a lot of couples. They decided not to, just to see who would win the game. The husband knew exactly what his wife wants, but he decided to play verbal games and not give it, and they hurt each other by their words, more and more. "So, you want me to love you more? You want me to stop watching football?" That kind of thing. And the wife gets angry, and he says, "Are you having your period?"

So, in one room there's that game, when they don't touch each other but they just abuse each other with words, and that's the game they play. And in the other room, you have a contrasting game, where they don't talk at all, they just make love.

But for the lovemaking to be a game, it has to be dirty. Because the maid went to all the trouble of going to the laundry room, stealing the suit of a customer and she put it in the room, and she hid in the bathtub. And her boyfriend, the bartender, comes up and changes to look like a guest. And they pretend they accidentally meet in the bathroom while she's cleaning, and then they start doing it. So to be a game, it has to be not normal, it has to be kind of dirty. In fact, the fucking is not so important, it's the game that's more important. The leading up to the fucking is more important. So, those scenes were deemed too dirty, although there's no nudity—a little bit.

**Topless nudity.**

But they were deemed dirty, so we were asked to cut. Of course, we just put in closer shots. But you don't see what is going on, you just see the reaction of the girl, so the idea of the game was completely destroyed. And it became like straight fucking, which is, for me, even more damaging. If you want to uphold the 'good values' of Thai society [*laughs*]. It becomes more damaging, because then there's no art, it's just fuck, fuck, fuck.

And, in fact, there's no reason why you have to stay on the scene for so long, and there's no reason to come back and forth between the two rooms many times. Because, in the uncut version, there were reasons to come back to the bartender and the maid from time to time, because the game was building up from just foreplay into intercourse, until in the end she lies there exhausted but happy, and she sings to us, straight to the camera. So, the progression in the script was coherent. In the censored version, you don't know why you keep coming back to the fucking. We know they're fucking! It's kind of horrible.

**It seems gratuitous.**

Right. The girl could have burst into song much earlier in the film. But I don't think the censors are aware of these kinds of things.

On the day of the premiere, the gala, the cinemas were crawling with police. Because when you premiere a film here, you might premiere a film at two or three cinemas at the same time. Or big films, like GTH films like *Pee Mak*, they would premiere in eight cinemas at one time, because there are so many people interested. But with my films, maybe two or three cinemas. But they were afraid that in one of the cinemas we might show the uncut version [*laughs*]. So, there were police everywhere.

**Nymph was released in two very different versions, and that was for commercial reasons?[294]**

Right. The version we went to Cannes with, we didn't really finish. In fact, it was really my worst experience of any film festival, *Nymph* in Cannes. In fact, we didn't even have the end credits.

**And there's no music.**

No music, not even end credits. It just ends. People were shocked [*laughs*]. "What is this?" It was terrible.

In fact, the commercial version is more like the director's version, because the one in Cannes wasn't finished. But it's so funny, because when we put the film in cinemas here, in Thailand, in Bangkok the cinemas asked my investors to put both versions in. I said, "But the other version is not a *version*. You cannot say that's a *version*. It was unfinished. The fact that it went to Cannes, it didn't mean it's a *version*." But they said a lot of people want to see the Cannes version. So that's why there were two different versions.

**Did *Headshot* have any censorship issues?**

One cut. The opening scene with the fake monk, the assassin dressed up like a monk. He goes to a politician's house to kill him. The guy comes to give the food, the alms to the monk. In the international version, the camera tilts down to the bowl of the monk, and he opens the bowl to wait for the food. In the international version, there's a gun in the bowl. For the one released in Thailand, we had to digitally remove the gun from the bowl.

**I saw that version.**

Again, I tried to reason with the censors. First of all, I tried to say that this is a fake monk. Number one, it's a fake monk. "Yeah, but the people don't know. A lot of stupid people go to cinemas, and they think a monk can kill people." I said, "Okay, perfect, that's why you should leave the gun there, because the gun in the bowl tells *everyone*, even idiots, that this is a fake monk. No real monk would own a gun [*laughs*]. So, this is the reason you should leave it there. Because people know, exactly, it's a fake monk. You must leave the gun in the bowl." And then they said, "No, we know your reason, and that makes perfect sense, but a gun and the alms cannot be together. The bowl is too sacred, and a gun is too evil."

**There have been problems with representations of monks doing lesser things than that, so I'm not surprised that it was changed here.**

Yeah. But it's funny, because all my films that are censored here, including what we'll talk about later on, *Paradoxocracy*, every time a film is censored, I'm not in a position like Apichatpong. He's free from commercial bounds. He can say, "Fuck you! I don't have to release the film." But in my case, the producers and the investors are all the time on my back, and I *have* to release the film.

But it's funny that, every time they censor my film, the meaning of the film after it has been censored not only changes, but it becomes against what they really wanted. It makes the film a bit stronger. In the case of *Ploy*, the meaning was stronger in the sense that it became like straight fucking [*laughs*], but it's supposed to be kinky and dirty. And in the case of *Headshot*, it becomes a real monk [*laughs*] shooting people. So, every time they try to censor, they shoot themselves in the foot.

**When you were making *Paradoxocracy*, did you expect that there would be any kind of censorship problems?**

Well, I was so naïve. I'm always naïve. Not *was*, I *am*. With *Ploy*, I thought, as long as you don't show pussy or cock, it's okay [*laughs*]. So I'm very naïve. With *Paradoxocracy*, I thought, as long as you don't attack the monarchy, as long as you don't say bad things about the monarchy, then you're fine. But, of course, the reality is not like that. You can't even *mention* it, you can't even *talk* about it. You don't even have to say bad things.

But stupidity or *naïvité*, not all the time, but sometimes, is also a blessing, because, all my filmmaking life, for sixteen years I've been making films, I've been able to do the things that I do because I don't really know what the rules are.

**You can break them, because you don't know what they are?**

I never paid attention to them, because I never knew what they were. So, you're free to experiment. I think I was more free to be honest. I could be honest. I could be sincere, because I didn't know what I had to avoid, or who I had to deceive. But, of course, many times it brought me trouble later on, but not *big* trouble. Small trouble.

No, I didn't think there would be any problem, when I was making it. I knew that the people that we interviewed would say some forbidden things, I knew that. But I thought I knew what the forbidden things were, so I'll just cut them out. Because half of the footage that we have, you can't show to people [*laughs*]. You'll just have to bury it in the ground somewhere [*laughs*].

I was surprised that the film opens with Pridi Banomyong's statement criticizing King Rama VII. It's a very strong opening, especially because it doesn't specify which king is being criticized.

But the original opening was that somebody was actually reading it. And again, here's a censorship contribution: they said, "Come on, please, you can't have the voice." So, we took out the voice. But it becomes even stronger when you take out the voice [*laughs*]. People are reading it themselves: "My God! They talked about the king this way!" Because if somebody was reading, as my original idea was, you would just be sitting there listening.

And it didn't cut. That first cut went on way too long, for a normal film cut that you would not have any voice or whatever, just a static piece of paper. No film would stay on that piece of paper that long. But the fact that it's so unusually long, you have to start reading it. Again, it just made it a stronger statement, by the censorship. But that letter, they didn't censor it because you can go and read it in the National Library, you can find it online.

It talks about King Rama VII. But, of course, once they seized power, they negotiated with the king, they brought him back from Hua Hin to stay on as a king under the constitution. Everything became normal again.[295] Perhaps two weeks after that coup, the coup-makers issued exactly the same kind of letter, but opposite: they apologized, and then they said, "You are such a wonderful king, and we are a bunch of dickheads, but we had to do this."[296] Again, the same kind of letter but an apology. But, of course, they never really wanted to apologize anyway. It was just a game. They tried to say, "We appreciate you. Please stay on as our king." But both sides, they never forgave each other.

**When the censors told you to cut some footage, why did you decide to mute the sound?**

This was the first film in my life that I made, that I actually had to go see the censors myself, because I had no investors, just me and my producer [Pasakorn Pramoolwong]. We paid for the film ourselves, and we made our personal thing. I had no buffer between me and them, so I had to go.

There were five people in that room. They watched the film, and then after that, they called us to go and meet them. And they said they liked the film a lot. They really liked the film, and then they said, "This film is going to be wonderful to show to people, and people need to see it."

But, of course, there are five cuts that they have to cut, because it's about the monarchy. So, I said, "But we didn't attack the monarchy. We didn't say bad things about the monarchy. We just said things about the monarchy that people know, like King Rama VIII was killed, was assassinated." One of the guys, whose day job was as an attorney, said, "In fact, people are going to sue you, if you show the film like this. There are going to be some people who will sue you. Because, starting with Abhisit [Vejjajiva]'s government, the *lèse-majesté* law, people have been using it left and right, to accuse people, to throw mud."

So, this attorney said, "Somebody will sue you if you show the film like this." But he admitted that, "You will win." He said, "Pen-ek, you will win the case. If they sue you, if you fight, you will win because whatever you say that we have to censor, later on in the film you explain what it means anyway, so you will be okay. But we must censor. And as an attorney, I have already over 10,000 cases of *lèse-majesté* [*laughs*]. Please don't add another one." So, I said, "Okay."

Again, you come up against something like this, you don't know whether to laugh or cry, because they're nice to you, but they're asking you to cut your baby's arm off, your baby's legs. But they're nice, and I think they were also shocked at my reaction, because most of the time when they try to censor films, usually the filmmakers are, "Don't touch it!" and they make it into a scandal, and the newspaper will cover it.

But I think they were shocked at my reaction, because I was really mild. I just sat there very quietly, trying to think what to do. Because this is the first time that I actually have the kind of power that Apichatpong has, that I don't have to show this film. I'd just put it away, it's okay. I'll show it in my house, and I'll bring friends to watch it and that's fine, I don't care. It's my own money.

So, I told them, "Then, what do I do?" And they said, "Well, you have to cut." But I think they were nice to us, because I didn't go in there like an activist. I tried to help them solve the problem. But I couldn't, so I said, "We'll just go home, and I'll think of what to do, and if I can't find any solution, I just can't cut the film." I said, "I cannot do it." So, I told them, if I come up with some solution, I'll propose to them, but just to cut the way they suggest, that's impossible. I would not do that. And I told them, "If I can't come up with any solution, do not worry about it. I will not make a big deal out of it. I would just put the film away, in my house, quietly, it's fine." So, I assured them of that, and they were really appreciative.

So, when we left the office, it was lunchtime. I went to have lunch with my producer. And that's when I had the idea, "Hey, this is not a fiction film. I didn't write a script. We just talked to people, and then we just put them together, to show that there's a journey of this thing called democracy in Thailand." So, I thought, "Okay, it is not a fiction, it's a documentary. The fact that the film itself is being censored, it is also a recording of what happened in our time."

So, after lunch, I called back the censors and said, "I don't have to cut the picture, right?" They said, "No, you don't have to. The picture's fine. There was nobody masturbating or anything, so it's okay." "So, you have a problem with the sound?" "Yes." So, I said, "Can I cut just the sound?" They said, "Sure." I said, "But, if I leave the picture, they'd be silent, with the mouth moving." They said, "Fine." I said, "This can't be. They don't understand what I'm saying." Because it would make them look like fools [*laughs*]. And the English subtitle would have a black bar over it.

So, I thought, it made it a better film, because now it's no longer a film. It's not a film anymore. It becomes like an art piece. Because the film itself is participating in this, becoming a victim. So, I thought, "Perfect. This is actually a much better film than before." And it worked, because when you saw it in the cinema, first of all, people gasped, but the second time—

**They laughed.**

They started laughing. And people knew right away what the deleted sound was about. They knew *exactly* what it was about. It made the point even stronger. It didn't matter what these people said, but it made the point. People understand what they were talking about: it has to be our monarchy. And then they became even more curious, the people watching the film.

The censors—in my opinion, anyway; you might not agree, a lot of people might not agree—but in my opinion, as a filmmaker, in this case, the censorship actually brought the film to another level. When you look at some people, you see the scars on the face, they're tough.

This guy has a story. "Where did you get that cut? Where did you get that scar?" "I was fighting with a motorcycle gang. And this scar here, I ran into some glass. I was thinking of something and smoking outside, one week before the film opened. And I got forty stitches." So, now this film became like a person.

And I told my producer, "They don't know what we're going to do. They agreed so quickly. So, let's call them back again" [*laughs*]. So, we called them back and I said, "But you know that you're going to look like a fool. You know what the film's going to look like." They said they knew. "But you'll look like a fool." And they said, "Yeah." But they wanted the film to be shown. And I think they agreed to this, even though they knew that they would look like a fool, partly because they—this is my guess, it might not be a fact—but my guess is that they were shocked at my manner, that I didn't say "Fuck you!" to them. I was as calm as a Buddhist monk when I talked to them. So, they felt that they had to accommodate me a little bit.

But, having said all this, this is a fluke, that I could have this solution. If I didn't come up with this solution, I wouldn't show the film. I would not cut the film; I wouldn't show the film. And this solution is a one-off thing. I'm making part two, and it will be done in about a year from now, and the hope of this one actually showing in Thailand is super-slim. Because we go deep into something that has to be talked about, like the coup d'état.

**The People's Alliance for Democracy?**

No, not so much. To be honest, we try to stay away from this 'red' and 'yellow,' because I find that, right now, this kind of thing seems like a big deal, being a 'redshirt' or a 'yellowshirt.' The country is so divided in this way. Even this mob here, with the whistles.[297] It seems like it's a big deal now. But a hundred years from now, eighty years from now, when we're all dead, when we look back into the journey of democracy, this thing will be like dust, almost.

I read a lot of research. There are so many incidents in our past that were such a big deal at the time, and nowadays we don't even know about. Like the coup d'état, it will always be examined. We've had twenty-one coups d'état. As many versions as *Nang Nak*! The coup d'état is exactly the same: they keep remaking it in different versions. Like *lèse-majesté*, you have to talk about it, why it exists. It must've had a reason in the beginning. Or the massacre on 6 October [1976].

**You covered that in *Paradoxocracy*.**

Very little. You want to *examine* it. To be honest, when I made *Paradoxocracy* part one, no such film had been made in Thailand before, in the history of our country. Television, maybe. Documentaries, maybe. But for a filmmaker to actually make a film about this and put it in a cinema, commercially, it was not done before.

So, when we made part one, a lot of people who we wanted to talk to were not interested. Okay, they knew who *I* was, most of the people knew who *I* was, but they didn't know we would be so serious about doing it. They thought it would be a half an hour documentary on TV. But when the first part came out, it was so well received, it was packed, every screening up to the front row. And with the second part, we got a lot more cooperation.

But if the country hasn't changed by the time we finish the film, the hope of it to see the light in this country will be so dim. I'm saying this to say that the idea that I came up with, to solve the problem of the censorship in the first part of *Paradoxocracy*, is a one-off thing.

It's like the Beatles' 'The White Album': you can only do 'The White Album' once. You can't do 'The White Album' twice.[298]

**So, are you thinking that maybe you wouldn't show it in Thailand, or at least not commercially in Thailand?**

I would *love* to show it here, but really it's not for me to say what can be shown and what cannot. But it's like, you have to do it. You've come this far. For somebody like me, who five years ago had no interest in politics at all—I was happily making my love stories here—to become *very* interested in politics. I have no choice. At least, you have to document it.

In fact, this is the country that needs to see the film most [*laughs*]. So, you would stop this petty arguing. Because I wanted to make this film, both parts—it's supposed to be a *sane* film, in a country that's so insane. It's supposed to be a steady kind of film. I had no intention of making it neutral, but that's because I'm not neutral. I have my own political standpoint, individually. But it's not about 'red' or 'yellow.' My standpoint is not about that. It's to be sober. Because, right now, my God, nobody is sober.

I went to vote [on 2 February 2014] but, of course, I couldn't, because my voting site was closed, because of not enough staff working. But I went to vote. And now, a lot of my friends are shocked that I went to vote, because they decided not to go to vote. Suddenly, a person who goes to vote has to explain themselves [*laughs*]. It should be the other way around!

**It's extraordinary.**

Suddenly, if you go to vote in the last election, or if you had the intention to go to vote, you supported the government. No, I don't support the fucking [Pheu Thai] government! This is a terrible government. And I *love* the fact that people came out in droves to protest against the government, but I'm against people who say that "We don't want elections" [*laughs*]. I'm against that. And I don't want a government elected by a group of people and not the whole country. I'm against that. I don't fucking care that these people are the 'good people' or not. I don't care. But if I go along with this shit then where do I base my principles? I don't know where.

At least I have to believe in something that is not emotional. If you play football, the rule is that you can't use your hands. And suddenly, we have a group of people who come out in droves, saying "But if we keep playing only with our feet and our heads, and without using our hands, then we can't win. The other guys will always win. So, let's stop this game and then decide, maybe we can use our hands sometimes or our elbows sometimes."

**Or the 'invisible hand.'**[299]

Or the 'invisible hand.' But then that's not football, that's volleyball. So, then, let's agree that we're going to play volleyball. But then, if you agree to play volleyball, then you can't use your feet, okay? "No, we want to use everything."

I don't like Thaksin [Shinawatra]. I don't like him. I cannot say that I don't like Yingluck [Shinawatra], because she has no interest in this thing at all. She's doing it for her brother. She'd rather go shopping. And I don't think she's more dumb than an average Thai woman. She's average. But she shouldn't become the prime minister [*laughs*]. The rice scheme thing is so terrible.[300] But let's protest issue by issue, and don't bunch all the issues together. I can't go along with that.

I don't like this government. And I agree, I like it when millions of people come out to protest against the government. I think that's the right thing to do, when you have a bad government. I even went to the mob, in the beginning. I even went, because I thought the ridiculous pardon thing—

**The amnesty.**

The amnesty thing. That they would pardon everybody, except the people who are accused of the *lèse-majesté* law—they will never come out. It should be the other way around [*laughs*]. These political prisoners, they didn't do anything. Like that guy [Somyot Prueksakasemsuk] who just published the article in the 'redshirt' magazine [*Voice of Taksin*]. And he's in jail. And Ah Kong [Ampon Tangnoppakul] is dead. So, this fucking amnesty bill—I went out on the street. But then afterwards, the government backed down.

**Right, but they didn't stop.**

They didn't stop. And now, suddenly, all these people who go to the protest with their Hermés bag and Prada shoes and outfit, and all their phones, they go, "You know, Pen-ek, we have to fight for the farmers. These poor farmers, they're being so cheated." And I'm going, "Have you seen a farmer in your life? You never left your fucking Mercedes. Have you seen a farmer?" Suddenly, they're going, "Poor farmers."

And now, the government is fucked, so the government is going around to every bank, to say, "Please loan us the money, so we can give it to the farmers." So, the protesters were like, "Any banks that would loan the money to the government, we'll go and shut them down." "But I thought you wanted the farmers to have the money?"

So now they don't want the farmers to get the money, because if the farmers get the money, the farmers will go home. And they would have no cause to cling to. So, these middle class now cling to the farmers: "Oh, Pen-ek, I feel so bad for these farmers." "When have you seen farmers in your life? Have you seen a farmer?" And these are my friends. Mostly, they're my friends, because I'm middle class. These are my friends, but I want to puke in their face.

**Sometimes I try to explain it to friends back in the UK, but how can you explain what's happening because it's so ridiculous? You couldn't make it up.**

Right. I tried to explain to some German people, about a month ago. Halfway through, I just had to give up, because I got confused myself. "What the hell is this?" So, I'm trying to stay sober from all this. And I can't talk about this to anybody. Because they would piss me off, or I would piss them off.

What people don't realize is that, as human beings, we're more complex than that, than just to belong to one group. We are more complex than that. I go to vote—"Oh, you're a 'redshirt.' " I don't know. Some days I'm 'red.' Some days I'm 'yellow,' depending on, that day, who pissed me off. In fact, if I'm going to be a 'redshirt,' it's not a disease. "If I'm going to become a 'redshirt' one day, it's because of people like you [*laughs*] who drive me there."

The only reason I haven't become a full-blown 'redshirt' at the moment is just because I don't like Thaksin. If the 'redshirt' people can separate themselves from Thaksin, then I would become completely a 'redshirt.' And if they stay sober. Anyway, let's get back to our censorship thing [*laughs*].

*The last question is about what happened with the cinemas that were showing Paradoxocracy.*

Oh, that's another form of censorship.

**Was there an active campaign to dissuade people from seeing it, or was it just a miscommunication?**

It was a campaign. Well, it started when we were editing the film. The two cinema chains that were friends of mine, they always say, "Whatever Pen-ek does, we'll always show."

**Major and SF?**

No, I didn't know Major well. It's another one: they own Siam, Lido, Scala.[301] They're good friends of ours, and they appreciate what I do, and my position in the Thai film industry, and they realize that they have to support it. And I think, if you're not so stupid, for commercial reasons or from a business point of view, to support somebody like me, or support somebody like Apichatpong, or Aditya [Assarat], it made them look good. They show this kind of film. They support this kind of filmmaker.

So, when we were editing the documentary, they said, "We'll definitely show it." "Okay, fine." And when we finished editing, we sent a rough cut to them. They just went quiet. Strangely quiet. And we planned to do the press conference in one of the cinemas. In fact, we'd already printed the posters with the date of the release. But that was just the rough-cut stage. We didn't lock the picture or the sound.

They went quiet, and then a few days before the press conference, they called my producer, and they said that the venue that they planned to give us to do this thing is not available. They had to do another press conference about the Oscar films that they were going to release in the next month, or something. That's strange. And so my producer called them and said, "So, what is going on?" And they said they don't think they could show the film.

So both of them pulled out. "So what do we do?" So we took it to Major. And the programmer of Major—I think there are two or three programmers, each of them operating independently—this guy liked the film. And he said, "Especially as it's Pen-ek's film, we're here to serve." I had a meeting with them. They were talking to me very respectfully. They said they are fans of my films. They were a bit *noi jai* [disappointed] that *Headshot* didn't play in Major. And they wanted to do this. "Great." And the film went through the censor, as we talked about. So everything was set.

And we had the press screening one night, in a small cinema, one of Major's. And unexpectedly, the film became quite a bit of a hit, over that night. Because I thought people would just fall asleep, watching people talking. And then it spread on the Internet that the film would go to cinemas on a certain day, in one week.

And after that press screening, I had to go to Israel. So, I went to Tel Aviv. There was a film festival there, and I had to teach a class. So, when the film opened, I was in Israel. And when I was there, I didn't know any news. So, when I came back, I realized that there was so much difficulty, because all my friends texted me, when I put my SIM back in my phone [*laughs*].

And you know the story. They didn't put the film on the website. When somebody called the cinema, they would either say, "We're not sure the film is showing tonight or not" or sometimes they would say that they were not showing. And there was one weekend when the 'redshirt' people were going to come and see the film, and they booked thirty-two seats, or something like that, and after that, they realized that those are the 'redshirt' people. At that time there was this 'white mask' movement.[302] They were afraid that they were going to clash. They told the people that somebody already bought out the cinemas that showed the film. And the programmer who booked the film disappeared. We couldn't contact him. He went outside of Bangkok.

So, this went on for ten days. We agreed to show the film for ten days. But it's funny because halfway through—five days—the cinemas realized that they were making quite a bit of money from this film. So now the battle between greed and fear [*laughs*], the inner battle.

**Greed wins, I guess.**

No, they operate on both planes. So, on one side they still continue to try to discourage people to come to the cinema. But the more they discourage, the more people came. So, in fact, it's a win-win situation for them [*laughs*]. But every day, I wanted to kill somebody. And I thought if I couldn't kill anybody by the end of day ten, I'd kill myself. I'm so depressed, every day. They did things that I felt were really disrespectful to me, and to the film, and to the *audience*.

So, one day, I just told my producer, "We have to meet with these Major people. I can't go on like this." So, the programmer came to meet us. And he looked like a wreck. And he said he's going to be fired. So, I said, "What happened?" He said that he thought he had the power to put the film in the cinemas, because he'd been working at Major for the last—I don't know—seven years. He'd put films into cinemas, even controversial films, and some films he even took out halfway through by himself, so he had the power. But with this film, he realized that he didn't have any power at all.

His big boss saw a trailer.[303] He didn't see the film, he saw a trailer. He said, "Is Thaksin in the film? How can you put a film with Thaksin in the cinema?" So, on the day before it was released, he was going to pull the film out. They switched the decision—"Pull out"/"No"/"Yes"—about five times before the noon showing, because my producer told them that, if they pull the film out, they have to answer questions to the journalists, because my producer said, "Pen-ek and I cannot answer. The journalists are waiting." So, they said, "Fuck, we cannot pull out." So, they had to go ahead with the film, but no promotion whatever. That became the situation.

So, the guy said he was going to be fired. In fact, I pitied him. I felt kind of bad for him. But in the meantime, the managers of the two cinemas loved it, because, "My God, it's making money!" So, every day, while they're blocking the people to see the film, they kept calling me and producer saying, "We want to put it in more cinemas. And, by the way, after the ten days, we want to extend one more week." So, I said, "No more cinemas. Just keep the two cinemas. And after the ten days, we don't want any more headaches." Because by that time, I had to kill somebody. I became so violent [*laughs*]. For somebody so calm, I became *so* violent. I became like a person I didn't like, actually. But they said, "But you can make a lot more money." I said, "Fuck the money! I don't care about the money" [*laughs*].

**Now you're doing it again, if you're making part two.**
Yeah, now I'm doing it again [*laughs*]. You never learn!

(The interview took place at a café in Bangkok on 11 February 2014.)

# THUNSKA PANSITTIVORAKUL

*"I decided not to show any of my films in Thailand."*

**In terms of censorship, your case is different because you don't show your films here.**

In 2009, my film *This Area Is Under Quarantine* was banned from the World Film Festival. Since then, I decided not to show any of my films in Thailand. But because Harit [Srikhao] is my close friend [*laughs*], and he has a new photography exhibit at Gallery VER, I'll show *Homogeneous, Empty Time*, that I made with Harit.[304] This film has something related with his photography, also.

**His photos are in the film.**

Yes. But his new work is about politics, and this film is a bit political and personal. So, I decided to show it in July [2017], not in Gallery VER but next to VER, at Tentacles, a small coffee shop with only maybe fifty seats. And I'll show it only once.[305]

**Can I start with your short films? Was it hard to show films like *Unseen Bangkok*?**

It was easier than now. At that time, I thought it was really hard. But that time was easier than now. That period had more freedom. I thought it was the time for something like this, because the technology changed—the Handycam. There was no mobile phone. The Handycam changed the world for the filmmaker. It was easier and so many filmmakers made movies about themselves. Me too. Trying to tell everything that we feel about Bangkok. But some topics I couldn't tell in public, like that guy, actually he used to be a model, a nude model. He was a prostitute.

I found a pirate VCD on sale in Pantip.[306] It's a video shot by some guy in a changing room in a swimming pool. And I was quite excited about that video, because most of them were about women or girls, but this one had men. So, I cut between that VCD and this guy.

**How have things changed since that period of underground filmmaking?**

In this time, we have a lot of platforms. We have Vimeo, YouTube, some channels can show short films. But at that time, you could show only in some places, and not so many people were going there, just maybe a hundred, fifty, twenty people. To watch a movie, you must go from your home to that place, but now everything is easier. For underground films, there's more freedom, because you can do anything and no censorship, because just a few people watch them.

**I remember at Gallery VER, you showed all your short films, and there was a small audience.**

At that time, I met Benedict Anderson, who came to see that also.[307] At that time, because I showed in just small places, some people called me to ask to watch. Sometimes, some of them told me that they're from a cultural center and they need to watch. And sometimes they said they can help sending to film festivals, but actually it's not that—they need to check what I will say in the movie. At that time, I didn't know who they were, and sometimes I got scared because I was not sure. Some people told me that they needed to watch because they needed to write a thesis, but sometimes it's not, sometimes it's from the government. At that time, I was quite low-profile. Until now.

**Apichatpong [Weerasethakul] said the same thing. Now he tries to stay off Facebook. He doesn't even want to promote his film.**

When I started on Facebook, I had around 3,000 or 4,000 Facebook friends. But now I deleted, and have only 200.

**So, these people from the government or somewhere, would they contact you before screenings, or would they turn up in the audience?**

They never came to the screenings, but they called me and asked me to show them. This thing is very hard, very tiring for me, because, sure, I need to show my films to an audience [*laughs*], but who are they? So, I just show in some events that I'm quite sure will not make problems for me.

But at the World Film Festival, when Kriengsak Silakong asked me to show at the Festival, he said he would not send it to the censors. But it's not what happened: he sent it to the censors.[308] Actually, my film was not officially banned, because when he sent it to the censors, they could not decide about this film, they could not give the rating.

So, finally that film couldn't be shown. And at that time, I was quite angry with them, so: "I will not show any more films in Thailand and I will do something harder than before."

Apichatpong told me that, when he got the award at Cannes, and he went to dinner with Abhisit Vejjajiva, Abhisit said to Apichatpong: "Your film is very good. It's good for filmmakers to make the world know about Thailand. Don't make a movie like that filmmaker who makes them about politics and nakedness." But he forgot my name. But Apichatpong knew who he meant. So Apichatpong thought maybe he watched some of my films, especially *This Area Is Under Quarantine*, because that one was sent to the censors.

But some people who work for the Ministry of Culture don't know anything about culture. They don't know anything about the art scene. They're from other ministries. When I got the Silpathorn award,[309] the officers couldn't use the Internet. They couldn't use email. At that time, I was in Phuket, and I said, "Can I send my picture, via my email?" And they said, "I cannot do via email. Can you send via fax?" How can I send a picture by fax? My God! And this kind of people work for the Ministry.

**You showed *Middle-earth* at around the same time that you won the award.**

The money for making *Middle-earth* was from that award. At that time, Apichatpong's film *Syndromes and a Century* was banned in Thailand. I knew an actor [Putthithorn Kammak] from that movie, so that actor is in *Middle-earth*. In that film, he is a guy who plays badminton, and has a problem with his brain. He was in the hospital in Apichatpong's film, and actually two years ago he killed himself, and I just knew it last year from Facebook.

One of them is him, and one of them [Tarueti Sriwatana] is the son of a politician. I knew him by accident. And he has a scar around here [*points to his thigh*] because he had a tattoo but his mother didn't like it. So, his mother told him that he must remove the tattoo. So, he went to the hospital to get it lasered, and he got that scar from that. This is not in the movie.

**Sure, but you see the scar in the movie.**

Yes, and because of this I selected the two of them for this movie. It's funny—I thought, as Thai people, we have so many rules, so many things we cannot do: I cannot do something, because my mother doesn't like it. I'm really fascinated by something like this, so I chose them for the film.

That short film is two guys who sleep, and sleep, and sleep. For me, that time is like a time that freedom was sleeping. After the period that Apichatpong's film was censored was the period that Thailand got the new law about ratings. But for me, it's worse than before, so my feeling is like freedom is sleeping.

**Why is it worse than before?**

Because you could sneak to show somewhere by not showing it to the censors, if you made an independent film. Actually, that law covers not only film. If you made a wedding video, by that law you must send the wedding video to the censors. Or you made a VCD that you gave for free with a magazine, you must send that VCD to the censors. Actually, they cannot check all of them, but if someone goes to a wedding, and saw that something was not good in the wedding video, he can tell the government to check it. Because the rule covers that also.

And that movie, I tried to make two people asleep, feeling like a good dream, with a white room. When the government made the rule, they said they made it because it is good for the people, and when they ban some movie it's because that movie is not good, it's bad for you. And some people like it. For me, it's like in a dream, the earth that everything is good and clean, no monsters or evil in this world.

**It's a fantasy?**
Yes. But finally, in the last part, I tried to say that we, as a people, are still alive. But still in a dream.

**Because he is still asleep.**
Yes.

**To go back to *This Area Is Under Quarantine*, did they ever say why they wouldn't give the rating? Was it because of Tak Bai?**
They didn't give any reason. They just said they cannot decide to show or not to show. I thought it was like their strategy to try to not show my film.

**Why did you want to show the Tak Bai clip?**
Actually, at that time, I didn't know anything about politics. I still hated Thaksin, like everyone, but I didn't question about the soldiers. But I started to learn about politics, because I got an award from the Taiwan Documentary Film Festival, and I had so many interviews in magazines, but one of the interviewers worked for *Image* magazine, and during the interview she asked me why I wasn't interested in politics. Actually, at the time, I wasn't interested in political issues. I tried to protest the government in lectures, about gay issues, and I

never knew anything about politics. And she gave me *Fah Diew Kan* [*Same Sky*].

**They had the VCD of Tak Bai.**
Yes. Actually, the Tak Bai clip is from that.

**From that VCD? I have that, too.**
It's the same clip. So, the method of making this film is the same method as *Unseen Bangkok*: I got footage from the VCD, and I interviewed some guys in the movie. But because at that time I never knew anything about politics, I asked them. The southern politics is different, so I shot them because one of them is Isaan and one of them is southern. Actually, my mother's family is southern, but I had never been to Isaan.

But finally, both of them said they also hated Thaksin, even though the Isaan boy said his family loved Thaksin. But at that time I wasn't interested in this issue. Something happened in that VCD that touched me, the first time that I watched it. It's something that I never knew from other media. And for the film, I tried to make the structure merge between documentary and acting.

**Reincarnate also seems to be partly documentary and partly acting.**
The film that changed my world is *Reincarnate*.[310] I knew something more than before. But I'm still living in Thailand [*laughs*]. How can I live here when I know the truth?

**This is the film that you wanted to be "harder" than *This Area Is Under Quarantine*?**

Yes. It tells something about politics and royalty. But I was still living in Thailand, so I could not say it directly, so I said it like a poem.

**There is also one of your most graphic sex scenes in that film.**

That was the first masturbation in my movies, *Reincarnate* and *The Terrorists*. For me, it's for the same reason. When you masturbate, you feel happy, but it's like a dream, it's just a short time. And after that, you wake up to reality [*laughs*]. When you wake up, everywhere around you is reality, and you cannot break out. You must live with it. For *The Terrorists*, it's a bit different, but for *Reincarnate* it's just like that. But for *The Terrorists* it's more than that, because I tried to compare with 6 October [1976].

**You show him masturbating and then you show the footage of 6 October.**

For me, it's like masturbation: that massacre is like masturbation.

**Why?**

Some people did it to make it better. They need to feel good and happy, but it's really cruel. And for me, it's more complicated than that. For the left wing, the people who died in that situation are like heroes, fighting for democracy. But for me, they are not heroes. They are losers. And when I say that to the left wing, they will think I'm really cruel.

We never win, and a lot of people die. So, when I showed *The Terrorists*, some left wingers hated that scene [*laughs*].

**Of course.**

But when I make films, I try to record the feeling that I feel to my country, that I feel during that time. And it's not easy to make a film. I make a feature every two years. So, during that time, I think again and again and again. And I don't need to make films and be a hero for the left wing. But I made it because I thought about them in that way, and I don't care [laughs] who will hate me or love me.

I must tell you that the first time that I got funding from Germany, from Jürgen [Brüning], for making a film was *The Terrorists*, but the first project that I told him was not *The Terrorists*. I forget the title of the film, but the project was beautiful men in various occupations in Thailand, like farmers [laughs], in every part of Thailand. So, I started going on a boat—

**Oh, with the fishermen?**

With the fishermen, on *The Terrorists*. I started from that. But I was on board on 10 April [2010], the first day that they shot the people on Khao San Road. On the boat, there was no Internet, no television, so I called to my friend in Bangkok and asked her about the situation, "What happened in Bangkok?" The day after that, I came back to Bangkok, and they had a small ceremony, with some people going there and lighting candles as a memorial, for the people who died in that situation. One of them that I met on that day, at Democracy Monument, was an eighteen-year-old guy, my friend's son. Some weeks after that, that guy was shot dead. After that, I emailed to Jürgen, "I need to change the topic and I need to know what happened, so I'm going there."

A year before that, 2009, in April's Songkran festival, they had a situation like that also, but it was short-term. At that time, I was still teaching at Bangkok University, and I watched television. Because of Songkran, I was not going to the university, but I watched television and every channel was Victory Monument. The camera from PBS showed Victory Monument, something burning, and smoke at the Monument.[311] Actually, at that time, I hated the 'redshirts,' because the television reported that they tried to burn the city. But a Facebook friend made a clip. She went there. It's the same clip shown on the news on television, but on TV they cut something out. So, if you watch that clip on the news on TV, you will really hate the two women who are 'redshirts.' They blame the soldiers, they're fighting with the reporter, and are really aggressive in that clip. But after that, when I watched the full clip that my friend shot, she said that in the morning she saw so many soldiers kill some 'redshirts,' and drag them to a truck. I was really shocked. It's the same again as in the clip that I watched on *Fah Diew Kan* [*Same Sky*]'s VCD.

So, after that I tried to read a lot of books, so many books about politics, and tried to talk with people who knew about politics. A year after that, when my friend's son died, I got involved by going to the area. I needed to know what happened. When I think about what I did at that time, at Soi Rangnam, I scare myself, because that area was really dangerous.

When I was shooting that clip at Soi Rangnam, I didn't know who they were, but they were shooting guns at the people. I saw a guy there in front of me [*holds up a finger at arm's length*], not so far, like across the road, and he just [*throws his head back*].[312] "My God! Why did I come here?" But at that time, I needed to keep shooting. I must keep shooting. And once, I remember something like that [*points to a pillar*], I hid behind that, and I found that above me someone was shooting. And nowadays I still ask myself why I went there, and why

I kept shooting. But my feeling was very strong at that time, so I put so much information about politics in that film.

**Let's move on to *Supernatural*. How risky is it to make a film like that in Thailand? Is it safe to do that, with references to 'the Leader' as in *Nineteen Eighty-Four*?**

I thought it's not obvious for a foreign audience. If you're living in Thailand, you will know, but I didn't show my films in Thailand, so I don't care. I could not do anything, and I needed to fight, but I didn't know how to fight, so I made this film. But one thing that I still think the same as in *The Terrorists* is, we will never win. Even in a hundred years, we will never win. So, I started from that point.

One thing is sure, that I cannot show the king's picture in my movie, because I would get problems. The film was made for DVD, so I showed other pictures, ancient pictures.[313]

**So, is that because the DVD could come back to Thailand?**

Yeah.

**Can you say more about that? Because Apichatpong [Weerasethakul] had the same situation.**

Every house in Thailand has the king and queen's picture. But I cannot put the picture of the king and queen in the movie, so instead I put Greek gods. In the story, I tried to compare the king with a Greek god or Hindu god. Because the film is fiction. In *Homogeneous, Empty Time*, because it's a documentary, if someone questions me, I can tell them, "You can see something like that everywhere." But when I make fiction, if I put that picture in the film, I thought I could get some problems.

But in *Homogeneous, Empty Time,* I was quite surprised, because the boys in that film are quite young, but they criticize Prayut [Chan-o-cha] and 'Bike for Dad.'[314]

But not all of them, actually just one of them. And a group criticizes the government.

This might be a strange question, but did their parents say anything about that? Because these are young people. Maybe they don't know the consequences.

Maybe they don't know. And they are living in a dorm, not with their families, so I think their parents didn't know.

Do you worry about the result of showing the film?

For this film, I will not make a DVD. I will show it once in July [2017],[315] but to just a few people, and I will check every guest [*laughs*].

(The interview took place at a restaurant in Bangkok on 1 May 2017.)

# NONTAWAT NUMBENCHAPOL

*"It would be hard to stay in Thailand, if I do something controversial."*

**I wanted to ask you about Boundary. Why did you decide to make a film on that subject?**

About the temple? At first, I wasn't planning to shoot in Cambodia at the temple. I wanted to shoot the conflict in Bangkok between 'redshirts' and 'yellowshirts.' And I focused on the Ratchaprasong situation at that time, because before that I'd never been interested in politics. I was a teenager, a young man not interested in politics so much.

But, at that time, it happened in the middle of Bangkok, and everything stopped and I couldn't go anywhere. I wanted to know what happened. I started to read lots of articles about that. I was a bit confused about the truth of it. Almost a hundred people died [in 2010]. After that, I met a soldier from the crackdown.

**That was Aod?**

Yeah. I talked with him, and I was interested in his experience, because I'd never had a life like him. He was in the real situation, in every political conflict in Thailand. Before Ratchaprasong, he was sent to the south of Thailand, then he was sent to the crackdown in Bangkok.

I wanted to know what the people in the real situation think. I talked with him, and he told me he'd be back to his hometown in Sisaket province on the border of Thailand and Cambodia for the [2011] Songkran festival. I asked him if it was okay to go with him and shoot. When I followed him to his hometown, Thailand and Cambodia were fighting at that time. It was very interesting for me, because this situation was like a chain reaction from the politics in Bangkok in the middle of Thailand. When I knew that this situation was because of the temple, an ancient temple which still had a conflict now, I chose this topic.

At first, I wanted to show more of him, but sometimes when I was shooting with him on camera, he panicked, and acted not natural. But when I talked with him, he could tell his story. With the war between Thailand and Cambodia at that time, I could not shoot in some places, because it was sensitive with the soldiers over there. They didn't want me shooting over there. I talked with people who got problems on the border, and that was fine. And then Thai people's opinions on the border conflict. And I wanted to cross the border to shoot in Cambodia, but because I'm Thai I could not cross and shoot over there. I had to spend one year looking for connections to bring me to shoot [*laughs*].

**It's quite brave to have not only one sensitive topic, Ratchaprasong, but also the temple in the same film.**

At first, when I had the idea, I was still young, and I didn't know what the problems were going to be. When I sent it to the censors, I didn't know it would happen like this. But now I know [*laughs*]. Thai society is very sensitive.

This year is the first year that Supannahong, the Thai film awards, were open for everyone to vote for the final nominations. But my film was not in the voting list. I didn't know why, and I asked the Supannahong members. Nobody knew why my film was not in that list. Finally, my film was put in, but it was too late for voting.

**So, you think it was too sensitive to be included?**
I think so.

**Some people might be surprised by the military draft lottery that you show in the film.**[316]
It's only in Thailand? England doesn't have it?

**Not in the last fifty years.**
Wow.

**How did you feel when you finally got access to the temple?**
I was really happy, because it was hard to go there. I was planning to finish this film around two years ago, but I couldn't shoot at the border. I had a rough cut, without shooting the Cambodian border side, but it wasn't a good film because it was a bit biased.

Finally, I was lucky because I found my coproducer [Davy Chou]. He is French-Cambodian, and he's a director, too. He helped me a lot with connections. Finally, I got a connection from New York, not in Cambodia. She [Tith Kanitha] is Cambodian, but she stayed in New York. But her hometown is Preah Vihear, so that's good for me. And she really wanted to help me shoot over there, because she wanted to show Thai people what happened to the Cambodian people. Finally, I could go. But she told me I could not tell anyone in Cambodia that I'm Thai, because it would be hard to shoot. I had to tell everybody I'm Chinese-American [*laughs*], a friend of hers. My name was Thomas in Cambodia.

Finally, when I wasn't Thai, it was so easy to shoot at Preah Vihear temple. Everybody in Cambodia was so nice, took care of me and helped me, and loved to talk about the situation. I was so happy, because finally I'd finished my film, and Preah Vihear temple is very beautiful. It felt like heaven, very high, in the clouds.

But one thing I was not happy about, I could not show my real identify. I was a bit panicked. I didn't want to stay a long time. I was there around five days, at the temple one day, and other places. But I wanted to stay over there more, because I wanted more footage.

**So, it's really like a coproduction between Thailand and Cambodia, if the producer is Cambodian?**

Yes. But he grew up in Paris. His family moved to Paris before the Khmer Rouge.[317] He emailed me: "I heard you're making a film about Thailand and Cambodia. We have to join up." So, I joined with him and he helped me on this project.

For the production in Cambodia, I was the only Thai because I could not take my Thai crew over there. I had a Cambodian team of two people with me.

**You finished the film and you had to submit it to the censor. What happened next?**

It premiered at the Berlinale, and I wanted to screen it in theatres in Thailand. I had to send it to the censors. I sent it, and they said,

"Wait one week." Then, someone called me and said, "You can come." And my film was banned: "Cannot show in Thailand." I said, "Why is it banned?" She said, "It's very sensitive." I asked her, "Which part is sensitive? Can I do something about it?" She told me, "You cannot edit, because it's the whole film." Then I called Kong Rithdee and Apichatpong [Weerasethakul].

I went back to my home and I wrote on Facebook, and posted about the ban. And I was surprised, because in one night there's around 2,000 shares about it. In the morning, I was phoned all day by TV and media around the world—*The Guardian*, AP—I was so surprised.

The censors called me again: "Okay, let's lift the ban." But they asked me about one scene with sound about the king. I asked my friends who saw the film. Nobody had heard this sound. It's like an ambient sound, celebrating the king and celebrating the new year at Ratchaprasong. They wanted to mute this sound. It was okay, because it was just two seconds. But Apichatpong told me it's not good, not the right thing. But okay [*laughs*].

**So, when they initially said it was banned, what reason did they give?**

I talked with people at the border, and the people there supported the 'redshirt' side. But I think the censorship members' attitude was on the other side. I think that's why. One thing they said: it's not a documentary, it's not the truth, it's opinion. They had a problem with the captions in the film. One reason they banned me is that my attitude doesn't match with the censors' attitude.

**But two days later, they changed their opinion. Was that because of the international media attention?**

I think so. They said it's a subcommittee, but the censorship process is not professional. There are two rooms for the censors. My film was sent to the DVD room. "If you want a quick result, you have to send it to another room, but only big films are sent there, like *Pee Mak.*" I asked them, "My film is not for DVD now, but I want to screen in theatres." And someone told me, "This film is not for theatres, just for DVD." The process is not professional. For big films, it's more easy. And I think they have money. I think when they saw my film, and they didn't like every scene, "Just ban it."

I didn't think people were interested in it, but it flew around the world. And I think the censors were surprised about this, too. I think, on that day, so many media called the censors to ask about this film. Have you seen Thunska [Pansittivorakul]'s film?

**Yes, sure.**

But that film has not only politics, it has—

**Sex, as well.**

Dick [*laughs*].

**But he said he would not show his new film in Thailand, only internationally.**

Have you seen it?

**Sure, *Supernatural*.**

It's good?

**Yeah, it's great. I think it's his best film, actually.**
Why doesn't he want to show it in Thailand?

**Because, I think, he knows it would be banned.**
It talks about the king?

**Not directly. It's set in the future, and everybody follows 'the Leader.'**
I don't know why Thai people are so crazy. I think there's too much propaganda on TV.

**You were given an 18 rating. How did you feel about that?**
I requested 18 because we can elect at eighteen-plus. You have to choose what you want to believe in my film. There is not one truth, and it's a sensitive thing. But after my film passed the censorship, the censors told me, "If you asked for 13," they will give me 13 too, but finally it's 18 [*laughs*]. Why are they talking like that? At first, they banned me, but finally they told me, "If you want that rating, you can, but you asked for 18. Okay, I give you 18."

**So, you don't want to change to a 13 rating?**
It's fine. I have to think a lot about my new projects. I'd love to do a controversial issue. But it would be hard to stay in Thailand if I do something controversial in the future, super-controversial. I think I cannot. I'm thinking about my life [*laughs*].

Thunska said he has a choice: do something conventional and show it in Thailand; or do something controversial and not show it in Thailand. And he chose to do something controversial. And Pen-ek [Ratanaruang] is making *Paradoxocracy* part two, and "the hope of this one actually showing in Thailand is super-slim," he told me.

But the best way is to show in Thailand, and it's very controversial. It's hard, but everybody will talk about it.

My new film, after *Boundary*, is still political and controversial, but it's more artistic. This film [*By the River*] is about toxins in the river. It captures the people who live around the river: their lives at that moment. Talking with Apichatpong, he said, "This film is more political."

Foreign audiences like my new film more, because they are touched by everything. But in *Boundary*, sometimes they don't know Thai politics, they're confused about what happened in Bangkok [*laughs*]. In Q&As afterwards, I have to tell everybody about 'redshirts' and 'yellowshirts.' It's very hard to explain about this. It's so complicated [*laughs*].

It doesn't have talking-head interviews. Some people think it's a fiction film. It looks like a fiction film.

**What happened about the distribution for *Boundary*? Because you had to show the film yourself?**

I had a problem. After the press screening at Major Cineplex, the programmer called to say, "We have to take it out. Major cannot screen this film anymore." We were shocked. "What happened?" They said that the owner of Major knew about my film. Not only my film, but Pen-ek's film, too.

**He said the same thing, the same problem.**

At first, the problem was Pen-ek's film, because the trailer had Thaksin [Shinawatra] in it. When people saw that the program didn't have Pen-ek's film, people talked like, "Banned again." They had to be like, "The show must go on." A lot of people called Major, and the media were still interested in this issue, and they had to screen Pen-ek's film.

But my film was just a press screening, and they took it out. And I changed to SF, because before this SF had called me: "We want to screen the film." But I'd told SF, "I already dealt with Major" so I had to say no to SF. But Major did that, and I wanted to change to SF.

I tried to call SF and talk about this. I thought I would stop the press screening that day, and change to SF the next week, but finally Major told me I cannot do that. If I stopped the press screening and changed to another distributor, the problem is that the media and everybody would ask why the press screening was stopped. Finally, I had to rent the theatres by myself. I had to sell tickets by myself, because I rented the theatres by myself.

(The interview took place at a restaurant in Bangkok on 11 February 2014.)

# CHULAYARNNON SIRIPHOL

*"I fight for the next film, the next project in the future."*

**Why did you start making films about politics?**

Around 2009, at that time, was a big riot in Bangkok. 'Redshirt' people blocked the streets.

**During Songkran.**

During Songkran, in April. I live in Bangkok, grew up in Bangkok. It affected my life. I questioned why they came to Bangkok, because most of the 'redshirt' people were from the countryside. And from that point, I turned to be interested in the political situation. And the first film that I made is *Karaoke: Think Kindly*. It's not only my work.

**That's right. Scene 22.**

Scene 22. My friends from university. We were film students. We graduated in 2008, so it's one year after. We worked together. There was a competition from a television program. They created a short film competition about Thai politics, so we made this *Karaoke* and submitted it.[318]

**Did it play on television?**

Yes, it premiered on television. The idea of the music video is quite sarcastic, making a relationship between Buddhism and politics. Because the image of Thailand is like a beautiful country, and a peaceful country, but from the conflict in 2009, it seems like maybe it's not true. We have a lot of violence, and we have big protests. And we see a big gap between rich and poor people.

The political situation in 2009 quite changed my perspective about how we understand our society. We had 'yellowshirt' people before 2009. From 2005 to 2008. I was interested, but it wasn't in my films. 'Yellowshirts' were mostly middle-class people. Okay, I am one of the middle-class people. And I think it seems like it's not the main problem. When the 'redshirts' were stronger, in 2009, it got to the point. Suddenly, I was interested in politics, and it appeared in the film.

**In *Karaoke*, you said that you wanted the two sides to come together. Did you think that was possible?**

I think, in 2009, it was possible. From my experience, I had a chance to interview a worker, and he was happy to talk about politics in 2009. But after the incident in 2010—

**Ratchaprasong.**

Ratchaprasong. I went back to interview the worker again, and he said, no, he didn't want to say anything. So, I think, in 2009 it was more positive to be open-minded and talk about what we are thinking. So, I think this film looked positively at the political situation, reconciliation between 'red' and 'yellow.' We can sing together through *Karaoke*, with this karaoke song [*laughs*].

**Can you say something about the ending of the film? You show the photo of the Democracy Monument under construction.**

I found this photo on the Internet. It's under construction, after the [1932] revolution. I think it's kind of symbolic of the unfinished democracy, even though it's past more than eighty years. But today there are many incidents that make us question: do we really have democracy? So, I think that image can represent our situation at this time.

**In *A Brief History of Memory*, you have a monologue from the mother of a 'redshirt' victim. How did you get in contact with her?**

In the beginning, one of my friends, who was an art student, lived in that community, in Nang Loeng. And she would like to create a relationship between art and community. And she would like to make a documentary film about her community. And she invited me and another five artists and directors to make short films or documentary films about the community.[319] I got selected, and in the process I tried to do many activities. For example, in the film, there is a health activity to clean the hair. That is one of the activities that I and my friend created for the children.

And, importantly, my friend's mother is a community leader. And I found out that, in 2009, there was a conflict between the community and the 'redshirt' people. And two people from the community died, shot by the 'redshirt' people at night. And so I think it's interesting to make the connection between personal memory and the Thai political situation at that time, because it's just one year after.

So, I asked the mother, who is a leader of the community, to make a connection between me and the mother who lost her son. As you see in the film, the mother who lost her son speaks quite openly. And many people asked me how I could make it. And I think the mother of my friend is quite powerful in the community, so she could be a bridge, to make her open-minded to talk about her pain and her memory. Because she said this project is a community project. And finally, the film will be screened in the community.[320] It seemed like I was not an outsider, but I am a part of the community, so the mother was open-minded to talk.

**The film ends with a 'redshirt' commemoration. Why is that?**

Because the film was made in 2010, around October, so it's five months after the Ratchaprasong incident in May. For me, it's unacceptable to have political victims. I support peace talks, and I support elections, and no violence, so I would like to talk about all the victims, 'redshirts' and also 'yellowshirts.' For the ending of the film, I didn't want to show the victims of only one side, because it seems that the Nang Loeng community are against the 'redshirts.' So, to make a balance, I also included the 'redshirt' victims from Ratchaprasong, to talk about the victims of politics. Not only to document what happened, but to expand the issue and make it bigger.

**You say that, in *Karaoke*, you wanted to make a connection between Buddhism and politics. Is *Myth of Modernity* a development of the same idea, linking religion and politics?**

I think it's not the intention, but maybe I kept being interested in this topic. But *Myth of Modernity* has one more element: it's not only Buddhism and politics, but also architecture. I made it in 2014, during the time of the right-wing PDRC protests on the street. That protest was quite long, six months or something. The end of 2013.

**Until the coup.**

Until the coup. So, it was a long time and a strong ideology. It's not only against Thaksin [Shinawatra], but [they characterized themselves as] *real* Thai, *real* Buddhists, against corruption. I think that statement was very strong and very radical. It can be like magical realism. Or weird [*laughs*]. I made the connection between the belief of Buddhism and the myth. And also the political ideology of the protesters. So, I combined everything, and the film was divided into two parts. The first part looked like a TV documentary. The second part suddenly changed to science fiction, with no dialogue. It reflects our society. We live in a society with something supernatural, but it really exists in our daily life. Maybe because I grew up in a Buddhist school. But now, can I say that I'm a Buddhist? I think, yes. But some rituals, I think, are only rituals. I don't believe in the rituals, but I still believe in the main idea and the core.

**What about *Here Comes the Democrat Party*? What was the idea behind that?**

It's the same time as the PDRC, but this work was for fun. It's not so complicated [*laughs*]. It's part of the short film project, *Thai Aurora at the Horizon*.[321] We questioned, what is the political ideology in Thailand? The producers made a group of independent Thai filmmakers, and asked them to make short films about politics. And I submitted this short film, just for fun.

It's a kind of music video, the song of the Democrat Party, but the image is the PDRC protesters. But it's quite fun, because the Democrat Party said they were not a part of the PDRC, but we saw that many politicians were part of the PDRC [*laughs*]. So, it's kind of sarcastic, to make fun of the protests and question the politicians.

It's just to reflect what happened at that time, not something deep [*laughs*].

**And *Thai Contemporary Politics Quiz* was also just for fun?**
This was also for fun [*laughs*]. I made ten questions about Thai politics, and four choices for each question. Some answers can all be correct, or none of them. And I don't have the final answer. Maybe some audiences are looking for the correct answer from me, but I said, "It depends on you, your perspective and your belief in political ideology."
It's a silent film, for ten minutes. For me, it's quite interesting to question, is this a film? To make it interactive with the audience. It's not only one-way communication, but the audience can react to the video, to the film itself. The moving image today can be everywhere, in the media, on the Internet. It's not only in the cinema. I try to expand the possibilities of making the moving image, not only short films. Sometimes in public spaces. It's a turning point that I changed from short films to art.

**I think *Planking* is my favorite of your short films. How did you develop the idea for *Planking* originally?**
It's also from a political movement. In 2010, a lot of people were shot in the center of Bangkok. There was one political leader [Sombat Boonngamanong] who supported the 'redshirt' people. He tried to make the government [face its] responsibility for the people who died in the center of Bangkok. He made a performance by inviting the people to lay down on the floor after the national anthem, in public, so you can see many people lay down on the floor, to represent the dead people. That was the first idea. And the second idea, in 2012, for young teenagers around the world, planking was a movement.

**A fad.**

Taking photos and uploading to the Internet. In strange locations. And so I made a connection between the national anthem and the people who lay down on the ground—people who are still alive and people who passed away. It's like a public intervention. When the body is controlled, do we have to follow the rules—follow the norms—or should we question and be against nationalism? Because I think one of the problems in 2010 was nationalism. And it's a simple action, but it's a strong statement.

**Absolutely.**

So, I can say this is like a video performance, like a public intervention. The video itself is the documentation, and the real work is the performance at that time. I was the videographer. My friend, who had the same political ideology as me, said, "Okay, we can do it." But we were worried that some people would be against us, and not understand what we were doing, so we promised that we would not meet after the end of the national anthem. We had to walk away [*laughs*], in different directions, and meet again ten minutes after, so it seemed that we had no connection [*laughs*]. And finally, we did ten places, and no one arrested us. But some places were quite scary, because when my friend lay down on the floor, some people shouted to a car to drive over my friend. But nothing happened.

**A very strong reaction!**

Yes, the most strong reaction from this project. Because the national anthem is at 8am and 6pm, I made an appointment with my friend to come in the morning at Lumpini Park. But at 8am, my friend just woke up, so I had to do it by myself [*laughs*]. Put the camera and perform.

But only one place. No one took care of the camera. Because I was face down, I didn't know what happened to my camera.

But some of my friends, nationalists or right-wing, unfriended me on Facebook [*laughs*]. That's what I got.

And for the places in the video, it's public spaces that the national anthem was announced through speakers. Like in a park or a bus station. In the SkyTrain. But some places were related to modern political history. Like in Thammasat University, the incident on 6 October [1976]. I think it's a good place to make a connection relating to history and the current situation.

**If we compare *A Brief History of Memory*, *Planking*, and *Birth of Golden Snail*, they're all about the history of a specific location. Is that something you're interested in?**

For *Birth of Golden Snail*, it's not related to politics directly. But the Thailand Biennale created an open call for artists to submit a proposal. And the Thailand Biennale is a site-specific art installation, so I made an installation in the cave in Krabi. And my idea was to make a relationship between early cinema—black-and-white film, no dialogue—and a Thai fairy tale written more than 100 years ago. It's about a boy born with a conch, a kind of shell. The film is about the myth and legend, and the origin of early cinema.

I got the approval from the Biennale committee. I finished the film and sent the preview to a different group, the group that censored my film. In the cave area is a Muslim community, and my film contains some nudity. "It shouldn't be screened in the Muslim community." So, in that sense, it's quite a political issue, in terms of gender and religion. Who has the power to decide if this film should be screened—I as an artist, or the curator, or organizer, or the community?

**And there was a problem about the girl in school uniform?**

Oh, I forgot. For the committee of the Biennale, it's not only the nudity, but also the schoolgirl's uniform.[322] Under eighteen years old. In the story, she gets pregnant with a snail and a Japanese soldier during World War II. And the committee said: "Oh, a schoolgirl shouldn't get pregnant under eighteen years old." So, I think it's the second problem, not only the nudity.

And the third one: I think the committee said, the representation of the Japanese soldier in World War II in my film looked violent, so it can make a bad relationship between Thailand and Japan [laughs]. I think it's three issues.

They wanted me to cut some parts of the film. And then, after cutting, I have to resubmit to the committee. But when I had a chance to talk with the curator, the curator said, it depends on me if I will follow them or not. But, for the curator, this film has no problem. And finally, I decided to keep the original version. And I said: "My work is finished. If you want to censor, it depends on the organizer. The organizer can censor the film." For example, they can block the light from the project in some scenes that they don't want the audience to see. Or draw with a black marker onto the film directly. And also, they can cut with scissors [laughs]. But finally, the committee [declined] "because it's the artist's work."

So, it's like a paradox, because after that they gave me a letter [saying] that this film is against article 29, which is that the film can be against national security. "The film is very harmful. It should not be screened." I have to re-edit by myself. Even though they gave me the letter, I still insist to not cut by myself. But the point is, they said I cannot finish my work, and they don't want to pay the last budget. And the last budget is quite big. And I advanced some money, so I need the money back. So, it's like playing a game between me and the organizer [*laughs*].

I said, "Okay, I will screen a white light in the cave. Only white light, in real time. The film is twenty minutes long, so I will screen a white light in the cave for twenty minutes. And I will give the screenplay to the audience, and the audience can read and imagine what should be on the screen [*laughs*]. So, in that sense, the film is in the mind, like imagination, and it depends on the audience." And the committee said, "Oh, it's not the same as you proposed, so we are not [going to] accept it."

That was the first attempt. For the second attempt, "Okay, I will not cut by myself, but I will show only short clips, about two minutes. It's not re-editing, but some parts of the film only." And now, it's [under discussion] if the committee will accept this or not. And I hope they accept this, so I get the money back.

But actually, I don't care so much about the money, but the point is if I cannot finish the work, the organizer can sue me, because it's tax. It's the government's budget, and it seems like I stole the money from the government. But actually, I finished my work, but they don't want to accept that. The worst case is, I have to pay more money than what I got. It's quite complicated, a long process. They think they have the power to do anything.

**But actually, they have no authority, according to the Film and Video Act. They aren't the Film and Video Censorship Committee, so they have no authority to make that decision.**

Yes. In the letter, they refer to article 29. But they are not the Film [and Video Censorship] Committee, they are the Thailand Biennale committee.

But I don't want to screen it, because there is another character in this [*laughs*]. There was a local person in Krabi. He had a chance to see my film, and he posted on Facebook [*adopts a very dramatic tone*]: "Do not look down on the cave, otherwise you will die!" The local people in Krabi commented, "What happened? What is the film about?" And he said, "It's an R film, some nudity. They look down on our community. It's a dangerous film." And it seems like the organizer—the government—tried to protect the community.

So, what is the role of the organizer, if this issue happens? Because now, they take sides, not protect me and the artwork. The organizer should have a public talk between me, the community, the curator, and the organizer. We have to understand each other. But now the organizer is kind of a dictator [*laughs*]. It's not fair for me, and it's not fair for the audience. It's not only the community audience, but foreigners and people from Bangkok who want to see the film in Krabi. But they don't get that chance.

What are we fighting for? A rating system under democracy. It can be a bigger issue, it's not only about the Thailand Biennale. And what is the standard of the ratings in Thailand? I use this film as a case study, to understand and question the system. I don't fight for myself, but I fight for the next film, the next project in the future.

**Let's talk about *Ten Years Thailand*. In 'Planetarium,' there's a link with *Planking*, when the protesters lie down.**

'Planetarium' is a combination of many short films. Not only *Planking*, but also *Myth of Modernity*. And also, did you see *Monk and Motorcycle Taxi Rider*?

**Yes.**

So, from my previous short films talking about Thai politics in different perspectives. But in 'Planetarium' I tried to make a connection between each short film, to show that they're connected.

And the main idea is belief, technology, and education. It seems like someone tries to control the people, to behave in the same way. And the question is, if someone cannot follow the rules, how should we manage? Is it possible to kill the enemy? If the ruler—the government, or someone who has power [*laughs*]—needs the people to behave in the same way.

**"Someone."**

Someone [*laughs*]. Do we have punishment, or do we let diversity happen? In the film, there is punishment. It's like suppressing, or killing. And at the end, it seems like the monk, who is in the upper class of Thai society, blesses the dictator, or someone, or ruler. Blesses and supports them: "What you did is good. Oh, you are a very good dictator" [*laughs*].

But the film has no dialogue, so I would like to hear different interpretations from the audience. But now, it's quite sarcastic. For example, in Khai Maew cartoons, there is no dialogue, so in the comments there are different interpretations. So, in my film, I expect to have more diversity. I hope that the audience can interpret that the dictator is a good person, if they support the dictator. At the end, maybe they think what the dictator did to the people is really great. But, on the other hand, if you're against the dictator, it seems like this film is sarcastic. So, I hope there is more diversity in interpretation.

**You mean, some people will see this and think it's optimistic?**

Maybe [*laughs*]. The pink lady, many people say, looks like someone important in society. I got this question when I went to Busan in Korea. The Korean audience asked me: "Does it look like the queen or not?" And I said, "No, it can be my mother, or my teacher when I was in school, or it can be some female military [leader]." It can be anyone who has power, so it's more flexible to interpret.

**I wasn't thinking about her face or her age, but about her Scout uniform. Is there a connection to the Village Scouts from 6 October [1976]?**

It's not only 6 October. There are many references. The Red Guard in China.[323] Also, during 6 October, there were Village Scouts, using the Scouts as symbolic of people's power, right-wing power. And also now, the current king has a symbol of the Scouts.[324] So, yes, there are many references for the Scouts.

And in my school, I also studied in the Scouts. As you see in the film, it's the young teenagers who are the Scouts, so it can be from my memory also. So, the audience can infer the culture of Scouts in many aspects. It depends on what you know [*laughs*], what you experience. To not make trouble, I can say "It refers to my memory, and my childhood in school."

**That's the safe answer.**

Yeah [*laughs*].

**I heard that you filmed two different versions of the monk, one with saffron robes and one with white robes. Is that true?**

It's true, but it's not my suggestion. It's my producers' suggestion, because they were scared of censorship against the monk's uniform. But we got 13 and everyone was so surprised. The producers [Aditya Assarat, Soros Sukhum, and Cattleya Paosrjiareon] worried about the first film, the black-and-white film.

**'Sunset.'**
Yeah, because of the police and soldiers. And also my film. But finally, we got 13. Maybe because *Thibaan: The Series* got cut. Maybe the Film [and Video Censorship] Committee didn't want to have trouble again in a short period, because people will [say], "Oh, why? What are you doing?" And maybe, if they censored or banned the film, it's going to be international news, because the film went to Cannes and other film festivals. It's not good for the Committee.

But the point is, there is some nudity. In Singapore, the film got 18. I think it makes sense.

**I think, in the UK, it would get 15 or 18.**
Right. But we got 13 with nudity [*laughs*]. So, what is the standard? We made fun, our filmmakers said: "Maybe the Committee slept? Or they think it's not a woman, it's a cat naked [*laughs*]?" I don't know what the reason is. I don't understand [*laughs*].

But the bigger question is, what is the standard of the ratings? If we have a standard—nudity: 15; violence: 18—the filmmakers will know the limits, and the producers will understand how much money they can get. But now we have a rating system, and we also have censorship and bans.

The rating system sounds good, but the rating depends on the consideration of the Film [and Video Censorship] Committee. And the consideration of the Committee, in each group, is different, so it's very flexible.

Secretly, the producer submitted the film on Monday, because there is a film critic that is [sympathetic] to us.

**A film critic on the Film and Video Censorship Committee?**

The film critic is one of the Committee giving the rating. He [Kittisak Suwannabhokin] is quite an old film critic. So, we submitted on a Monday, because we knew that he would come on a Monday.

But after we got the 13, we knew that the Film [and Video Censorship] Committee that considered our film did not include the film critic. Because on Mondays, there are two groups of the Film [and Video Censorship] Committee. And the Committee who considered *Ten Years Thailand*, the main Committee [member] is the former director of the Office of Contemporary Art and Culture, who I got banned by [*laughs*].

**In Krabi.**

In Krabi. So, I don't know what the standard is. It's like playing the lottery [*laughs*].

(The interview took place at a restaurant in Bangkok on 14 December 2018.)

# SURASAK PONGSON

*"I will fight for what I believe is right."*

**Why is the monk crying at the funeral in *Thibaan: The Series* 2.2 such an important sequence in the film?**

The crying monk scene, as written in the screenplay, is important because it represents the falling action.[325] I had already decided that the falling action, as portrayed by that character, must be in that scene. In the screenplay structure, I had planned the climax in which Bai Khao dies. When Bai Khao dies, it leads to the falling action of the [monk's] character. He can't deal with the situation, and his falling action is that he must accept it. To create the most emotional scene, it needs to focus on his humanity, regardless of his role as a monk. This is what I intended.

**When did you learn that the film had been rejected by the censors?**

When we showed them this scene, they gave their feedback. Actually, we have to blame ourselves because we were pretty late in submitting the film to the censorship board. In the Thai film industry, the release date must be set first. Nowadays, they will fix the release schedule first, otherwise international films will dominate.

The release schedules of international films at the cinema are predetermined, whether in summer or whatever season. If we don't want to clash with these blockbuster films, we need to set an alternative release date. Once we've set it, we have to start the marketing strategy to promote the film. Due to the low budget, we needed to promote the film quite early. GTH's marketing strategy is to promote the film just one month before it opens at the cinema. But in our case, we started promoting early because, first of all, we have a small budget. Secondly, the promotion for our film is quite straightforward.

When it was delayed, time was running out. On 19 November [2018], we were told that the censorship committee did not approve our film, and on the next day, 20 November, we had to arrange a press screening.[326] When we knew that, we were shocked because in our opinion, after we had time to think about it, it should not have been that severe. We didn't expect that to happen.

**Did you have an opportunity to negotiate with them?**

We tried to solve the problem by negotiating with them, asking them not to cut this scene, and saying that a higher rating was acceptable to us. But it wasn't successful. We would have to request an appeal in order to negotiate further.

We asked them if we could still hold the press screening, because cutting the scene would take a long time. The press screening was scheduled for the next day, the guests were already invited, and the event had been organized. We tried hard, negotiating with them up until the last minute.

I also apologized to the fans, announcing that the film had not been passed by the censors. I knew that many of the sponsors might not feel comfortable, so I took responsibility and postponed the release.

**How long did it take to edit the scene?**

I spent two full days, because there was the process of converting the files and making the DCPs again. Once the file conversion was done, we could go back for censorship approval. Once it passed, we had to make the DCPs again.

**So, you worked overnight?**

Well actually, before show time, we worked two consecutive weeks, day and night. The post-production for this film took around three weeks.

**What did the censors tell you?**

They told us that this scene needed to be removed, otherwise they wouldn't approve it. We asked if they could consider a higher rating. They said they couldn't do that because it was rated 18 already. Even if this scene was cut off, it would remain at an 18 rating.[327]

I couldn't make a decision at that moment because, firstly, I had many partners. I had to ask them first whether it could be removed. And if it was removed, would there be any impact or not? I couldn't make a decision at that time, and I needed time to analyze the situation. The point is that I didn't have time to make a decision.

Firstly, from the director's perspective, I felt sad because we designed this scene to make the audience feel emotional. It's the climax of the film. If we cut it, the film will be meaningless. And the second point is, if we didn't cut it, there would be a financial impact. As it's also a business decision, I had to evaluate the situation.

If we didn't cut it, and appealed, the whole process would take six months. By that time, we would lose everything, because if the later release date was in blockbuster season, our income would be affected. Even postponing for a few days, we would lose millions of baht.

**Who decided to post the uncensored video clip online?**
We sent the file to the Thai Film Director Association to get their feedback. But what they did with the video was up to them, it wasn't our decision. They could do whatever they wanted with it, and I was okay with that.

**How do you feel about slapstick comedies featuring monks, most of which are not censored?**
I don't feel anything, because I don't compare my film with others. I will fight for what I believe is right. If the result is that other films are approved but mine isn't, I don't feel anything. I don't feel offended.

(The interview took place at a gallery in Bangkok on 7 December 2018.)

# TANWARIN SUKKHAPISIT

*"They regarded this film as immoral,*
*and hazardous to national security."*

**What happened when *Insects in the Backyard* was shown at the World Film Festival?**

At the time this film was shown at the World Film Festival there was no problem. But the promoters were afraid that there could be a problem, so the film was rated for people aged twenty-one or older, whereas the highest official rating is 20.[328]

**When the ban was first announced, did the censors explain their decision?**

When the ban was decided by the censors, an officer explained briefly that they regarded this film as immoral, and hazardous to national security. When we asked for an explanation, they agreed to have the words 'hazardous to national security' crossed out, leaving only the word 'immoral' remaining, with no more details. When we asked the committee who considered the film which scenes constituted immorality, they simply said that they thought every scene is immoral, and they didn't give us any more details.

**Did you have an opportunity to meet the censors and discuss the film?**

After the film was banned, we appealed against the decision and explained our intentions in producing the film. However, we were told by one of the committee members that we should have made the film in a 'good' way. This was said as if we did not know how to produce a good movie, and no clear explanation was given.

**Why did you decide to sue the censors in the Administrative Court?**

We decided to sue them in the Administrative Court because we realized that this law was newly issued so both the enforcers and the subjects might not completely understand it. We hoped that this would be a test case. Also, we wanted to highlight the weak points of the law to them, so that the law could be improved in order to promote and support Thai films, as opposed to using the law to deprive Thai people of their rights and freedoms, forcing film producers to censor their creative processes and destroying their imaginations.

**Do you get any support from the film community when you started the lawsuit?**

When we decided to take legal action against them, iLaw took on our case and filed the lawsuit for us, as they regarded this is a case of human rights violation.[329] But only a few people in film circles lent us a hand in this case. Most of them didn't want to get involved.

We tried to explain to the public, and to professionals in the film industry, that the banning of this film would have serious consequences for film producers and audiences, because the right to watch or not watch a film is a fundamental right in a free society. The agencies that stood by us throughout were the Thai Film Director

Association led by Songyos Sugmakanan, and the Movie Audience Network in Thailand.

**While your appeal was being considered, were you asked to give evidence?**

The evidence we delivered to the court for consideration was the film itself. The film shows our intention to present the problems of contemporary Thai society that have been overlooked and dismissed for many years. If the audience open their mind without prejudice they will see that the film wants to present this clearly, and it's lucky for us that the Administrative Court recognized and understood the content and style of this movie better than the officers who are directly responsible for films, the censors themselves.

**But the Administrative Court ruled that the film must be cut.**

It's true that the Court's decision was that the three-second pornographic scene is unlawful, and that caused us to lose the lawsuit. But the Court gave us the option that, if we made this three-second cut, the film could be released with a 20 rating. The Court's verdict was that there are no immoral scenes in the film, as it's a film focusing on problems in Thai society.

**Will you appeal again, to the Supreme Court?**

As the Administrative Court's judgment was that only three seconds of one scene should be cut, we considered that we had won the case, because the cut doesn't have an impact on the rest of the film, and we could finally release the film. So, there's no appeal to the Supreme Court.

**Are you still determined to show the film uncut in Thailand in the future?**

The movie is scheduled to open on 29 November [2017],[330] but it will be the version that's cut by three seconds to meet the legal requirement.

(The interview was conducted via email on 2 August 2017.)

# KANITTHA KWUNYOO

*"I cut the film through my tears."*

**When you were making *Karma*, did you expect that it would cause any controversy, and were you trying to make a provocative film?**

I thought that when *Karma* was released, it would be interesting to people and go viral because I created it from something close to home. It's presented as a horror movie that most Thai people can easily understand and enjoy. But I never thought that the movie could cause controversy or problems in society. Then it was banned.

**Did the studio [Sahamongkol] have any concerns about the film's subject matter?**

Of course. Ever since I wrote this movie, the investors wanted to lessen and cut some content that may lead to public misunderstanding or anger, such as the scene of the novice monk (Sun) kissing the girl (Fai). As director and writer, I didn't want to do that. I thought it wasn't exploitative but necessary to the story. We had many fights until the investors and the studio eventually allowed me to keep this scene. Finally, when the movie was finished, the scene became a problem and had to be cut to get permission to be released.

**Did you meet the censorship board to discuss the film?**

On the judgment day, Prachya Pinkaew, the producer, went to listen to their decision. As for me, I was at a promotional event. Shortly after the verdict, the producer informed me that the film was banned. But he only found out after the censorship board had told the media. At first, he wasn't even told that it had been banned, even though he was there during the censors' deliberations.

The producer went to talk to the board about the reasons for the ban on my behalf. Everything happened so fast. Our team never thought that it would be banned. They just expected an 18 rating.

**What comments did the censor board give you about the film, or what reasons did they give for the ban?**

*Karma* was banned in Thailand because of romantic scenes between monks and women, drugs, and scenes showing clutter in monks' living quarters. The censorship board told us that the film disrespected Buddhism, and violated moral and cultural norms. They felt that it would be hard to cut those scenes, so the film was banned.

The producer didn't accept the judgment, because they never asked us if we would agree to any cuts. It turned out that they banned the film and told the media without talking to our team.

**Was it possible to negotiate with the studio about cutting the film?**

Yes, it was. I was called by the investors to discuss about cutting the scenes so that the film could be released, to minimize the damage.

**The new version was ready after only a few days. Was it hard to edit and retitle the film so quickly?**

I was called to edit the film that night. After the meeting, I went to the film editing room immediately. As regards editing the film, it was not difficult. Our team stood by to edit the film and change the title according to the censors' verdict. Our team was called to finish the version I edited immediately.

For me, the difficult part was my emotion when making cutting decisions because I had to be conscious at that moment of how to cut. I wanted to love this film no matter what happened. I didn't want anything to interfere with my inspiration and I had to make it acceptable for the censors.

It was so hard at that moment. Every decision happened so fast. I would say that I cut the film through my tears.

**The film's title was changed. Was this required by the censors?**

It was part of the censors' verdict. If you wanted to get a new verdict, you would have to change the film's title. That was the only reason they gave me.

**Are there any differences in meaning between the two titles?**

No, there are not. In terms of Buddhism, *arbat* and *arpat* have the same meaning. Most people are more familiar with *arbat*.

**Did retitling the film cause any problems with the poster or the advertising campaign?**

No, although the name change was quite ironic. Anyway, most people still understand that the film was the same. In terms of the text, only one letter was different. The meaning didn't change. It didn't have much impact.

**How do you feel about the rules regarding monk characters in films? For example, *Syndromes and a Century* and *Headshot* were also edited because of their portrayals of monks.**

It seems that, regarding monks in films, there are different rules for comedies and dramas. So, there is no consistency, and we don't know what the rules are. I have to consider the studio and do what's necessary to get the film passed. But we need freedom of artistic expression.

**Congratulations on being selected as Thailand's Oscar candidate.[331] Is it ironic that your film was once banned and is now celebrated?**

Thank you, but I still wonder why. I'm not really proud because our film is not the complete version and some scenes were cut according to the censors' verdict. When it was selected, I was not confident about our film.

A thought popped into my head that maybe our film didn't deserve it. But I'd like to thank you for being interested in our film.

(The interview was conducted via email on 18 May 2017.)

# ING KANJANAVANIT

*"Our lobby is not strong. But at least it exists."*

**Are you optimistic that there will ever be a time when *Shakespeare Must Die* can be shown in Thailand? If so, what type of political atmosphere would be necessary for that to happen?**

I think it's futile to focus on 'political climate,' etc. which are vague and beyond our control. The whole world is imploding. We can't be optimistic or pessimistic over such things. If you take action, you can stop wasting energy on abstract anxieties (like Hamlet). We should focus on reforming film legislation, which is something we can do (but which unfortunately not enough filmmakers do).

Because of the lack of numbers, and no backing from a trade union or equivalent (the Thai Film Director Association is under the Federation of National Film Association of Thailand), our lobby is not strong. But at least it exists.

The whole point of ending the banning of films is so we would never have to worry about toxic politics and tyranny ever again as far as censorship is concerned. At long last we would have the sense of security and respect that other professions enjoy as a matter of course. We have to keep on pointing out this ridiculous fact: that filmmakers are the only people without a legal right to freedom of expression. The only people who must submit their work to government inspection before being allowed out into the world.

Amend the law, scrap § 26(7),[332] give us some measure of security. Why should the law empower seven people to judge what Thai cinema is allowed to be?[333] It's preposterous. How can we make truthful, organic films (fictional or not) if we have to look over our shoulders all the time and wonder who's in power? And work years on a project to which we're devoting heart, soul, health and money, only for it to be banned by a bunch of trembling morons with the power of life and death over our films.

**How would you compare the experiences of submitting *Citizen Juling* and *Shakespeare Must Die* to the censors? Were you equally concerned about possible censorship before submitting both films, and were the censors' decisions equally unexpected?**

I was amazed and delighted when *Citizen Juling* passed the (pre-rating system) censors. I thought it should pass but I was nervous. The film had to be so long because I had to show everything and tell nothing. People either thought it was extremely anti-royalist or fanatically royalist. The truth of course is it is neither. It just shows what the camera saw.

I don't understand this compulsion to categorize. Perhaps it's the age of branding, literally. People feel threatened if they can't dismiss you as some tribe or type, the voice of this or that. The censors are the same way, that's why they always give me such a grilling. But *Juling* flew right by them. Amazing!

As for *Shakespeare Must Die*, Manit [Sriwanichpoom] and I really didn't think it would be banned. First, it was half-funded by the

Ministry of Culture. It's true that it had been reluctantly approved—we were the only film that had to present script pages, so yes, I suppose they found it dicey from the first with the regicide scene.[334] It was the very last project to be greenlighted, but it was approved. (This was the *Thai khem khaeng* [strong Thailand] under the Abhisit [Vejjajiva] government; *Uncle Boonmee* was the first beneficiary of the promotional fund for its trip to Cannes.) But since *Juling* made it through, there was no reason for this one not to. Then again, it was impossible to predict as the atmosphere was imminent civil war.

We thought we'd get a rating of 13 or 15. It's a play taught to school children! We didn't expect the level of fear. How can you be this fearful of a Shakespearean horror movie that your Ministry half-funded? It shocked me how scared they were of both the (Yingluck [Shinawatra]) government and the film. It shocked a lot of people that the film was banned.

**In *Censor Must Die*, I thought the most revealing sequence was the video at the Ministry reception, teaching how to sit in a respectful and traditional Thai way. Do you think that the Ministry of Culture is becoming more open in embracing a wider definition of Thai culture, or do you think that it's still too old-fashioned?**

The Ministry of Culture question is best answered by Manit, who helped to found it with other misled and over-optimistic people who then find themselves fighting the Frankenstein's Monster that they'd spawned.[335] Their good intentions, their best-laid plans and dreams for this country, have been hijacked by the bureaucrats.

For me, this country will never be free until we've publicly disowned Luang Wichit's cultural indoctrination. Thanks to him, culture is a dirty word for Thai people, laden with the stench of propaganda. The very word *watthanatham* [culture] invokes the fascist regime of Field Marshal Phibun Songkhram. From our years of personal experience of fighting for freedom of expression, over and over again it's the bureaucrats who defeat all attempts at progress and reform, including in this round. They can defeat anyone, even the military, even the monarchy (see Rama VII's attempt to cut expenses to prevent national bankruptcy). They're a brick wall. They only care for their own survival.

I'm glad you like the comic relief of the Ministry of Culture lobby video scene. They had it on a loop and I had to watch it over and over while waiting for Manit to come out of his meeting with the appeals board. We always get a good laugh for that scene. Thai audiences know that *Censor Must Die* should be experienced as a comedy. When it went to a film festival in Beirut, the audience there was really solemn, probably because a lot of them had personally gone through similar arbitrary oppression. It's funny if you're not in it.

I used the exact same tactic that got *Juling* past the censors. They knew that legally they had no basis on which to ban it. So, they ruled it as news footage and refused to rate it (which incidentally means no cinema would show it, effectively banning it).

However, this ruling has set a marvelous legal precedent for all documentary films. I'm going to use this ruling to exempt my next film (another *cinéma vérité* documentary, called *Bangkok Joyride*) from the censorship process. Then it's a matter of finding a cinema. This is a whole other question we're dealing with.

**My Teacher Eats Biscuits has become almost a mythical film now. Is it true that a screening was raided by police, and could you explain what happened on that day?**

*My Teacher Eats Biscuits* was banned as an insult to all religions. This is like banning John Waters' *Pink Flamingos* for bad taste.

The police raid incident was at the Saeng-Arun Arts Centre [in Bangkok], during the screening of *Bugis Street*, a Singaporean gay film which had also been banned from showing at the first Bangkok Film Festival in 1998 (the original Bangkok Film Festival, not the scandal-plagued, FBI investigated and convicted Bangkok International Film Festival).[336] Two films had been banned: *Bugis Street* and *My Teacher Eats Biscuits*. This was under Chuan Leekpai's government.[337]

Two lecturers from the Film Department at Chulalongkorn University's Faculty of Communication Arts decided to stage the (very first) gay film festival in Thailand called the Alternative Love Film Festival and *Bugis Street* was on the bill. Armed with a video camera in case of trouble, I was in charge of security. We showed a tape of my meeting with the censors over *My Teacher Eats Biscuits* on a TV in front of the theater, but *My Teacher Eats Biscuits* wasn't shown.

The police raided the *Bugis Street* screening which opened the festival. They went inside the auditorium, lights came up, all blinked, and then they apologized and left. The head cop (I think the deputy chief of Bangrak [in Bangkok] or maybe even the top guy himself) said "Sorry, clearly there's been a misunderstanding. We received a complaint from the censorship board that immoral films were being shown" (implying they were expecting a gay orgy) "but we can see that there are many respectable people in the audience. So sorry, please carry on."

The censors' complaint was based on an anonymous fax sent to the censors. We traced the fax to a member of the censorship board. She was notorious for her zealousness as a film censor. Soon after that, she became instrumental in refusing permission for the Jodie Foster, Chow Yun Fat *Anna and the King* to shoot in Thailand. She was really vicious to *My Teacher Eats Biscuits*, and the other censors all bowed to her. Film censorship was still under the police then. But the other censors—two cops and a studio head—were much more reasonable.

It shocked me that it was the academic who was the fascist, which just shows how naïve I was. This discovery turns out to be nothing surprising in our subsequent encounters with enemies of reform and freedom of expression.

(The interview was conducted via email on 24 March 2016.)

# YUTHLERT SIPPAPAK

*"If you show this movie, somebody burns the theater."*

**You're filming something at the moment, aren't you?**

Yeah, *Seven Boy Scouts*. It's a political satire [*laughs*]. Finding a way to fight back in a film in the mainstream. I put the names of the politicians, seven boys. The names are like the prime minister [Prayut Chan-o-cha] and all the bad people, [they] become scouts. The name of the girl scout is the ex-prime minister.

**Yingluck [Shinawatra].**

Yeah [*laughs*]. Nobody knows the plot yet. Some people know it's a political issue. We're just worried it's gonna have [a problem] with censorship. Try to let the audience imagine: when the bad boy becomes prime minister, what's gonna happen. But I kill them all.

**Oh really?**

Yeah [*laughs*]. No one grows up, because I kill them all! That's my film [*laughs*].

**How can you kill kids in a film, though?**

I can kill them! The kids did a bad thing. If you kill people, but you're young, nobody kills you. No, it's wrong: if you kill someone, you must die. That is the law of karma. It's gonna be fun. And it's a horror [film].

**It sounds like it!**

So, when I do horror, I can go anywhere.

**Can I ask about *Fatherland*? It was based on a book, *Promdaen*?**[338]

Yes, from Vasit Dejkunjorn.

**He died recently [in 2018].**

He wanted to see the movie, but I didn't have a chance to show him.

**Before he died?**

Right. I can say it's not exactly like the book, but I keep the characters and I change in my own way.

**Was it your idea to make the film?**

No. Before this, in Yingluck's government, it seemed like [conflict] between Yingluck's government and the military. This project happened because the government and military tried to make peace, and [with] this project I had to make Thai people get together, get to understand each other. If people go to watch this movie, and come out like, "I need peace." Something like that. They wanted to do that.

First, it was not *Fatherland*, but my idea was *Motherland*. *Motherland*, I needed THB 300 million to make it. I was gonna do the plot by myself. I was gonna make a story about a big issue in Thailand, the conflict of 'red' and 'yellow', but they didn't allow me to do that. They needed a love story or something, and they didn't give me THB 300 million.

They gave me *Promdaen*. I liked it, because [there are] many things that Thai people didn't know what happened there [in the south]. Because the propaganda—government propaganda or military propaganda—tries to make that place so scary. In the book, they didn't say that, they say something opposite the military propaganda, Information Operations. I think this project is against the I.O.

So, after I finished the film, the government changed [in 2014]. I went to talk to Tu [Prayut Chan-o-cha]. He asked me, "Why [did] you do this film?" And many questions. I just said, "I cannot change, because I did it from the book." But I went to the army; I needed them to be a sponsor. I used everything, like warships, helicopters. But they asked me, "If you show this movie, somebody burns the theater. Who's gonna [take] responsibility for that?" They asked me, "Can you?" I said, "I cannot!" So I froze it.

Right now we are in a military government. My film is not about censorship, it's about the person who controls censorship [*laughs*].[339]

**He told you directly?**

No, he sent like a secretary or something to talk to me. But he wrote everything to ask. They showed me the questions, many questions. The questions were stupid questions. I'll just keep it, and wait until they're gone. It might take ten years or five years. I think ten years.

**Was it commissioned by the military, or commissioned by the government, or both?**

Both. Because I used all the military [equipment] free. But if they asked, "Who signed for the helicopter?" the people who got involved with my film would get a problem. If they cannot do anything to them, they'd come to me [*laughs*].

**Did they see the script before you started the film?**

[*Shakes head*] Because my producer negotiated. They gave me the book. I made a screenplay. I went to the south. I shot [the film]. That's all I know. But when it was gonna launch, "Hey, hold on!" The producer is gone.

**So, who made the decision to cancel the screening?**

Me. I didn't mean to cancel; I just need time. Because I got a problem with the military government. So, I decided to freeze for a while, maybe ten years. The film is still there. I like it.

**What is it about the film that's so sensitive?**

The one word that's so sensitive is *het kan sa-ngop, ngop mai ma*: 'if no war, no money.' Money is power. And the person who created the war is the military. I said that, and I don't want to take that out. That's the truth. And they don't want the truth. I want the truth.

**So, they want to keep the war going because it means more money for them.**

Yes! No conflict, no power. If there's peace there, they don't need soldiers. They try to [say] the conflict in the south is because of religion. No! Because they just wanna make the conflict there. Asking me, "Just change the plot." I said no. Because I cannot say something that I really wanna say.

When I have enough money, I will come back to this project. I don't have to show in theatres in Thailand. I might talk to Netflix. If you show here, that's kind of dangerous. If the military's still here. I'll find a way.

**I saw you at the *Uncensored* event [on 7 July 2019]. Why did you want to speak there?**

First, the guy [Headache Stencil] who [organized] that session is close to me.[340] And the Future Forward Party are kind of close to me. I never gave a shit about politics. But right now, it's too much. I just wanted to express that 'what you did is not right.' On Twitter, I'm not talking about the film, I'm talking about politics issues. I got a problem.[341]

**With the court.**

With the court [*laughs*].

**You had to apologize.**

I went there and they tried to help me. "Yuthlert, say like this, please." It's no problem to apologize. But I'm going to keep doing the same thing.

We are in a jail of imagination. We are like painting in prison. Yes, we can paint, but painting in prison.

(The interview took place at a café in Bangkok on 22 November 2019.)

# NOTES

## Introduction

1. Thunska Pansittivorakul, quoted by Kong Rithdee (2005), 'Underground Experience,' *Real.Time*, *Bangkok Post* (4 March).
2. Four journal articles examine recent film controversies: Rapeepan Sayantrakul (2007), 'ตัด-เบลอ-ดูด-เตือน-เฉือน-ระงับ! "เซ็นเซอร์แบบไทยๆ" ยังน้อยไป หรือมากเกินพอ' [cut-blur-bleep-warn-slice-ban! Thai censorship: not enough, or too much?], *Sarakadee*, vol. 23, no. 266 (April), pp. 110–17; Pongsawee Supanonth (2013), 'การควบคุมเนื้อหาภาพยนตร์กับสาระที่เปลี่ยนไป' [regulating a changing film industry], *Siam Communication Review*, pp. 37–50; Aekkachai Suttiyangyuen (2018), 'Thai Films (Un)censored,' *GQ* (Thailand), no. 46 (July), pp. 21–25; and Itthipol Waranusupakul (2014), 'Film Regulation in Thailand,' *The Journal of Social Communication Innovation*, vol. 2, no. 2 (July–December), pp. 36–46. For an English-language Thai cinema bibliography, see Adam Knee (2012), 'Scholarly Resources on Thai Cinema in English: A Bibliography in Progress,' *Thai Film Journal*, vol. 16 (June), pp. 18–22.

## Part One
## Chapter 1. A History of Thai Film Censorship

3. Parinyaporn Pajee (2013), 'Freedom on the Big Screen,' *The Nation* (6 June), p. 16.
4. Vajiravudh (King Rama VI) reigned from 1910 to 1925.
5. Chalida Uabumrungjit (2008), '*Suvarna of Siam*: The Mindset of Censorship before the 1930 Film Act,' 10th International Conference on Thai Studies (9 January).
6. สัมพันธ์ไทย [Thai matters] (1923), quoted by Kong Rithdee (2006), 'Historical Inspiration,' *Outlook*, *Bangkok Post* (29 March).
7. Scot Barmé (2002), *Woman, Man, Bangkok: Love, Sex, and Popular Culture in Thailand*, Chiang Mai: Silkworm Books, p. 57. Prince Dhani Nivat later acted as

regent for Bhumibol Adulyadej (Rama IX), who reigned from 1946 to 2016. Chulalongkorn (King Rama V) reigned from 1868 to 1910.

8.  Censors' comments, quoted in *Diseases and a Hundred Year Period* (2008). The film is included on the French DVD release of *Syndromes and a Century*.

9.  Thunska Pansittivorakul, quoted by Kong Rithdee (2007b), 'Cat Among the Pigeons,' *Real.Time, Bangkok Post* (14 September), p. 1.

10. Surasak Glahan (2016), 'Sex Scene Lands French Movie Film Fest Ban,' *Bangkok Post* (8 July), p. 8. After its rejection from the Thailand International Film Destination Festival, *Happy Hour in Paradise* was shown by the Friese-Greene Club in Bangkok. Although it was withdrawn from the Thailand International Film Destination Festival in 2016, *Detective Chinatown* was eventually screened at the festival on 27 March 2019.

11. Barmé (2002), p. 57. Prajadhipok (King Rama VII) reigned from 1925 until his abdication in 1935. The film's original title, อำนาจมืด, translates as 'dark forces.'

12. *Bangkok Daily Mail* (20 April 1923), quoted by Boonrak Boonyaketmala (1992), 'The Rise and Fall of the Film Industry in Thailand, 1897–1992,' *East-West Film Journal*, vol. 6, no. 2 (July), p. 64.

13. The Film Act (1930), quoted in *ibid*. p. 66.

14. The Film Act (1936), quoted in *ibid*. p. 73.

15. Quoted by Rebecca Townsend (2019), 'The Adulterer: Censorship, Morality, and Foreign Films in Thailand,' *Journal of Women's History*, vol. 31, no. 1 (Spring), p. 96.

16. Ministry of Education, quoted by Annette Hamilton (1993), 'Video Crackdown, or The Sacrificial Pirate: Censorship and Cultural Consequences in Thailand,' *Public Culture*, vol. 5, no. 3 (Spring), p. 520.

17. Boonrak (1992), pp. 73–74.

18. The Revolutionary Council's announcement no. 205, quoted by David Streckfuss (2011), *Truth on Trial in Thailand: Defamation, Treason, and Lèse-Majesté*. Abingdon: Routledge, p. 271. Thanom Kittikachorn was prime minister during an extended period of military rule, from 1963 to 1973. He staged a coup in 1971, and his junta was known as the Revolutionary Council.

19. Philip Cornwel-Smith (2020), *Very Bangkok: In the City of the Senses*, Bangkok: River Books, p. 312.

20. The series is สารวัตรใหญ่ [chief inspector], broadcast by Channel 7.

21. This caption appeared in the Thai theatrical version, though it was removed for the VCD and DVD releases. Other films have also been required to insert warnings discouraging inappropriate activities. *Mercury Man* (2006) contains a caption about the dangers of gambling. *In the Shadow of Naga* (2008) was released in two versions: one, rated 18, featured a caption explaining that it is not appropriate for monks to be tattooists; another, rated 20, did not require captions. Pen-ek Ratanaruang's *Invisible Waves* (2006) includes an anti-smoking warning. The erotic film เธอชื่อลินดา [her name is Linda] (1993) ends

with a voice-over discouraging suicide as the eponymous character walks into the sea.

22. Quoted by Sakdina Chatrakul na Ayudhya (1989), 'Direction Unknown,' *Cinemaya*, vol. 4 (Summer), p. 60.

23. Ministry of the Interior (1991), quoted by Streckfuss (2011), p. 271.

24. Director Rattana Pestonji was a notable exception to this trend, and his *Black Silk* (1961) was artistically and technically superior to other films of the period. For a history of 16mm Thai films, see 'ภาพยนตร์ไทยในยุค ๑๖ ม.ม.' [Thai films in the 16mm era] (1997), *Feature Magazine*, vol. 13, no. 150 (August), pp. 120–25. See also Aliosha Herrera (2015), 'Thai 16mm Cinema: The Rise of a Popular Cinematic Culture in Thailand from 1945 to 1970,' *Rian Thai: International Journal of Thai Studies*, vol. 8, p. 28: "These 16mm quickies … perpetuate a former theatrical entertainment tradition by engaging one or more persons to perform the voices and other foley sound effects at the point of their public projection."

25. Chalida Uabumrungjit (2001), 'Cinema in Thailand: 1897 to 1970,' *Film in South East Asia: Views from the Region—Essays on Film in Ten South East Asia-Pacific Countries* (ed. David Hanan), Manila: SouthEast Asia Pacific AudioVisual Archives Association, p. 138.

26. Dome Sukwong and Sawasdi Suwannapak (2001), *A Century of Thai Cinema*, London: Thames and Hudson, p. 14.

27. Anchalee Chaiworaporn (2001), 'Thai Cinema Since 1970,' *Film in South East Asia: Views from the Region—Essays on Film in Ten South East Asia-Pacific Countries* (ed. David Hanan), Manila: SouthEast-Asia Pacific AudioVisual Archive Association, p. 142.

28. Philip Jablon (2019), *Thailand's Movie Theatres: Relics, Ruins and the Romance of Escape*, Bangkok: River Books, p. 173.

29. *Ibid.* Sirichai lost a libel case against one of the corrupt officials he featured in his *Serpico* voice-over.

30. Constitution of the Kingdom of Thailand (1997), § 39.

31. Wisit Sasanatieng, quoted by Kong Rithdee (2010c), '*The Red Eagle* Has Landed … Again,' *Real.Time, Bangkok Post* (1 October), p. 1.

32. Apichatpong Weerasethakul, quoted by Andrew Pulver (2016), 'Apichatpong Weerasethakul: "My Country Is Run by Superstition,"' *The Guardian* (12 April).

33. Issariya Praithongyaem (2015), 'Thai Film Director Decries Censorship,' BBC News (15 October).

34. Thunska Pansittivorakul, quoted by Matthew Hunt (2012), 'Thai Movie Censorship,' *Encounter Thailand*, vol. 1, no. 7 (October), p. 39. Thunska released a new version of *This Area Is Under Quarantine* on the Vimeo website in 2017. In the revised version, the film is played in fast-forward, with a 'CENSORED' banner obscuring almost all of the frame. The only uncensored sequences are the opening titles and the footage of the Tak Bai incident.

35. *Syndromes and a Century* was shown at the Alliance Française from 16 to 17 November 2007. *Cemetery of Splendour* was shown in Chiang Mai on 23 February 2018, without any publicity. *Ploy* was shown at the FCCT on 2 October 2008. *Censor Must Die* was shown at the BACC on 1 June 2013 during a 'Freedom on Film' ['สิทธิหนังไทย'] seminar featuring Nontawat Numbenchapol, Apichatpong Weerasethakul, Tanwarin Sukkhapisit, and Nonzee Nimibutr. Later in 2013, *Censor Must Die* was shown at Silpakorn University (on 22 August), the Friese-Greene Club (from 5 to 9 November), and the Thai Film Archive (on 11 December). Ing Kanjanavanit and Tanwarin Sukkhapisit took part in 'Art, Politics, and Censorship,' a discussion at the FCCT, on 5 July 2012. Tanwarin organized a similar discussion, 'Freedom Thai Film' ['ทำไมผู้หญิงน่ารัก มักมีแฟนแล้ววว้า'], with Surasak Pongson and Chulayarnnon Siriphol at the BACC on 7 December 2018. The *Shakespeare Must Die* university screening took place on 28 June 2012, and the film was also shown at a members-only screening at Ing's Cinema Oasis in Bangkok on 16 December 2018.

36. Genevieve Jolliffe and Andrew Zinnes (2006), *The Documentary Film Makers Handbook*, New York: Continuum, p. 221.

37. According to the censors, they were unable to process the rating application as the correct documentation had not been included when the film was submitted. The film's de facto ban was announced on 30 October 2009.

38. Thunska Pansittivorakul, quoted by Yu Sen-lun (2004), 'The 4th Taiwan International Documentary Festival: A Sweet and Sour Slice,' *Taipei Times* (13 December).

39. Thunska organized *Inside Out, Outside In*, a retrospective of his films, from 18 to 20 April 2008. *Endless Story* features a slideshow of Thunska's photographs, some of which are sexually explicit. *Life Show* was shown as part of the exhibition *The Bangkok Invisible Landscapes* [ลักปิดลักเปิด] at the Chulalongkorn University Art Center in Bangkok from 11 March to 15 April 2005. *Life Show* was also the title of Thunska's photography exhibition held in Bangkok in 2008. There were two screenings of *This Area Is Under Quarantine*: 27 August and 1 September 2008. *The Terrorists* was screened on 23 July 2011 as part of the 'Morbid Symptom' ['แก้หมัน'] season at the *Dialogic* [ตรรกะสังสรรค์] exhibition. The *Homogeneous, Empty Time* screening took place on 2 December 2017. Thunska distributed his explicit photobook *Quasi una fantasia* (2018), Bangkok: Linga Project 2018, equally carefully, in an edition of only thirty copies. *Quasi una fantasia* was accompanied by a short film, *A Season in Hell* (2018).

40. For an eyewitness account of the police raid, see Megan Sinnott (2004), *Toms and Dees: Transgender Identity and Female Same-Sex Relationships in Thailand*, Honolulu: University of Hawai'i Press, pp. 182–83: "The police arrived shortly before the screening of the first film. The officer seemed somewhat embarrassed about being there. He meekly walked to the front of the theater, followed by boos and catcalls. He said he was sorry but there had been a report of immoral

films being shown and he would have to watch a bit to see if that were true. The lights were dimmed, and *Bugis Street*, a film about a male transgendered community in Singapore, began. The opening happened to be a rather graphic and vivid scene of a drunken sailor having sex with a transvestite, and I was worried that this chance scene would bode ill for the struggle against censorship. However, after the scene, the policeman discreetly left the theater, saying quietly as he walked out that he did not see anything wrong in what he saw. The audience applauded, and the festival continued uninterrupted thereafter."

41. See also Kong (2005), p. 1: "The only reason he's not controversial (or blacklisted by the Ministry of Culture) is because the 31-year-old is hardly known outside the tiny circle of Bangkok cinephiles—the few screenings of his eye-opening movies, always at alternative cinema venues, were done with minimum pride or publicity."

42. Abhisit Vejjajiva was prime minister from 2008 to 2011.

43. Prabda Yoon, quoted by Monruedee Jansuttipan (2016), 'TrueVisions Pulls Prabda Yoon's "*Motel Mist*" from Cinemas Straight After Premiere,' *BK* (17 November). *Motel Mist* was press-screened at Bangkok's Scala cinema on 14 November 2016.

44. Email from Prabda Yoon to Matthew Hunt (30 October 2019).

45. Prabda Yoon, quoted by Ludmila Cvikova (2016), 'Tiger Talk: Prabda Yoon about *Motel Mist*,' International Film Festival Rotterdam (31 January). See also Thunska Pansittivorakul, quoted by Jolliffe and Zinnes (2006), *The Documentary Film Makers Handbook*, p. 221: "Even when we put our feet on a table, it is against our gracious culture, so there will be a mosaic screen on those feet too." This blurring of forbidden imagery even extends to plastic bags. At a press conference organized by the government's Department of Environmental Quality Promotion on 18 December 2019, eight TV stations (NBT, MCOT, Thai PBS, Workpoint TV, ONE31, GMM25, Channel 8, and Channel 7) agreed to censor plastic bags from their entertainment programs.

46. Soopsip (2013), 'Stuck with a Troublesome Film, Yuthlert Builds His Own Cinema,' *The Nation* (18 November), p. 16.

47. Yuthlert Sippapak, quoted by Pravit Rojanaphruk (2013), 'Despair Over Move to Stop Film about the South Being Screened,' *The Nation* (30 April), p. 2. In lieu of the film itself, an exhibition of photographs from the making of the film— *The Land We Call Home* by Sira Twichsang—was held at the Jam Factory in Bangkok from 6 to 28 September 2014.

48. Sasiwan Mokkhasen (2016), 'Lack of Competition Stifles Thai Film Industry,' Khaosod English (15 March).

49. Pen-ek Ratanaruang, quoted by Patrick Brzeski (2013), 'Thailand's Pen-ek Ratanaruang on Risking It All to Film the Paradoxes of Thai Democracy,' *The Hollywood Reporter* (8 July).

50. Ing Kanjanavanit, quoted by Parinyaporn Pajee (2018), 'Where Equality Counts,' *The Nation* (16 March), p. 8.
51. The song, 'ฟ้าต่ำแผ่นดินสูง' [low sky, high earth], is from the soundtrack to the classic film *A Man Called Tone*.
52. The original title, ผู้ชายขายตัว [the male prostitutes], was changed to ผู้ชาย...? [male...?].
53. The original title, อำนาจมืด [dark forces], was changed to ชะนะพาล [defeat of the hooligans].
54. *One Take Only* was shown at the Bangkok Film Festival on 25 November 2001 in its original version, and went on general release in 2003 after being edited and retitled.
55. The typeface exploits the visual similarity of อื (in the original title) and วิ (in the replacement).
56. The ban was announced on 12 October 2015. After being edited and retitled, the film was passed four days later. The original title was อาบัติ (*arbat*). The revised title was อาปัติ (*arpat*). Both words refer to karma, though *arbat* is Thai and *arpat* is Pali.
57. Townsend (2019), pp. 100–01.
58. *Ibid.* p. 101.
59. For an analysis of foreign films censored before the rating system, see Satien Chantimatorn (1972), 'Thai Cencorships and the "Ban Movies"' [sic], *The Social Science Review*, vol. 10, no. 3 (March), pp. 26–43.
60. Thunska Pansittivorakul, quoted by Jolliffe and Zinnes (2006), p. 221.
61. Foreign Correspondents' Club of Thailand (2018), 'Programme Cancellation.' The screening was originally scheduled for 4 July 2018.
62. Chattan Kunjara na Ayutthaya, quoted by Reuters (2007), 'Thailand Pulls Iranian Cartoon from Film Festival' (27 June).
63. Surasak (2016), p. 8.
64. Nontawat Numbenchapol, quoted by Vaschol Quadri (2013), 'Interview: "*Boundary*" Director Nontawat Numbenchapol on the Censorship Controversy,' *BK* (26 April). The International Court of Justice ruled in 1962 that the temple grounds were part of Cambodian territory, and the ownership debate was reignited in 2008 when the temple was designated a World Heritage Site. The governing People's Power Party was a reincarnation of former prime minister Thaksin Shinawatra's Thai Rak Thai Party, and the foreign minister who signed the joint communiqué, Noppadon Pattama, had previously acted as Thaksin's personal lawyer. Thus, the anti-Thaksin 'yellowshirts' saw Preah Vihear as symptomatic of Thaksin's continuing influence on the country.
65. Drew Dowdle, quoted by Alison de Souza (2015), 'Shot in Chiangmai, but no Trace of Thailand,' *The Straits Times* (26 August). *No Escape*, inspired by Thailand's 2006 coup, was filmed in 2013. (Its working title was *The Coup*.) During the film's post-production in 2014, Thailand experienced another coup.

66. The press conference took place on 26 April 2006.
67. Linnie Blake (2018), 'Ghost Game,' *Thai Cinema: The Complete Guide* (ed. Mary J. Ainslie and Katarzyna Ancuta), London: I. B. Tauris, p. 127.
68. *The Nation* (2006), 'Film Brings Shame Upon Thai Society' (30 April).
69. This took place on 13 October 2006.
70. Phibun Songkhram, quoted by Nicholas Grossman (2009), *Chronicle of Thailand: Headline News since 1946*, Singapore: Editions Didier Millet, p. 88. Phibun was prime minister from 1938 to 1944 and again from 1948 to 1957.
71. Thepmontri Limpayom, quoted by John Aglionby (1999), 'Thai Censors Ban "Insulting" Remake of *King and I* Film,' *The Guardian* (29 December), p. 2. Rama IV reigned from 1851 to 1868. Permission to film *Anna and the King* in Thailand was refused in 1998, and filming took place in Malaysia instead. That same year, permission to film another Hollywood drama, *Brokedown Palace* (1999), in Thailand was also refused as the film depicts a convicted drug smuggler requesting a royal pardon from the king (notwithstanding the fact that such pardons are routinely requested, and many are granted).
72. Censors' comments, quoted by Noy Thrupkaew (2003), 'The King and Thai,' *The American Prospect* (20 August). Noy observes that the focus on Leonowens' Indian heritage "betrays a kind of racism of its own—one that also surfaces in the Thai insistence on calling Indian immigrants *kak*, or guests, with the implied notion that all polite guests will eventually leave."
73. Kong Rithdee (2008), 'The Long Road Home,' *Real.Time*, *Bangkok Post* (4 April), p. 1. This decision was announced in April 2007. The film premiered on 30 August 2006 at the Venice International Film Festival.
74. The Free Thai Cinema Movement [เพื่อเสรีภาพของภาพยนตร์ไทย] organized a press conference at House Rama on 23 April 2007. This was followed by a seminar on film censorship, 'From Censorship to Rating System: The Way Forward?' ['จาก เซ็นเซอร์สู่เรตติ้ง ทางออกที่เป็นไปได้'], at Bangkok Code on 29 May 2007, organized by the Thai Film Foundation. For transcripts of the conference proceedings, see 'สำรวจเส้นทาง พรบ. ภาพยนตร์ 2473 กับกรณีศึกษา' [exploring the path forward from the Film Act (1930), with case studies] (1997), *Thai Film Journal*, vol. 14 (November), pp. 25–53; and 'จากเซ็นเซอร์สู่เรตติ้ง ทางออกที่เป็นไปได้' [from censorship to rating system: the way forward?] (1997), *ibid.* pp. 157–232. Another seminar, 'จาก YouTube ถึงแสงศตวรรษ การเซ็นเซอร์สื่อในยุครัฐบาล คมช.' [media censorship from YouTube to *Syndromes and a Century*], was held at Chulalongkorn University on 27 April 2007. *Bioscope* magazine distributed a short black-and-white film (directed by Pimpaka Towira) featuring various directors speaking out against censorship. Pimpaka also directed *The Silent Melody* (2018), part of the *Cut It Out: Films Against Censorship* series of short films.
75. Chalida Uabumrungjit (2007), 'Free Thai Cinema Movement,' Petition Online.
76. Chalida Uabumrungjit, quoted by Kong Rithdee (2007a), 'Time to Move Forward,' *Bangkok Post* (4 May), p. 1. The National Legislative Assembly (NLA)

was the body appointed by the leaders of the coup in 2006 as a replacement for the elected House of Representatives and partially elected Senate. It was dissolved following a general election in 2007.

77. Apichatpong Weerasethakul (2007a), 'A Hidden Agenda that Deems Us Morons: The Folly and Future of Thai Cinema Under Military Dictatorship,' *Bangkok Post* (25 September), p. 10.

78. Nontawat Numbenchapol, quoted by Vaschol (2013). The ban was confirmed on 17 April 2013, and Nontawat announced it publicly on 23 April 2013.

79. Several sequences in *The Sweet Gang* were replaced with "SENSOR !!!" [*sic*] flashing on a black screen. One of the interviewees in *The Six Principles*, Anuthee Dejthewaporn, is briefly interrupted by the Ministry of Information and Communication Technology's Internet blocking screen and a short burst of Muzak. Similarly, Manit Sriwanichpoom's video installation *Program Will Resume Shortly* (2020) recreates the caption transmitted by cable TV company TrueVisions, which blocks the signals of international news channels when they broadcast reports about Thailand's monarchy or military.

80. Each audience member received a postcard with links to the censored clips on the YouTube website: doctors drinking whiskey (https://www.youtube.com/watch?v=yyKTE8TytA), a monk playing a guitar (https://www.youtube.com/watch?v=POcyqNMxcow), a doctor kissing his girlfriend (https://www.youtube.com/watch?v=rocSdWvmZaY), monks playing with a remote-controlled UFO toy (https://www.youtube.com/watch?v=p3Bz6dGxzAs), a statue of Princess Srinagarindra (https://www.youtube.com/watch?v=-fPCYKNtlZk), and a statue of Prince Mahidol Adulyadej (https://www.youtube.com/watch?v=yGFj4JJNciU). For a reproduction of the postcard, see Hunt (2012), p. 39. On 10 April 2008, Apichatpong took part in a panel discussion about film censorship at the Paragon Cineplex.

81. Rama VIII acceded to the throne as a child in 1935. In 1946, he died from a gunshot wound to the head. The book accompanying the film (Pokpong Chanan, Bangkok: Matichon Publishing, 2013) was also censored, with black lines struck through parts of the text (pp. 42, 275, 285, 286).

82. Quoted by Chris Baker and Pasuk Phongpaichit (2000), *Pridi by Pridi: Selected Writings on Life, Politics, and Economy*, Chiang Mai: Silkworm Books, p. 71. Pridi, leader of the People's Party, was one of the revolutionaries who organized a coup on 24 June 1932. Within a few days of the coup, the king agreed to the abolition of absolute monarchy and democratic institutions were established. Pridi himself wrote and produced a propaganda film, *The King of the White Elephant* (1941). The film was intended as an anti-war statement for an international audience, and it ends with a pacifist speech by the fictional King Chakra (whose name is a barely disguised reference to Thailand's ruling Chakri dynasty).

83. Manopakorn Nititada, prime minister from 1932 to 1933, quoted by Rebecca Townsend (2017), *Cold Fire: Gender, Development, and the Film Industry in Cold War Thailand*, Ithaca: Cornell University Press, p. 41. The film, การเปลี่ยนแปลงการปกครองเมื่อวันที่ 24 มิถุนายน [administrative changes on 24 June], was confiscated and director Manit Wasuwat was paid THB 4,000 in compensation. See also Charnvit Kasetsiri (1999), ภาพยนตร์กับการเมือง เลือดทหารไทย พระเจ้าช้างเผือก บ้านไร่นาเรา [film and politics: *Undaunte Sons of Siam, The King of the White Elephant, our farmland] [sic], Bangkok: P. K. Group.

84. Thunska Pansittivorakul, quoted by Curtis Winston (2009), ' "*Quarantine*" Under Lockdown,' *Daily Xpress*, vol. 2, no. 450 (30 October), p. 2.

85. Sudarat Musikawong and Malinee Khumsupa (2017), 'State Censorship of Thai Cinema: Right of Expression or Enemy of the State,' 13th International Conference on Thai Studies (17 July).

86. Anyone providing proof of marriage is also eligible to view films rated 20, and marriage in Thailand is legal at age seventeen.

87. Film and Video Act (2008), § 26(7).

88. Guillaume Boutigny (2006), 'Thai Cinema and Censorship,' *Thai Cinema* (ed. Bastian Meirsonne), Lyon: Asiexpo Edition, p. 248.

89. Kong (2007a), p. 1.

90. Apichatpong Weerasethakul, quoted by Matthew Hunt (2013), 'Exclusive Interview with Apichatpong Weerasethakul,' *Encounter Thailand*, vol. 2, no. 13 (May), p. 38.

91. Film and Video Act (2008), § 29.

92. *Ibid.* § 4(1).

93. *Ibid.* § 4(2).

94. Manit Sriwanichpoom, quoted by Kong Rithdee (2012a), 'Censors Ban "Shakespeare" Film,' *Bangkok Post* (4 April), p. 1. The ban was announced on 3 April 2012.

95. Monruedee (2016).

96. Parinyaporn (2013), p. 16.

97. Film and Video Act (2008), § 27(1).

98. *Ibid.* § 7.

99. *Ibid.* § 29. The Office of Contemporary Art and Culture wrote to Chulayarnnon on 1 November 2018, citing the Film and Video Act as justification for its refusal to approve the film.

100. Apichatpong (2007a), p. 10.

101. Quoted by Kong (2007a), p. 1.

102. Ladda Tangsupachai, quoted by Simon Montlake (2007), 'Making the Cut,' *Time* (Asia), vol. 170, no. 16 (22 October).

103. *Ibid.*

104. On 15 June 2017, a group of soldiers visited Harit's *Whitewash* exhibition at Gallery VER, and asked the curator to remove three photographs: 'Chosen

Boys,' 'Cadets,' and 'Heaven Gate.' The exhibition represented Harit's response to the 2010 massacre of 'redshirt' protesters.

105. Anand Panyarachun (1998), 'Getting to Know You,' *Outlook, Bangkok Post* (9 November), p. 1.

106. Manit Sriwanichpoom, online message to Matthew Hunt (21 April 2018).

107. Keith B. Richburg (2000), 'Not Playing: "*Anna and the King*," ' *The Washington Post* (7 January).

108. Eakachai Chunhackeewachaloke, quoted by David Lamb (2000), 'Thai Movie Ban Shows Respect for King Supersedes Freedoms,' *Los Angeles Times* (12 February).

109. Apichatpong (2007a), p. 10.

110. Prayut was speaking during his weekly address to the nation, *Return Happiness to the People*, broadcast on all radio and television stations.

111. May Adadol Ingawanij (2008), 'Disreputable Behaviour: The Hidden Politics of the Thai Film Act,' *Vertigo*, vol. 3, no. 8 (Winter).

112. Kong Rithdee (2019), 'Until the Abyss Stares Back,' *Koschke*, no. 2, p. 145.

113. Streckfuss (2011), p. 233.

114. These two films are *Undaunte Sons of Siam* [*sic*] (1935) and บ้านไร่นาเรา [our farmland] (1942). In the latter example, a farmer enlists with the army, and the film highlights the patriotism of Thai farmers and the role of the military as a pillar of the nation.

115. National News Bureau of Thailand (2014), 'The Twelve Core Values for a Strong Thailand.' The propaganda films proposal was announced in 2020 by the Fine Arts Department.

116. Connors (2005), p. 543.

117. Boonrak (1992), pp. 83–84. Thanin Kraivichien was prime minister from 1976 to 1977.

118. Apichatpong Weerasethakul (2008), 'Influence: Today and Tomorrow,' *ArtAsia Pacific Almanac*, vol. 3, p. 269.

119. Karl Schoonover and Rosalind Galt (2016), *Queer Cinema in the World*, Durham: Duke University Press, p. 159.

120. Dianne Daley (2008), 'In the Frame of Mind to Take Control: Politics Surrounding the Banning of Apichatpong Weerasethakul's *Syndromes and a Century*,' 17th Biennial Conference of the Asian Studies Association of Australia.

121. Ing Kanjanavanit (2011), 'Poses from Dreamland,' *Manit Sriwanichpoom: Phenomena and Prophecies*, Bangkok: Srinakharinwirot University, p. 19. *Homogeneous, Empty Time* also serves as a counterpoint to films such as ท้องนา สะเทือน [shaking the paddy fields] (1976) and หนักแผ่นดิน [burden of the land] (1977), which celebrate the Village Scouts as national heroes. For an analysis of how movies such as these function as "a vehicle for anti-communist propaganda," see Rachel V. Harrison (2010), 'The Man with the Golden

Gauntlets: Mit Chaibancha's *Insi Thorng* and the Hybridization of Red and Yellow Perils in Thai Cold War Action Cinema,' *Cultures at War: The Cold War and Cultural Expression in Southeast Asia* (ed. Tony Day and Maya H. T. Liem), Ithaca: Cornell University Press, p. 197.

122. Sondhi Limthongkul, quoted by Nattaya Chetchotiros (2008), 'Sondhi Explains His "Final War," ' *Bangkok Post* (26 August), p. 3.

123. Similarly, Chulayarnnon Siriphol's 'Planetarium,' his science fiction segment of the anthology film *Ten Years Thailand*, depicts a near future in which the country's leader and her minions all wear Scout uniforms. For Chulayarnnon's performance art event and short film *Parade of Golden Snail* (2019), actors dressed as Scouts marched through a gallery, and the director explained that the costumes are "symbolic of people's power, right-wing power." In his dystopian vision, the entire country has been taken over by this royalist militia. The performance took place on 30 April 2019 at the BACC. The short film begins with the text of the letter banning *Birth of Golden Snail*.

124. Goppong Khunthreeya (2015), 'Critical Discourse Analysis of Thailand's Film Acts,' The Asian Conference on Media and Mass Communication (15 November).

125. Quoted by Jocelyn Gecker (2010), 'Thailand Bans Film about Transgender Father,' The Associated Press (24 December).

126. Film and Video Act (2008), § 26(1).

127. Jutatip Thitisawat (2015), 'From Censorship to Rating System: Negotiations of Power in Thai Film Industry,' The Asian Conference on Media and Mass Communication (15 November).

128. Thunska Pansittivorakul, quoted by Hunt (2012), p. 38.

129. Naresuan (Samphet II) was king of Ayutthaya from 1590 to 1605. The junta also proposed the production of a state-sponsored romantic comedy film (working title *Lost in Bangkok*) to attract tourists to Bangkok, announced in a National Legislative Assembly speech by Prayut Chan-o-cha on 12 September 2014.

130. B. J. Terwiel (2011), *Thailand's Political History: From the 13th Century to Recent Times*, Bangkok: River Books, p. 28.

## Chapter 2. *Nang R*: Sex and Sexuality on Screen

131. Kong Rithdee (2010b), 'To Show or Not to Show,' *Real.Time*, *Bangkok Post* (27 August), p. 1.

132. See also Dome Sukwong (1996), หลงทางและคดีหลงทาง [how *Going Astray* lost its lawsuit], Bangkok: Film House.

133. For more on the changing role of the *dao-yua* character, see Chanchana Homsap (2013), 'ตำนาน "ดาวยั่ว" กับความโป๊เปลือยในสื่อบันเทิงไทย ช่วงปี 2500–2520' [the story of the *dao-yua* in Thai erotic entertainment 1957–1977], *Read*, vol. 4, no. 3 (January–March), pp. 152–69.

134. Sopida Rodsom (2017), 'The Evolution of Sex in Thai Movies,' *Time Out Bangkok* (1 February).
135. ตัณหานักบุญ [lustful saint] (1976) features a lesbian kiss. For an analysis of Thai cinema's increase in sexual frankness after the 14 October incident, see Wimonrat Aroonrojsuriya (2000), 'หนังโป๊กับเสรีภาพหลัง 14 ตุลาคม' [freedom for pornographic films after 14 October], *Thai Film Quarterly*, vol. 2, no. 8 (April–June), pp. 34–43.
136. The film is ชู้ [the adulterer] (1972), quoted by Rebecca Townsend (2019), 'The Adulterer: Censorship, Morality, and Foreign Films in Thailand,' *Journal of Women's History*, vol. 31, no. 1 (Spring), p. 89.
137. *Ibid.* p. 102.
138. Thai erotic films are reviewed on the ThaiWorldView website (https://www.thaiworldview.com/tv/tv28.php). The directors of erotic films, including *Just a Friend 2* and *Girls Girls Girls*, amongst others, were often credited using pseudonyms.
139. Chatrichalerm Yukol, quoted by Thomas Richardson (2006), 'Interview with Chatrichalerm Yukol,' *Medium* (14 October). The interview was conducted in 1993.
140. Kong Rithdee (2012b), 'Never Mind Nipples, the Law Is an Ass,' *Life, Bangkok Post* (29 September), p. 9.
141. The masturbation and tattoo sequences occur in a segment titled 'ปรารถนา' [desire].
142. *Eternity* was rated 15, though a longer and more sexually explicit director's cut was released on DVD, rated 18. The international version of *The Scar*, rated 20, is forty-five minutes longer than the Thai version.
143. Pen-ek Ratanaruang, email to Matthew Hunt (1 March 2018).
144. Thunska Pansittivorakul, quoted by Kong Rithdee (2007b), 'Cat Among the Pigeons,' *Real. Time, Bangkok Post* (14 September), p. 1.
145. Arnika Fuhrmann (2016), *Ghostly Desires: Queer Sexuality and Vernacular Buddhism in Contemporary Thai Cinema*, Durham: Duke University Press, pp. 191–92.
146. Eighteen-year-old cadet Phakhapong Tanyakan died on 17 October 2017. Chaiyaphum Pasae was shot by a soldier at a checkpoint in Chiang Mai on 17 March 2017. *Santikhiri Sonata* premiered at the Doclisboa International Film Festival in Lisbon on 17 October 2019.
147. Linda Napapan's single, 'คนร้อยเล่ห์' [trickster], was released in the 1970s.
148. Oradol Kaewprasert (2005), 'The Very First Series of Thai Queer Cinemas: What Was Happening in the 80s?' Southeast Asian Cinema Conference: Cimema at the Borders (16 August).
149. B. Ruby Rich (2013), *New Queer Cinema: The Director's Cut*, Durham: Duke University Press, p. 23.

150. For its domestic release, *Beautiful Boxer* was cut by fifteen minutes for pacing reasons, though the international director's cut was later released in Thailand on VCD and DVD. The Singaporean film *Pleasure Factory* (2007), by the same director, includes an explicit male masturbation scene that was cut in both Thailand and Singapore.

151. Sucheera Pinijparakarn (2004), 'Call to Limit Gay Presence on TV', *The Nation* (5 June).

152. Tanwarin Sukkhapisit, quoted by Kong Rithdee (2010d), 'Insect in the Backyard', *Real.Time, Bangkok Post* (26 November), p. 1. *Insects in the Backyard* was submitted to the censors on 4 November 2010, and an 18 rating was requested. This request was denied on the day of submission. On 22 November 2010, Tanwarin resubmitted the film and requested a 20 rating; she also proposed that the film could include a disclaimer emphasizing that its characters are fictional, and a warning that viewer discretion is advised. This request was also rejected on the same day. The next day, Tanwarin appealed to the National Film Board, which rejected her appeal on 22 December 2010 and issued its written judgment to that effect on 28 December 2010. A restaurant called *Insects in the Backyard*, named after the film, opened in Bangkok in 2017.

153. Peter A. Jackson (2002), 'Offending Images: Gender and Sexual Minorities, and State Control of the Media in Thailand', *Media Fortunes, Changing Times: ASEAN States in Transition* (ed. Russell H. K. Heng), Singapore: Institute of Southeast Asian Studies, p. 215. The film, ผู้ชายขายตัว [male prostitutes], was banned at the last minute, after the police intervened on the day of its scheduled release, 12 October 1974. The poster is reproduced in Free Thai Cinema Movement (2013), p. 59.

154. Its title is ครั้งแรก [the first time].

155. The song is 'บ้านบนดอย' [home on the hillside], by Jaran Manopet, from his album โฟล์คซองคำเมือง [Kham Muang folk songs] (1979).

156. Tom Waller, quoted by Asaree Thaitrakulpanich (2019), 'Thai-Farang Romance in "*Soi Cowboy*" Still Rings True: Producer', Khaosod English (19 August).

## Chapter 3. The Untouchables: Film and Politics

157. Thai PBS World (2019), 'Thai Politics Getting Faster and More Furious' (11 June).

158. Kittinun Klongyai (2017), '*Love Missions*: Junta's New Soapie Reflects Military Fantasy', Prachatai (22 June).

159. Araya is also known for performance videos in which she addresses corpses in the morgue. This series began with *Reading for One Female Corpse* (1997).

160. The Thai title is รอ ๑๐ [waiting for ten], a reference to the regnal number of Rama IX's successor, Crown Prince Vajiralongkorn, who became Rama X.

161. Kong Rithdee (2010b), 'To Show or Not to Show,' *Real.Time, Bangkok Post* (27 August), p. 1. For further discussion of politics and cinema, see Sirichai Leelertyuth (2012), 'ภาพยนตร์สนทนา ข้อสังเกตว่าด้วย "การเมือง" ในหนังไทย' [talking about politics in Thai films], *Prachatai* (28 June).

162. Apichatpong Weerasethakul (2007a), 'A Hidden Agenda that Deems Us Morons: The Folly and Future of Thai Cinema Under Military Dictatorship,' *Bangkok Post* (25 September), p. 10. Pibulsongkram is an alternative Romanization of Phibun Songkhram's name.

163. The film was provisionally titled *2482 นักโทษประหาร* [1939: on death row].

164. Twenty minutes of footage from the film was shown at the School of Oriental and African Studies in London on 6 October 2017. The film features interviews with historians and dramatic reconstructions of the lives of Phibun and Pridi, particularly their time spent in exile. Based on new research by the director, the documentary reassesses the legacies of both men. See also ' "*Frienemies*" สารคดีชีวิต ปรีดี-จอมพล ป. สะท้อนมิตรภาพและความขัดแย้ง จาก 2475 ถึง ปัจจุบัน' [*Frienemies*, a documentary on the lives of Pridi and Phibun, reflecting on their friendship and conflict since 1932], BBC News.

165. Field Marshal Sarit Thanarat became prime minister after staging a coup in 1957, and died in 1963. The biopic was provisionally titled จอมพล [marshal]. Sarit was portrayed briefly in the horror film *Zee Oui: The Man-Eater* (2004). In the film, Sarit orders the swift execution of the eponymous cannibalistic murderer, the implication being that capital punishment was carried out for political expediency before the investigation was complete.

166. The film's title, ไอ้ซ่าส์ ... จอมเนรคุณ [the leading betrayer], begins with the insulting prefix *ai* [ไอ้]. Veera also wrote a book with the same title (Bangkok: Bhannakij Publishing, 1978), and its cover features a silhouette and a question mark, to convey a mystery identity. Like the film, the book uses a sound-alike name—"สกัด สุนทรีเวทย์" [Sagat Suntareewayt], p. 101—instead of naming Samak directly.

167. Tom Waller, online message to Matthew Hunt (28 August 2019).

168. *Ibid.*

169. *Ibid.*

170. The numbers are printed on a boiler suit worn by one of the actors in the music video. The song, 'Remember' by the Subtitle Project, appears on their album *Ordinary People* (2018). The video is dedicated (in a braille caption) to poet and 'redshirt' activist Kamol Duangpasuk, who was murdered in 2014.

171. Director Arin Rungjan has said: "The numbers are related to significant political events that happened in Thai history, which I'll leave for people to decode themselves." Quoted by Gail Piyanan (2018), 'Interview with Arin Rungjang,' *Time Out Bangkok* (1 January).

172. Apichatpong Weerasethakul, quoted in the documentary *On Cemetery of Splendour*, included on DVD and blu-ray releases of *Cemetery of Splendour*.

For a similar analysis—"sleep for Weerasethakul can also be a political metaphor"—see Dana Linssen (2017), 'Un/Folding: If Light Was the Measure of Time,' *Apichatpong Weerasethakul* (ed. Marente Bloemheuvel and Jaap Guldemond), Rotterdam: nai010.

173. The short film *The COUPle's Place* (2018), also set in a high school, puns on the 2014 coup in its title.

174. Quoted by Wassana Nanuam (2014), 'Yingluck Saw the Coup Coming,' *Bangkok Post* (24 November), p. 3.

175. Anocha Suwichakornpong (2010), 'Interview: Anocha Suwichakornpong—*Mundane History*,' International Film Festival Rotterdam (3 February).

176. See also Carmen Gray (2012), *Mundane History*, Second Run DVD, p. 5: "Rejection of the father figure has broader symbolic implications in Thailand's patriarchal society, in which power was destabilised by a military coup; the conflict in Ake's household a microcosm of the unrest between the rulers and ruled at large."

177. Nick Pinkerton (2020), '*Krabi, 2562*,' *Sight and Sound*, vol. 30, no. 5 (May), p. 73.

178. Graiwoot Chulphongsathorn (2010), 'Thoughts on Contemporary Experimental Films in Thailand,' EX!T 2010. For a history of earlier experimental Thai films, see Panu Aree (1997), 'ประวัติภาพยนตร์ทดลองในประเทศไทย' [the history of experimental films in Thailand], *Bangkok International Film Festival*, pp. 11–21. For a survey of Thai short films, see Jit Phokaew, Kanchat Rangseekansong, Wiwat Lertwiwatwongsa, Chulayarnnon Siriphol, and Chayanin Tiangpitayagorn (2012), 'Mysterious Object from Thailand,' *Experimental Conversations*, no. 9 (Summer).

179. *Friendship Ended with Mudasir Now Salman Is My Best Friend* was shown at the *Internet Universality Beyond Words* exhibition at the Thailand Creative and Design Center (TCDC) in Bangkok, from 28 September to 14 October 2018. It includes extracts from the documentary *October 14 Thai Student Uprising 1973* (1993) and the *Tom and Jerry* cartoon 'Jerry's Cousin' (1951).

180. Paige Lim (2018), 'In the Spotlight,' *Tatler* (Thailand), vol. 26, no. 320 (April), p. 102.

181. Alexandra Genova (2019), 'The Director Speaks: Apichatpong Weerasethakul on the Future of Film in Thailand,' *Huck* (6 March).

182. Thunska's short film *2060*, an extract from *Supernatural*, also includes this caption, and it was shown during the 'Design Nation' event at the Pridi Banomyong Institute in Bangkok on 14 October 2012. Pallop Pinmanee was also responsible for ordering the 2004 massacre at the Krue Se Mosque.

183. *Democracy after Death* was screened at Thammasat University on 7 October 2016. The English subtitle translating the soldier's comment was not censored. The photograph shows coup leader Sonthi Boonyaratglin meeting King Rama IX in the middle of the night, and was initially circulated by the junta to demonstrate the military's fealty to the monarch and the king's acceptance of

the coup, in an attempt to reassure the public and justify the military's actions. It is reproduced in *Time* (2006), vol. 168, no. 14 (2 October), p. 20.

184. Ampon Tangnoppakul was convicted of *lèse-majesté* in 2011. He died of cancer in 2012 while serving a twenty-year prison sentence. The *Cemetery of Splendour* diary entry expresses the hope that Ah Kong (Ampon's nickname) will be released: "ขอให้อากงได้ออกมา" [hoping that Ah Kong will get out]. The text was taken from รักเอย [love Oey] (2012), a memoir by Ampon's wife, Rosmalin.

185. Somyos Praeksakasemsuk is an alternative spelling of Somyot Prueksakasemsuk, editor of *Voice of Taksin* [เสียงทักษิณ] magazine, who was jailed for *lèse-majesté*. Somyot was sentenced to ten years in jail in 2013, and this was reduced to seven years in 2017. He was released in 2018.

186. The subtitles read: "in the story there are XXXXXXXXXXX and XXXXXXXXXXX." Weeranan's girlfriend, Prontip Mankong, was sentenced to two years in jail, alongside a fellow student, Patiwat Saraiyaem, for their production of *The Wolf Bride* [เจ้าสาวหมาป่า] (2013). The pair were jailed in 2015 and released in 2016. Patiwat appears in 'Song of the City,' Apichatpong Weerasethakul's segment of the anthology film *Ten Years Thailand* (2018).

187. Thunska submitted an extract from *Supernatural*, titled *Narayana's Arrow Spaceship*, to the Short Film and Video Festival, though it was submitted anonymously. Some of its dialogue was self-censored and its credits were replaced by black stripes. The credits of *Democracy after Death* (2016) were also self-censored. Each crew member was credited as 'anonymous,' and the production company was listed as Anonymous Films.

188. The film's set design includes a wall calendar featuring a photograph of Rama IX, an item found in millions of Thai houses though conspicuous by its absence from many films with domestic settings. One shot is carefully composed so that the king's photograph on the calendar is visible through a door left ajar.

189. Tom Waller, online message to Matthew Hunt (23 July 2017). The second part of Ing Kanjanavanit's *Bangkok Joyride* (2017) includes a few bars of the royal anthem, though she did not submit it to the censors. Also, *Krabi 2562* (2019) begins with schoolchildren being instructed to sing the royal anthem in the playground. (2562 BE is equivalent to 2019.)

190. Drew Dowdle, quoted by Alison de Souza (2015), 'Shot in Chiangmai, but no Trace of Thailand,' *The Straits Times* (26 August), Rama IX was born on a Monday, the day on which yellow is traditionally worn.

191. At a New Years' Eve countdown event at Ratchaprasong in downtown Bangkok, the announcer told the crowd: "Let's countdown and celebrate H.M. the King's 84th anniversary." Quoted by iLaw (2013), 'Case #472: *Boundary*,' The original Thai passage, "เรามาร่วมเคาท์ดาวน์และร่วมฉลองให้พระบาทสมเด็จพระเจ้าอยู่หัวมีพระชนมายุครบ 84 พรรษา," is quoted by May Adadol Ingawanij (2013), 'กับดักของฉันทามติ' [the consensus trap], *Read*, vol. 4, no. 4 (April–June), p. 140. Apichatpong commented on the censorship of Nontawat's film: "I think he shouldn't have cut that out. He should fight."

192. Apichatpong wore a tee-shirt with the slogan 'NO 112' at the opening ceremony for the World Film Festival of Bangkok on 16 November 2012. For a photograph of the director wearing it, see Curtis Winston (2012), '10th WFFBKK: Victor Is Awarded,' Wise Kwai's Thai Film Journal (18 November).

193. Manote Tripathi (1998), 'The King and Us,' The Nation (29 November). Manote also itemizes the censors' specific objections to the revised script.

194. The Shadow of History includes footage filmed by Chin Klaiparn (อนุทินวีรชน 14 ตุลาคม) [diary of 14 October heroes] and Taweesak Wiriyasiri (วันมหาวิปโยค) [the tragic day]. See also Chalida Uabumrungrit (2013), 'หนัง 14 ตุลาคม การเขียน ประวัติศาสตร์ประชาชนด้วยกล้องถ่ายหนัง' [14 October films: writing social history with a movie camera], Thai Film Journal, vol. 18, (November), pp. 87–96.

195. The uncut trailer is available online (https://www.youtube.com/watch?v=nU-QB1A4BUU) and on the film's DVD release.

196. One student says: "For our rector to accept a post in this cabinet is a total disgrace," a reference to Sanya Dharmasakti, Chancellor of Thammasat University, who was prime minister from 1973 to 1975.

197. Dome Sukvong [sic] (2013), A Century of Thai Cinema Exhibition's Handbook [sic], Salaya: Thai Film Archive, p. 160. (Dome's surname is more conventionally Romanized as Sukwong.)

198. The front page of Dao Siam 6 October 1976 is rarely reproduced in its complete form, as the combination of the strapline—"แขวนคอหุ่นเหมือนเจ้าฟ้าชาย" [hanging the prince in effigy]—and photograph is still considered highly provocative. However, it does appear in Thongchai Winichakul (2020), Moments of Silence: The Unforgetting of the October 6, 1976, Massacre in Bangkok, Honolulu: University of Hawai'i Press, p. 29. The students were also demonized in films such as เก้ายอด [nine peaks] (1977). In one sequence, the Hindu demon Tossakan is superimposed over footage of student protesters from 1976 as he mocks the students and denounces them as agitators.

199. Patporn Phoothong, quoted by Kong Rithdee (2017a), 'Massacre's Memory,' Life, Bangkok Post (20 July), p. 1. Respectfully Yours was first shown, in a shorter version, in 2016. It was also shown at a discussion about cultural representation of the massacre, 'The Forgotten,' as part of 'The Strange Facts of an Estranged Land' event at the 13th International Conference on Thai Studies on 17 July 2017.

200. Teerawat Rujenatham, quoted by Kong Rithdee (2017b), 'The Inciting Incident,' Life, Bangkok Post (6 October), p. 1.

201. The song is by Chatree, from their album ชะตารัก [love destiny] (1981).

202. The photograph, depicting Lt Col. Salang Bunnag, is reproduced in Nicholas Grossman (2009), Chronicle of Thailand: Headline News since 1946. Singapore: Editions Didier Millet, p. 212.

203. The film is titled นครพนมมือบ้าง นครไม่พนมมือบ้าง [Nakhon Phanom: some pray, some don't].

204. The Appeals Court's verdict was announced on 11 August 2017.
205. Ing Kanjanavanit (2014), Southeast Asian Film Festival 2014 (2 May). Neal Ulevich's photograph of the man preparing to hit the hanging corpse is reproduced in Thongchai (2020), p. 29. For her *Where Are They Now?* [ไทยมุง] series (2008), Ing painted portraits of onlookers in the background of Ulevich's photograph; reproduced in *Flashback '76: History and Memory of October 6 Massacre* (2008), Bangkok: Pridi Banomyong Institute, pp. 1–3, 6. Manit Sriwanichpoom appropriated Ulevich's photograph for his *Horror in Pink* (2001) series, in a commentary on viewers' desensitization to political violence. The series also included photographs of the 14 October 1973 and 'Black May' 1992 protests; reproduced in *Manit Sriwanichpoom: Phenomena and Prophecies* (2011), Bangkok: Srinakharinwirot University, pp. 61-67.
206. The meeting took place on 3 May 2012, and the culture minister at the time was Sukumpol Kunplome. The description of the proceedings was provided by a reliable source who wishes to remain anonymous, interviewed in Bangkok on 30 July 2019.
207. The clip is from an episode titled 'A Milhouse Divided' (1996), available on the DVD *The Simpsons: The Complete Eighth Season* (2006).
208. 'Democrazy' appears on Dogwhine's EP *Dog of God*.
209. The film's Thai and international versions are compared on the Movie Censorship website (https://www.movie-censorship.com/report.php?ID=451668).
210. Its title is ช่างมันฉันไม่แคร์ [forget it, I don't care].
211. Dana Linssen (2017).
212. Chulayarnnon Siriphol, quoted by Cicada Channel (2019), 'Issue 3: *Monk and Motorcycle Taxi Rider*.'
213. Prabda Yoon, quoted by the Institute for Ideas and Information (2019), Kembara Festival (7 February).
214. Vasan's other videos include the Actionism-inspired *There Must Be Something Happen* [*sic*] (1993), in which he defecates on a gallery floor.
215. Sunchinda's predecessor as prime minister, Anand Panyarachun, was asked by Rama IX to return as prime minister following 'Black May.' (Anand had been appointed prime minister in 1991. He resumed office in an interim capacity until elections were held later in 1992.) He told his biographer that the king implored him with a quotation from the Hollywood western *Shane* (1953): "Shane! Come back!" Quoted by Dominic Faulder (2018), *Anand Panyarachun and the Making of Modern Thailand*, Singapore: Editions Didiet Millet, p. 343. The king's implication was that, like the town in the movie, Bangkok had descended into lawlessness and needed a white knight to rescue it.
216. The film, พฤษภาทมิฬ [black May], was originally titled สัตว์เลือดเย็น [cold-blooded animals].

217. One such documentary, บันทึกสีดำ [black record] (1992), unusually features the five-note motif from Steven Spielberg's Hollywood blockbuster *Close Encounters of the Third Kind* (1977) on its soundtrack.
218. The subtitle reads: "Gen. Su*****da." Note that four letters have been removed from Suchinda's name, though there are five asterisks.
219. Apichatpong Weerasethakul's four *Photophobia* prints incorporate photographs of Tak Bai victims; reproduced in *Apichatpong Weerasethakul: The Serenity of Madness* (2016), Hong Kong: Para Site, pp. 38–39. 'Black Air' (2008), an installation by Pimpaka Towira, Akritchalerm Kalayanamitr, Koichi Shimizu, and Jakrawal Nilthamrong, is another artistic response to the massacre. Viewers press buttons that display still images from Tak Bai footage.
220. *Same Sky* (2004), vol. 2, no. 4 (October–December) featured a cover mounted VCD, ความจริงที่ตากใบ [the truth about Tak Bai], of Tak Bai footage.
221. Thunska Pansittivorakul, quoted by Curtis Winston (2009), '"Quarantine" Under Lockdown,' *Daily Xpress*, vol. 2, no. 450 (30 October), p. 2.
222. The National Administrative Reform Council (the 1976 junta) produced their own propaganda documentary shortly after the massacre—a short, black-and-white film that emphasized the alleged Communist sympathies of the students and showed weapons purportedly discovered at Thammasat. A documentary commemorating the massacre's twentieth anniversary, ชำระประวัติศาสตร์ ๖ ตุลา ๒๕๑๙ [settling history: 6 October 1976] (1996), begins with brief historical context, then replays raw footage of the massacre, and concludes with a caption calling for an end to state violence against civilians. It was released on VHS as ปณิธาน 6 ตุลา วิถีคนกล้าแห่งยุคสมัย แม้ 20 ปีล่วงไปไม่เคยจางความทรงจำ [6 October resolution: a time of bravery]. In 2001, it was extensively re-edited and reissued for the twenty-fifth anniversary, with much of the raw archive footage replaced by new interviews with academics and relatives of the victims. Another documentary, พ.ศ. 2519 [2519 BE] (1996), consists only of raw footage from the massacre. (2519 BE is equivalent to 1976.) This documentary concludes with the same caption mentioned above, suggesting that it originates from the same production team. It was released on VCD in 2001, alongside a documentary on the 14 October 1973 massacre, as เหตุการณ์จริง 14 ตุลา [real events of 14 October] and 4 ถึง 6 ตุลา [4 to 6 October].
223. William A. Callahan (1992), *Imagining Democracy: Reading "the Events of May" in Thailand*, Singapore: Institute of Southeast Asian Studies, pp. 19–20.
224. It was also released on VCD in 2001 as เหตุการณ์จริง 14 ตุลา [real events of 14 October] and 4 ถึง 6 ตุลา [4 to 6 October]. Also, episodes of the historical documentary series บันทึกเมืองไทย [save Thailand] relating to 14 October were released on VCD as บันทึกจากเหตุการณ์จริง 14 ตุลา สงครามปัญญาชน [actual events of 14 October: war between intellectuals] (2001).
225. These VCDs include ฝากกระจายด้วยนะครับ ! [spread the news !] (2008), ตำรวจฆ่าประชาชน [police killing people] (2008), and ความจริงประเทศไทย [the truth about

Thailand] (2010). The National Library of Australia's collection includes various DVDs and VCDs documenting anti-'redshirt' violence, listed on the Library's website (https://www.nla.gov.au/sites/default/files/udd_finding_aid.docx).

226. The song is 'Masochist' ['แผลเป็น'] from Yokee Playboy's album *YKPB* (2000).

227. According to Mirjam Kooiman (2017), 'Infected Memories,' *Foam*, no. 47, p. 233, Thunska's *Homogeneous, Empty Time* codirector had a similar experience after the 'redshirt' crackdown in 2010: "The events represent the catalyst for Harit Srikhao to research his country's political history." Sayan Daengklom (2011), 'ห' [or], *Read*, vol. 3, no. 2 (January–March), p. 215, links Tanwarin Sukhapisit's *Insects in the Backyard* to a wave of socially conscious "Post-Ratchaprasong art," following the 'redshirt' massacre at Bangkok's Ratchaprasong intersection.

228. Yuthlert criticized the Constitutional Court in a tweet from his personal Twitter account on 27 August 2019—"สงสัยว่าศาลรัฐธรรมนูญ เลือกอะไรกับประชาชน ก็ได้เหรอ?" [what gives the Constitutional Court the right to intrude on its citizens?]—and was summonsed to apologize for contempt of court. On 20 April 2020, via his NMG Twitter account, Yuthlert blamed the Digital Economy and Society minister for an equine disease outbreak: "รัฐมนตรีเฟคนิวส์ อยู่เบื้องหลังสาเหตุของการตายของม้าในประเทศไทย" [the minister of fake news is behind the horse deaths in Thailand]. As a result, Puttipong Punnakanta, whose ministry launched a campaign against fake news, filed a complaint against him under the Computer Crime Act.

229. Vasan explained the Artist Party's policies in a 2005 video manifesto [สารคดี พรรคศิลปิน]. His paintings include 'This Is the Buddhism Country' [*sic*] ['นี่แหละ หนอเมืองพระพุทธศาสนา'], a recreation of a photograph of the 6 October 1976 massacre by photojournalist Neal Ulevich; reproduced in *Vasan Sitthiket: Blue October* (1996), Bangkok: Sunday Gallery, p. 26. Later, Vasan painted 'Death for Democracy 1992' ['ตายเพื่อประชาธิปไตย 2535'] (2010), illustrating the violence against the 'Black May' protesters in 1992; reproduced in Luckana Kunavichayanont (2018), *I Am You*, Bangkok: Bangkok Art and Culture Centre Foundation, p. 77. His paintings of religious subjects are as controversial as his political works. His dystopian 'Buddha Returns to Bangkok '92' ['พระพุทธเจ้า เสด็จกรุงเทพ 2535'] (1993), depicting the Buddha surrounded by scenes of chaotic sex and violence (including a masturbating monk), was a reaction to the 1992 'Black May' massacre; reproduced in Joyce van Fenema (1996), *Southeast Asian Art Today*, Singapore: Roeder Publications, p. 250. His *Obsessive Compulsive* [ย้ำคิดย้ำทำ] (2011) exhibition included 'Take Care Only Oneself Not Anyone Else' [*sic*] ['ตัวใครตัวมันนะโยม'], depicting a monk having sex, with monks' robes appliquéd to the canvas; reproduced in Andrew J. West (2011), 'Obsessive Compulsive,' *Fine Art*, vol. 8, no. 79 (May), p. 71.

230. Tom Plate (2011), *Conversations with Thaksin: From Exile to Deliverance— Thailand's Populist Tycoon Tells His Story*, Singapore: Marshall Cavendish,

p. 74, speculated on the nature of a Hollywood biopic about Thaksin: "if they were critics of our self-exiled PM, they might make the *Thaksin* movie by taking *The Godfather* and putting it together with a bit of *Bonnie and Clyde*.... A pro-Thaksin screenplay would emphasize sports themes. It'd blend the gritty and inspirational *Chariots of Fire* with Kevin Costner's ultra-cool *Tin Cup*." In fact, a hagiographic *lakhon* biopic of Thaksin's pre-politics life was produced by Channel 7 during his first term as prime minister, though the series, ตาดูดาว เท้าติดดิน [feet on the ground, looking at the stars] (2005), was never broadcast as anti-Thaksin protests had begun by the time production was completed. It was later adapted as an animated series with the same title (2014), a vanity project distributed via YouTube. The *lakhon* and cartoon series were both based on Thaksin's autobiography; as Pasuk Phongpaichit and Chris Baker write in *Thaksin: The Business of Politics in Thailand* (Chiang Mai: Silkworm Books, 2004, p. 60), "Thaksin has mythologized his life story as a poor boy made good." Before he entered politics, film distribution was one of Thaksin's first business ventures, and he bought the rights to the hit film *Sai Tong* (1979), as dramatized in the second episode of the animated Thaksin series.

231. The director was interviewed by the police on 9 June 2004. Tellingly, he was asked to provide evidence of the source of the film's funding, indicating that the police suspected a political motivation for its release. The film also features a character based on Thaksin, with the punning name "เจ้าสัวรักสิน," which combines a slang term for a rich Chinese person (*chao sua*, a reference to Thaksin's wealth and heritage), and the sound-alike *rak sin*.

232. *Tossaliam* depicts Thaksin with a square face and a Hitler moustache. Its title compares Thaksin to Tossakan, a demonic figure from Hindu mythology (also known as Ravana). The title also refers to Thaksin's derogatory nickname Na Liam [square-face].

233. The VCD documentary is ความจริงประเทศไทย [the truth about Thailand].

234. The Short Film and Video Festival event, *Spoken Silence*, was held on 24 August 2007 at the EGV Grand Discovery cinema in Bangkok. *3-0*'s title refers to Anocha's age, and how military interventions represent milestones in her life: she was born in 1976, the year of the 6 October massacre; she was fifteen years old during 'Black May'; and she was thirty at the time of the 2006 coup.

235. *I'm Fine* won the first prize at the 2008 Short Film and Video Festival. Melalin Mahavongtrakul (2017), 'Redefining What's "Appropriate,"' *Life, Bangkok Post* (27 November), p. 1, praises it for "capturing the postcoup atmosphere in the country."

236. Lennon's single 'Imagine' was released in 1971, and has become a worldwide peace anthem. A television documentary on the 'Black May' massacre, broadcast by Channel 9 on 24 May 1992, also ends with 'Imagine.'

237. Songkran is the traditional Thai new year festival, celebrated annually on 13 April. The army used tear gas, and fired live rounds, to disperse the protesters

at Din Daeng, an intersection in Bangkok, on 14 April 2009. The attack on Abhisit's motorcade is shown in the documentary *Democracy after Death* (2016).

238. Wisit Sasanatieng, quoted by Kong (2010c), p. 1.

239. The series, เหนือเมฆ 2 มือปราบจอมขมังเวทย์ [beyond comparison 2: fighting black magic], was broadcast by Channel 3.

240. The film's teaser poster featured a news photograph of naked corpses on a beach, victims of the 2004 Indian Ocean tsunami. The exploitative poster led to public criticism and the film flopped. For a reproduction of the poster, see 'เลื่อนฉาย "สึนามิ" ' ["*Tsunami*" postponed] (2009), *Thai Rath* (26 April).

241. The director provided a translation of the censors' verdict: "The film's content is a threat to national security and international relations. The film presents some information on incidents that are still being deliberated by the Thai court and that have not yet been officially concluded." Quoted by Nontawat Numbenchapol (2013), '*Boundary* Banned by Censors, Screening Not Permitted in Kingdom of Thailand,' Facebook (23 April).

242. The documentary *Democracy after Death* describes the massacre with a similar statistic: "soldiers surrounded and killed 100 people." Similarly, the film *Young Bao* features a mockup of a newspaper headline about the 6 October 1976 massacre that also refers to 'almost 100' victims: "Almost 100 people have been effected from 6th Oct In Thailand" [*sic*]. In that case, 'almost 100' was arguably an exaggeration as the official death toll was forty-six, though it is consistent with unofficial estimates. Either way, the headline was not challenged by the censors.

243. Malinee Khumsupa and Sudarat Musikawong (2016), 'Counter-memory: Replaying Political Violence in Thai Digital Cinema,' *Kyoto Review of Southeast Asia*, vol. 20.

244. Yuthakarn Joichoichos was shot on 13 April 2009. *A Brief History of Memory* was released on the *Human Frames: Fanaticism* (2012) DVD.

245. Part one covers the buildup to the PDRC's campaign, from July to 9 December 2013. Part two covers 22 December 2013 to 15 January 2014. Part three covers 15–26 January 2014. Part four covers 26 January to 8 February 2014. Part five covers the aftermath of the 2014 election.

246. The song, 'Lao Duang Duen' ['ลาวดวงเดือน'], was composed by Prince Benbadhanabongse.

247. The song is 'ถามหาความรัก' [asking for love] by Carabao (https://www.youtube.com/watch?v=t6lnfpaCRus), from their album กัมพูชา [Cambodia] (1984).

248. The documentary บันทึกสีดำ [black record] features the song 'ผู้ทน' [endurer] by Carabao (https://www.youtube.com/watch?v=ZyPTYTG5DnU), from their album ประชาธิปไตย [democracy] (1986).

249. The song, 'Echo' ['แว่ว'], was written in 1965.

250. Prayut's second term as prime minister began in 2019. He appears as a minor character in Tom Waller's film *The Cave* (2019), a drama based on the true

story of a young football team rescued by divers from a cave. The character, who has a close physical likeness to Prayut, serves no narrative purpose other than giving gift baskets to the divers. He also provides comic relief. Additionally, the music video for the song 'Sud-Swing Ringo Eto Bump,' on the *Stand Up Comedy 11* [เดี่ยวไมโครโฟน 11] (2015) DVD, features a Prayut look-alike, as does Hockhacker's music video for his single 'Citizen.'

251. Chulayarnnon also produced a six-volume book (Bangkok: Bangkok CityCity Gallery, 2020) with the same title, featuring collages of newspaper headlines and press photographs made every day from the 2014 coup to the 2019 election.

252. The film, *The Hunger Games: Mockingjay—Part 1*, premiered on 20 November 2014.

253. Richard Lloyd Parry (2014), 'Thailand's Big Brother Bans Orwell's *1984*,' *The Times* (11 June). The screening at Chiang Mai's Punya Movieclub was originally scheduled for 14 June 2014.

254. The planned screening of *By the Time It Gets Dark* on 6 October 2017 at Warehouse 30 in Bangkok was cancelled due to military pressure. The *Boundary* screening was originally scheduled for 24 April 2015 as part of Burapha University's 'Bangsaen Rama' film festival.

## Chapter 4. Saffron Cinema: Monks in the Movies

255. Ronald Green (2014), *Buddhism Goes to the Movies: Introduction to Buddhist Thought and Practice*, Abingdon: Routledge, p. 128.

256. *The Light of Asia* was shown at the Scala cinema on 6 June 2012.

257. Kong Rithdee (2011), 'Monks in the Movies,' *Outlook, Bangkok Post* (9 February), p. 1.

258. The documentary 'Thailand's Tainted Robes' (2014) notes that respect for monks "has been challenged as a series of scandals shake the public's faith in the monkhood."

259. Manat Kingjan, quoted by Kong (2011), p. 1.

260. Ing Kanjanavanit (2014), Southeast Asian Film Festival 2014 (2 May).

261. Graiwoot Chulpongsathorn (2009), 'Love Letters,' Criticine (15 December). Another reason for the ban was that the censors misinterpreted a character as a substitute for Princess Galyani, King Rama IX's sister.

262. It was shown on 8 September 2018.

263. Its Thai title is หลวงตา 3 ศึกข้างวัด [Luang Ta 3: a woman lives next to a temple].

264. Jesse Sessons (2018), '*The Holy Man*,' *Thai Cinema: The Complete Guide* (ed. Mary J. Ainslie and Katarzyna Ancuta), London: I. B. Tauris, p. 175.

265. Suphin Thongtara, quoted by Parinyaporn Pajee (2006), 'A New Spectre: Insensitivity,' *The Nation* (4 August), p. 12.

266. Poj Arnon, quoted by Soopsip (2016), 'Poj Lines up Another Romp for His Monks of Mirth,' *The Nation*, p. 16.

267. The monk, Phisan Dhammavadhi, withdrew his demand for a ban after viewing a cut version of the film.
268. Nasorn Panungkasiri, quoted by Kong Rithdee (2010a), 'Robed in Controversy,' *Real.Time, Bangkok Post* (19 February), p. 1.
269. *Ibid.*
270. Amnaj Buasiri, quoted by Kong (2011), p. 1.
271. Pen-ek Ratanaruang, email to Matthew Hunt (1 March 2018).
272. Monruedee Jansuttipan (2016), 'TrueVisions Pulls Prabda Yoon's "*Motel Mist*" from Cinemas Straight After Premiere,' *BK* (17 November).
273. Apichatpong Weerasethakul (2007b), 'Who Can Save My Flying Saucer?' *Film and Music, The Guardian* (14 September). Prince Mahidol Adulyadej and Princess Srinagarindra were the parents of Rama VIII and Rama IX.
274. Some of the censored shots were included in the music video for 'คนสุดท้ายของหัวใจ' [the last person in my heart] (2018), a song by Boy Phanomphrai from the film's soundtrack.
275. Justin McDaniel (2010), 'The Emotional Lives of Buddhist Monks in Modern Thai Film,' *Journal of Religion and Film*, vol. 14, no. 2 (October).
276. The music videos 'Remind' (2018) by Room39 and 'เธอบอก' [you say] (2015) by MJTD feature monks mourning their former girlfriends. In 'Remind,' tears trickle down the monk's cheek. In 'เธอบอก,' the despondent monk is physically shaken by the spirit of his deceased ex-girlfriend. In the music video 'Xnatta. soulless.nirvanA' (2019) by Yiaz, a monk cries while mourning his dead boyfriend.
277. The sequence was uploaded to YouTube (https://www.youtube.com/watch?v=9EgmiRH71vQ). It was also screened by the Thai Film Director Association during a press conference at the BACC on 21 November 2018.
278. Kanittha revealed this in a discussion about the ban, 'อย่าจองเวรจองกรรมซึ่งกันและกันเลย' [don't hold a grudge], on 17 October 2015 at the BACC. *Karma's* trailer is available online (https://www.youtube.com/watch?v=FY1FPFov3hg), though it was not approved for the film's DVD release.
279. *Pret Arbut* includes ten minutes of additional material. Its title is based on *Karma's* original title, อาบัติ (*arbat*), rather than the revised title imposed by the censor, อาปัติ (*arpat*).
280. The Thai national anthem video without monks was broadcast between 3 May and 16 June 2019, and its replacement—with monks—debuted on 17 June 2019. The complaint about the anthem video came from Charoon Wonnakasinanont.
281. These groups were the Thailand Bible Society, the Thailand Protestant Coordinating Committee, the Evangelical Fellowship of Thailand, and Catholic Social Communications of Thailand.
282. After the 'birth' of the snail, the girl's Japanese captors run away, leaving the gold they hid in a nearby cave. The girl dips the shell in molten gold, which is tinted yellow in this otherwise black-and-white film.

283. Niwat Wattanayommanaporn's death threat ["อย่าหมิ่นความศักดิ์สิทธิ์ของเขาขนาบน้ำ ให้กระทำสิ่งที่ไม่เหมาะสมได้ตายยกหมู่แน่นอน"] was posted on Facebook on 1 November 2018.

284. Chulayarnnon Siriphol (2018), 'My Biennale 006' ['เบียนนาเล่ของฉัน 006'], Facebook (7 November). The preview screening took place on 17 October 2018.

285. Translation of a letter from the Office of Contemporary Art and Culture (1 November 2018), quoted in *Hotel Art Fair Bangkok* (Bangkok: Farmgroup, 2019). The letter was displayed at the entrance to the Khao Khanabnam cave to explain the film's absence from the exhibition. It was later shown at the *Field Trip Project Asia* exhibition at the BACC, from 9 April to 5 May 2019. *Birth of Golden Snail* had its premiere on 29 November 2019, at the Singapore International Film Festival. It was first screened in Thailand on 14 December 2019, during the Short Film and Video Festival at the Thai Film Archive. The event also included an uncut screening of Apichatpong Weerasethakul's *Syndromes and a Century*, on 16 December 2019.

## Part Two
## Apichatpong Weerasethakul

286. *Blissfully Yours* was released on DVD in Thailand, though it was rather heavily cut. In addition to the sexual content cut from the theatrical version, eight minutes of footage of the male protagonist and his mother driving was removed. Apichatpong's website (http://www.kickthemachine.com) included a warning about the Thai DVD edition.

287. *Tropical Malady* features potentially dramatic subject matter—a tiger and a gay relationship—though the tiger is largely an ethereal presence and the relationship remains chaste.

288. Apichatpong was speaking at his home in Chiang Mai in 2016.

289. A Digital Cinema Package (DCP) is a hard disk containing a digital copy of a film, supplied to cinemas. (DCPs are the digital equivalent of analogue 35mm reels.)

290. *Cemetery of Splendour* was shown at the Thai Film Archive on 19 November 2018.

291. Apichatpong directed the short film *The Anthem* in 2006. The film is presented as a sound check for cinemas to play before showing their main feature, though its title implies that it could also serve as an alternative to cinema performances of the royal anthem. In 2008, Chotisak Oonsong faced a *lèse-majesté* charge after he refused to stand up during a performance of the royal anthem at a cinema in Bangkok. Kornkritch Somjittranukit (2016), 'The Royal Anthem: Shaping Thai Political Views Through Cinemas Nationwide,' Prachatai English (22 November), analyzes the subtexts of the royal anthem videos played at all Thai cinemas: "While the palace previously emphasised the King's commitment

to his duties as 'Father of the Land', anthem videos now push the Thai people's duty to love the monarchy as 'good children'."

292. At the height of the Cold War, Thai military rule was effectively propped up by the US, providing a significant impetus for Sarit Thanarat's anti-Communist agenda.

## Pen-ek Ratanaruang

293. Five seconds of film footage is equivalent to 120 frames.

294. *Nymph* (2009) premiered at the Cannes Film Festival in an unfinished form. The theatrical version was considerably shorter, and the Cannes version was given a limited release in Thailand alongside the theatrical version. Some sequences, such as Korn leaving his wife, and Korn and May praying to a tree, were removed in the shorter version because they are already referred to in the dialogue. We hear a loud noise and later see Korn's bandaged hand, though without the shot of the broken glass (present in the longer version), it is not clear that Korn smashed the window of May's car. Also, to enable the characters to reach the forest as quickly as possible, several early scenes were deleted in their entirety. These include sequences in a photography shop (where Nop discusses his plan to visit the forest), a hotel (where May surreptitiously telephones Korn), and the car journey to the forest (during which May ignores Nop and answers telephone calls from work). The result is that May and Nop's relationship seems to deteriorate only when they reach the forest, whereas in the longer version their marriage was on the rocks even before they began their trip.

295. Rama VII was staying at his summer residence, Klai Kangwon Palace in Hua Hin, when the 1932 coup took place. The palace subsequently became the summer residence of Rama IX.

296. Pen-ek is, of course, paraphrasing the announcement. Pridi and the other coup leaders had an audience with Rama VII on 26 June 1932, at which he agreed to their democratic reforms.

297. Rather than wearing colored shirts (as the PAD and UDD had done), the PDRC protesters blew whistles.

298. *The Beatles*, an album released by the Beatles in 1968, is known as 'The White Album' due to its plain white packaging.

299. After the 2006 coup, Thaksin Shinawatra, borrowing a phrase from economist Adam Smith, euphemistically accused an 'invisible hand' of interfering in the democratic process. After much speculation, in 2009 Thaksin eventually named this figure as Prem Tinsulanonda, President of the Privy Council.

300. Yingluck Shinawatra's flagship policy was a rice subsidy scheme intended to boost incomes for rice farmers. Her government bought rice from farmers at up to 50 percent above market prices, intending to stockpile it and thus drive

up the potential export price by reducing supply. However, Thailand was unable to sell its stockpiled rice, the government defaulted on its payments to the farmers, and Yingluck was charged with negligence and dereliction of duty. She was sentenced in absentia to five years in prison in 2017, after fleeing the country shortly before the Supreme Court was due to deliver its verdict.

301. These Bangkok cinemas were owned by Apex. They are photographed, along with other pre-multiplex Thai cinemas, in Sonthaya Subyen and Morimart Raden-Ahmad (2014), *Once Upon a Celluloid Planet: Where Cinema Ruled— Hearts and Homes of Films in Thailand*, Bangkok: Filmvirus. The Siam cinema was destroyed by arsonists in 2010. The Lido cinema closed down in 2018, and reopened as a cinema and performance venue (Lido Connect) the following year. Scala closed in 2020.

302. In 2013, a relatively small group of protesters wearing white masks demonstrated in Bangkok against the government of Yingluck Shinawatra.

303. The trailer is available online (https://www.youtube.com/watch?v=vKcTjM 72iuQ) and on the film's DVD release.

## Thunska Pansittivorakul

304. Thunska's relationship with photographer Harit Srikhao is explored in their autobiographical films *sPACEtIME* (2015) and *Avalon*. Harit's exhibition *Whitewash* was held from 3 June to 22 July 2017. 'Sunset,' a segment of *Ten Years Thailand* in which an exhibition is censored by a group of soldiers, is based on the military's censorship of *Whitewash*.

305. Thunska had intended to show *Homogeneous, Empty Time* in July 2017, though he cancelled the screening.

306. Pantip is a shopping mall in downtown Bangkok, specializing in electronics. *Unseen Bangkok* features clips from a bootleg VCD and an interview with a male hustler filmed by Thunska.

307. *Homogeneous, Empty Time*'s title is a phrase used by Walter Benjamin and Benedict Anderson, and the film is dedicated to Anderson's memory.

308. Kriengsak Silakong founded the World Film Festival of Bangkok.

309. The Silpathorn was a prestigious award given to outstanding Thai artists. Thunska received the director's award in 2007, which included a prize of THB 100,000.

310. Thunska released a new version of *Reincarnate* on the Vimeo website in 2017. It has brighter and more vivid color grading, and Thunska added a haze effect in some of the point-of-view shots of the lead character. At times, this effect represents the director's voyeuristic gaze, though later it suggests the ethereal presence of the daughter that the man seemingly gives birth to. One shot is shorter than in the original: he says "I think I am pregnant" and the revised version cuts immediately to a montage sequence symbolizing his labor pains,

while the original version included a moment of contemplative silence before the cut. There is also a minor change to the soundtrack: chirping crickets have been added to one sequence. The most substantial change is the addition of a new sequence—an outtake from *sPACEtIME*—of a man swimming naked, filmed underwater.

311. Thai PBS is a non-commercial public-service television channel.

312. Channarong Polsrila was shot dead by the military on 15 May 2010 at Soi Rangnam.

313. *Supernatural* was released on DVD in America in 2015. An extract from the film (*Liquid*), edited to remove a brief shot of an erection, was released on the Vimeo website in 2017.

314. In *Homogeneous, Empty Time*, teenagers make comments during television news coverage of the 2015 'Bike for Dad' cycling event in Bangkok led by Crown Prince Vajiralongkorn. They also make critical comments, including *ai hia*, a strong insult, while watching a televised speech by Prayut Chan-o-cha.

315. As already noted, the planned July 2017 invitation-only screening of *Homogeneous, Empty Time* was cancelled.

## Nontawat Numbenchapol

316. Thai men aged twenty-one are required to take part in an annual military draft lottery. Those who draw a red card must complete two years of military service, while those drawing black cards are exempt. Those who volunteer for six months' military service are excused from the lottery.

317. The Khmer Rouge, led by Pol Pot, ruled Cambodia from 1975 to 1979. The regime carried out a genocide and buried thousands of victims in mass graves known as 'the killing fields.'

## Chulayarnnon Siriphol

318. The *Thai People Theater* [โรงหนังประชาชน] competition was organized by Rangkid TV. *Karaoke* won the first prize of THB 50,000.

319. The project, *E-Lerng, I Love You* [อีเล้งที่รัก สมประกอบ ไม่สมประกอบ], was organized by Nawarat Welployngam.

320. *A Brief History of Memory* was shown at an outdoor screening for the Nang Loeng community on 9 October 2010.

321. *Thai Aurora at the Horizon* [การเมืองไทยในอุดมคติ], a program of fifteen short films about Thai politics, was shown on 20 and 27 July, and 10 August 2014.

322. Similarly, scenes of female students in uniform were cut from เพื่อเพื่อน เพื่อฝัน เพื่อวันเกียรติยศ [for friends, for dreams, for days of honor] (1997), as the censors felt that the girls were behaving inappropriately.

323. The Red Guards were a student paramilitary organization, active in the 1960s and endorsed by Chairman Mao Zedong.
324. In *Homogeneous, Empty Time* (2017), Thunska Pansittivorakul filmed a group of Village Scouts receiving their neckerchiefs, and their leader announced: "The royal scarf ceremony is a ceremony blessed by the King Himself."

## Surasak Pongson

325. 'Falling action' refers to the penultimate element in a dramatic narrative structure, following the climax.
326. The censors' rejection of *Thibaan: The Series 2.2* was announced on 20 November 2018, two days before the scheduled release date. The producers held a press conference at the BACC on 21 November 2018, to publicize the censors' verdict.
327. The film was ultimately rated 15 in its cut version.

## Tanwarin Sukkhapisit

328. *Insects in the Backyard* was shown at the World Film Festival of Bangkok on 6 and 8 November 2010, following its world premiere at the 2010 Vancouver International Film Festival. For the World Film Festival screenings, audiences were restricted to those aged twenty-one or above, and audience members were required to show their identity cards or passports as proof of age. This policy was a preemptive measure and was not related to the official rating system.
329. iLaw is a civil society organization promoting freedom of expression.
330. The film was released on 30 November 2017, in its cut version and rated 20, at House Rama. Before the rating system was introduced, House Rama occasionally showed films that had not been submitted to the Thai censors, such as György Pálfi's Hungarian film *Taxidermia* (2006).

## Kanittha Kwunyoo

331. *Karma* was chosen as Thailand's submission for the Foreign Language Film category in 2016.

## Ing Kanjanavanit

332. The Film and Video Act, § 26, lists the various categories into which films are classified. The final category, § 26(7), represents films that are prohibited from distribution.
333. The Film and Video Censorship Committee is comprised of four government representatives and three representatives of the film industry.

334. Just as the regicide in William Shakespeare's *Macbeth* (1606) occurs offstage, the act in *Shakespeare Must Die* takes place off screen.

335. Manit Sriwanichpoom answered via online message to Matthew Hunt on 21 April 2018: "Thai Ministry of Culture is normally conservative in nature. The officials there tend to think they own & protect 'Thai culture' from bad elements, and Thai people just merely follow them." Michael Kelly Connors (2005), 'Hegemony and the Politics of Culture and Identity in Thailand: Ministering Culture,' *Critical Asian Studies*, vol. 37, no. 4 (December), p. 523, describes the Ministry as "a site of contestation between conservative royalist-nationalist perspectives on Thai national identity and progressive localist and international understandings of Thai national identity."

336. The Bangkok Film Festival, which took place annually from 1998 to 2002, was organized by Nation Multimedia. In 2003, the event was renamed the Bangkok International Film Festival and was jointly sponsored by Nation Multimedia and the Tourism Authority of Thailand (TAT). Later that year, Nation Multimedia organized a rival festival, the World Film Festival of Bangkok. Meanwhile, the Bangkok International Film Festival, organized by TAT alone, continued annually until 2009. Being run by a government tourism department rather than a culture or media organization, the festival often prioritized glitz and glamor over cinematic quality. Juthamas Siriwan, a former TAT governor, was found guilty of receiving $1.81 million in bribes linked to the festival. She was jailed for fifty years in 2017, though she was not required to forfeit the money. Kong Rithdee (2009), 'The Sad Case of the Bangkok Film Festival,' *Dekalong 3: On Film Festivals* (ed. Richard Porton), London: Wallflower Press, p. 122, called the scandal "one of the most shocking infamies in the history of international film festivals."

337. Chuan Leekpai's first term as Thai prime minister was from 1992 to 1995, and he served a second term from 1997 to 2001.

## Yuthlert Sippapak

338. Vasit Dejkunjorn's novel *Promdaen* [พรมแดน] (2008) is set amid the separatist insurgency in southern Thailand.

339. Yuthlert was speaking in 2019, when Prayut was prime minister.

340. Yuthlert was a guest speaker at the one-day *Uncensored* exhibition held at the Jam Factory in Bangkok.

341. In 2019, on the day before Future Forward Party leader Thanathorn Juangroongruangkit was due to take his seat in parliament, the Constitutional Court began an investigation into his alleged violation of electoral law. The case was widely viewed as political as the Future Forward Party's manifesto included curbs on the military's political influence. Yuthlert criticized the investigation and was accused of contempt of court. Thanathorn organized a

protest outside the BACC on 14 December 2019. Coincidentally, Thunska Pansittivorakul was filming a performance art event (*Streaming*) inside the venue while the protest was taking place. The protesters are visible through the windows at several points during the film.

# FILMOGRAPHY

อำนาจมืด [dark forces] (1927)
    revised title: ชะนะพาล [defeat of the hooligans]
การเปลี่ยนแปลงการปกครองเมื่อวันที่ 24 มิถุนายน
    [administrative changes on 24 June] (1933)
    director: Manit Wasuwat
บ้านไร่นาเรา [our farmland] (1942)
    directors: Thongin, Neramit (Umnuai Klatnimi)
ชู้ [the adulterer] (1972)
    director: Somboomsuk Niyomsiri
ผู้ชาย...? [male...?] (1974)
    director: Warin
    original title: ผู้ชายขายตัว [the male prostitutes]
ตัณหานักบุญ [lustful saint] (1976)
    director: Rotjana Namwong
ท้องนาสะเทือน [shaking the paddy fields] (1976)
    director: Supachai Tosampan
หนักแผ่นดิน [burden of the land] (1977)
    director: Sombat Methanee
เก้ายอด [nine peaks] (1977)
    director: Supan Prampan
ไอ้ซ่าส์ ... จอมเนรคุณ [the leading betrayer] (1977)
    director: Veera Musigapong
ช่างมันฉันไม่แคร์ [forget it, I don't care] (1987)
    director: Bhandevanov Devakula
หลวงตา 3 สีกาข้างวัด [Luang Ta 3: a woman lives next to a temple] (1991)
    director: Permpol Choei-arun
บันทึกสีดำ [black record] (1992)
พฤษภาทมิฬ [black May] (1992)
    original title: สัตว์เลือดเย็น [cold-blooded animals]
เธอชื่อลินดา [her name is Linda] (1993)

สารวัตรใหญ่ [chief inspector] (11 May–6 July 1994)
    broadcaster: Channel 7
    director: Nirattisai Kaljareuk
ชำระประวัติศาสตร์ ๖ ตุลา ๒๕๑๙ [settling history: 6 October 1976] (1996)
    alternate title: ปณิธาน 6 ตุลา วิถีคนกล้าแห่งยุคสมัย [6 October resolution: a time of bravery]
พ.ศ. 2519 [2519 BE] (1996)
เพื่อเพื่อน เพื่อฝัน เพื่อวันเกียรติยศ [for friends, for dreams, for days of honor] (1997)
    director: Sarawut Wichiensarn
บันทึกจากเหตุการณ์จริง 14 ตุลา สงครามปัญญาชน [actual events of 14 October: war between
    intellectuals] (2001)
    series title: บันทึกเมืองไทย [save Thailand]
ชำระประวัติศาสตร์ ๖ ตุลา ๒๕๑๙ [settling history: 6 October 1976] (2001)
ครั้งแรก [the first time] (2003)
    director: Tanwarin Sukkhapisit
ความจริงที่ตากใบ [the truth about Tak Bai] (2004)
ตาดูดาวเท้าติดดิน [feet on ground, looking at the stars] (2005)
    broadcaster: Channel 7
สารคดีพรรคศิลปิน [Artist Party documentary] (2005)
    director: Vasan Sitthiket
ฝากกระจายด้วยนะครับ! [spread the news!] (2008)
ตำรวจฆ่าประชาชน [police killing people] (2008)
ความจริงประเทศไทย [the truth about Thailand] (2010)
นครพนมมือบ้าง นครไม่พนมมือบ้าง [Nakhon Phanom: some pray, some don't] (2010)
    director: Manussak Dokmai
เหนือเมฆ 2 มือปราบจอมขมังเวทย์ [beyond comparison 2: fighting black magic]
    (14–30 December 2012)
    director: Yuthlert Sippapak
    broadcaster: Channel 3
ตาดูดาวเท้าติดดิน [feet on ground, looking at the stars] (2014)
    Part 1: 'หัวใจแห่งความกล้า' [brave heart]
    https://www.youtube.com/watch?v=UTENAlSWZxs
    Part 2: 'ชีวิตที่เลือกบทได้' [choosing life's next chapter]
    https://www.youtube.com/watch?v=udp8tPEcJgA
    Part 3: 'ตกเหวคอนโดมิเนียม' [the fall of the condominium business]
    https://www.youtube.com/watch?v=3VjStKuvnEw
    Part 4: 'เปิดโลกคอมพิวเตอร์' [the world of computing]
    https://www.youtube.com/watch?v=imCnwFa9Yp8
    Part 5: 'ชีวิตคือการเรียนรู้' [life is learning]
    https://www.youtube.com/watch?v=Bcoub6AWWJk
    Part 6: 'บทเรียนจากวิกฤต' [lessons from a crisis]
    https://www.youtube.com/watch?v=QyJ4eQjWl9c
    Part 7: 'สู่ธุรกิจโทรคมนาคม' [into the telecommunications business]
    https://www.youtube.com/watch?v=X_nCdCvszfw

'เธอบอก' [you say] (2015)
    director: Pat Boonnitipat
    https://www.youtube.com/watch?v=IihTA6HYWTU
'คนสุดท้ายของหัวใจ' [the last person in my heart] (2018)
    director: Nattawut Sanyabut
    https://www.youtube.com/watch?v=DnEfs4IZEvo
เพลงชาติไทย [Thai national anthem] (3 May–16 June 2019)
    https://www.youtube.com/watch?v=v86OlB4f2QY
เพลงชาติไทย [Thai national anthem] (17 June 2019)
    https://www.youtube.com/watch?v=3TL13tZ3W78

**A**

*The Age of Anxiety* [รอ ๑๐] (2013)
    director: Taiki Sakpisit
*Agrarian Utopia* [สวรรค์บ้านนา] (2009)
    director: Uruphong Raksasad
*Angel* [เทพธิดาโรงแรม] (1974)
    director: Chatrichalerm Yukol
*Anguished Love* [รักทรมาน] (1987)
    director: Pisan Akaraseni
*Angulimala* [องคุลิมาล] (2003)
    director: Sutape Tunnirut
*Anna and the King* (1999)
    director: Andy Tennant
*Anna and the King of Siam* (1946)
    director: John Cromwell
*The Anthem* (2006)
    director: Apichatpong Weerasethakul
    https://www.youtube.com/watch?v=hKA4iLL89hl
*Ashes* (2012)
    director: Apichatpong Weerasethakul
    https://mubi.com/films/ashes
*Auntie Has Never Had a Passport* [ดาวอินดี้] (2014)
    director: Sorayos Prapapan
*Avalon* [แดนศักดิ์สิทธิ์] (2020)
    directors: Thunska Pansittivorakul, Harit Srikhao
*Awareness* [ภาษาที่เธอไม่เข้าใจ] (2014)
    director: Wachara Kanha

**B**

*The Bangkok Bourgeois Party* [ความลักลั่นของงานรื่นเริง] (2007)
    director: Prap Boonpan
*Bangkok Dystopia* [บางกอก ดิสโทเปีย] (2017)
    director: Patipol Teekayuwat

*Bangkok Joyride* [บางกอกจอยไรด์]
    director: Ing Kanjanavanit
    https://www.youtube.com/watch?v=ivMLl1eDRVI
    Part 1: 'How We Became Superheroes' ['เมื่อเราเป็นยอดมนุษย์'] (2017)
    Part 2: 'Shutdown Bangkok' ['ชัตดาวน์ประเทศไทย'] (2017)
    Part 3: 'Singing at Funerals' ['เพลงแห่ศพ'] (2018)
    Part 4: 'Becoming One' ['เป็นหนึ่งเดียว'] (2019)
    Part 5: 'Dancing with Death' ['ร้าวงพญายม'] (2020)
*Bangkok Love Story* [เพื่อน ... กูรักมึงว่ะ] (2007)
    director: Poj Arnon
*Bangkok Tanks* (2007)
    director: Nawapol Thumrongrattanrit
*Bar 21* [เทพธิดาบาร์ 21] (1978)
    director: Euthana Mukdasanit
*Bat in May* [ค้างคาวเดือนพฤษภา] (1992)
    director: Hamer Salwala
*Beautiful Boxer* [บิวตี้ฟูลบ็อกเซอร์] (2003)
    director: Ekachai Uekrongtham
*Belly of the Beast* (2003)
    director: Ching Siu Ting
*Birth of Golden Snail* [กำเนิดหอยทากทอง] (2018)
    director: Chulayarnnon Siriphol
*Black Silk* [แพรดำ] (1961)
    director: Rattana Pestonji
*Blinding* (2014)
    director: Chulayarnnon Siriphol
*Blissfully Yours* [สุดเสน่หา] (2002)
    director: Apichatpong Weerasethakul
*Blue Sky of Love* [ฟ้าใสใจชื่นบาน] (2009)
    directors: Krekchai Jaiman, Napaporn Poonjaruen
*Boundary* [ฟ้าต่ำแผ่นดินสูง] (2013)
    director: Nontawat Numbenchapol
*A Brief History of Memory* [ประวัติศาสตร์ขนาดย่อของความทรงจำ] (2010)
    director: Chulayarnnon Siriphol
    https://vimeo.com/86748910
*Brokedown Palace* (1999)
    director: Jonathan Kaplan
*Brown Sugar* [น้ำตาลแดง] (2010) director: Coffee Prince
    'โสบนเตียง' [a hooker in bed] director: Phanumad Disattha
    'รักต้องลุ้น' [expecting love] director: Zart Tancharoen
    'ปรารถนา' [desire] director: Kittiyaporn Klangsurin
*Bugis Street* [妖街皇后] (1995)
    director: Yonfan

*Bus Lane* [เมล์นรก หมวยยกล้อ] (2007)
    director: Leo Kittikorn
*By the River* [สายน้ำติดเชื้อ] (2013)
    director: Nontawat Numbenchapol
*By the Time It Gets Dark* [ดาวคะนอง] (2016)
    director: Anocha Suwichakornpong

## C

*Cadaver* [ศพ] (2007)
    director: Dulyasit Niyomgul
    original title: อาจารย์ใหญ่ [principal]
*The Cave* [นางนอน] (2019)
    director: Tom Waller
*Cemetery of Splendour* [รักที่ขอนแก่น] (2015)
    director: Apichatpong Weerasethakul
*Censor Must Die* [เซ็นเซอร์ต้องตาย] (2013)
    director: Ing Kanjanavanit
'Citizen' ['ผู้อาศัย'] (2020)
    https://www.youtube.com/watch?v=VMAHkBlgxWw
*Citizen Juling* [พลเมืองจูหลิง] (2008)
    director: Ing Kanjanavanit
*Close Encounters of the Third Kind* (1977)
    director: Steven Spielberg
*Colic* [เด็กเห็นผี] (2006)
    director: Patchanon Thumjira
*The COUPle's Place* [รัตนาวรรณ งามวงษ์] (2018)
    director: Rattanawan Ngamwong
*Criminal Without Sin* [สุภาพบุรุษเสือไทย] (1949)
    directors: Sukrawandit Ditsakul, Tae Prakartwutisan

## D

*Damaged Air* (2013)
    director: Nil Paksnavin
    https://vimeo.com/59506915
*Dang Bireley's and Young Gangsters* [sic] [2499 อันธพาลครองเมือง] (1997)
    director: Nonzee Nimibutr
*The Da Vinci Code* (2006)
    director: Ron Howard
*Delete Our History, Now!* [อำนาจ/การลบทิ้ง] (2008)
    director: Vasan Sitthiket
*Demockrazy* [ประชาทิปตาย] (2007)
    director: Duangporn Pakavirojkul

*Democracy after Death: The Tragedy of Uncle Nuamthong Praiwan* [ประชาธิปไตยหลังความตาย เรื่องเศร้าของลุงนวมทอง] (2016)
    director: Neti Wichiansaen
    https://www.youtube.com/watch?v=RICxpq-ReLo
'Democrazy' (2019)
    director: Jung
    https://www.youtube.com/watch?v=cc3aEWwOo4I
*Democrazy.mov* (2019)
    directors: Thunsita Yanuprom, Sarun Channiam
    https://vimeo.com/350989734
*Detective Chinatown* [唐人街探案] (2015)
    director: Chen Sicheng
'The Devil of Time' ['ปีศาจร้ายแห่งกาลเวลา'] (2019)
    director: Matichai Teawna
    https://www.youtube.com/watch?v=4A-ELHsVrQg
*Different Views, Death Sentence* [ต่างความคิด ผิดถึงตาย ๖ ตุลาคม ๒๕๑๙] (2011)
    producer: Suthachai Yimprasert
*Diseases and a Hundred Year Period* [โรคร้ายในรอบหนึ่งร้อยปี] (2008)
    director: Sompot Chidgasornpongse
*Don't Forget Me* [อย่าลืมฉัน] (2003)
    director: Manussak Dokmai
*The Duck Empire Strike Back* [*sic*] (2006)
    director: Nutthorn Kangwanklai

**E**

*Endless Story* (2005)
    director: Thunska Pansittivorakul
*Eternity* [ชั่วฟ้าดินสลาย] (2010)
    director: Bhandevanov Devakula

**F**

*Father and Son* [พ่อและลูกชาย] (2015)
    director: Saravuth Intaraprom
*Fatherland* [ปิตุภูมิ] (2013)
    alternate title: *Rachida* [ราชิดา]
    director: Yuthlert Sippapak
*Friendship Ended with Mudasir Now Salman Is My Best Friend* [สิ้นสุดกับ Mudasir ตอนนี้ Salman คือเพื่อนที่ดีที่สุดของฉัน] (2018)
    director: Tewprai Bualoi
*The Frienemies* [เพื่อนรัก เพื่อนชัง] (2017)
    director: Pasakorn Pramoolwong
*Fun Bar Karaoke* [ฝันบ้า คาราโอเกะ] (1997)
    director: Pen-ek Ratanaruang

## G

*Galanusathi* [กาลานุสติ] (2010)
    director: Sittiporn Racha
*Gaze and Hear* [สายตา รับฟัง] (2011)
    director: Nontawat Numbenchapol
*Ghost Game* [ล่า-ท้า-ผี] (2006)
    director: Sarawut Wichiensarn
*Ghost of Centralworld* (2012)
    director: Viriyaporn Boonprasert
    https://www.youtube.com/watch?v=JQZJnAZPY2s
*Ghost Rabbit and the Casket Sales* [กระต่ายผีกับคนขายโลง] (2015)
    alternate title: *Ghost Rabbit and the Casket Sales*
    director: Arnont Nongyao
*Girls Girls Girls* [สาว สาว สาว] (1992)
    alternate title: ค่ายสวาท [love camp]
    director: Jacky Chuan
*Give Us a Little More Time* [ขอเวลาอีกไม่นาน] (2020)
    director: Chulayarnnon Siriphol
*Going Astray* [หลงทาง] (1932)
    director: Sanga Kanchanakphan
*The Golden Riders* [มากับพระ] (2006)
    director: Udom Udomroj
*Grounded God* [เทวดาเดินดิน] (1975)
    director: Chatrichalerm Yukol

## H

*The Hangover Part 2* (2011)
    director: Todd Phillips
*Happy Berry* [สวรรค์สุดเอื้อม] (2004)
    director: Thunska Pansittivorakul
*Happy Hour in Paradise* [Prästen i paradiset] (2015)
    director: Kjell Sundvall
*Haunted Universities* [มหาลัยสยองขวัญ] (2009)
    directors: Banjong Sintanamonkolgul, Suthiporn Tabtim
    'Stairway' ['ป๊อกๆ ครืด']
    'The Morgue' ['ห้องดับจิต']
    'The Toilet' ['ศาลห้องน้ำหญิง']
    'The Elevator' '[ลิฟต์แดง']
*Headshot* [ฝนตกขึ้นฟ้า] (2011)
    director: Pen-ek Ratanaruang
*Here Comes the Democrat Party* [ประชาธิปัตย์มาแล้ว] (2014)
    director: Chulayarnnon Siriphol
*His Name Is Karn* [เขาชื่อกานต์] (1973)
    director: Chatrichalerm Yukol

*The Holy Man* [หลวงพี่เท่ง] (2005)
    director: Note Chern-yim
*The Holy Man 2* [หลวงพี่เท่ง ๒] (2008)
    director: Note Chern-yim
*The Holy Man 3* [หลวงพี่เท่ง ๓] (2010)
    director: Note Chern-yim
*Homogeneous, Empty Time* [สุญกาล] (2017)
    director: Thunska Pansittivorakul
*The Hunger Games: Mockingjay—Part 1* (2014)
    director: Francis Lawrence
*Hush, Tonight the Dead Are Dreaming Loudly* (2019)
    director: Kong Pahurak

## I

*I Am a Man* [ฉันผู้ชายนะยะ] (1987)
    director: Bhandevanov Devakula
*I'm Fine* [สบายดีค่ะ] (2008)
    director: Tanwarin Sukkhapisit
    https://www.youtube.com/watch?v=ycZeXFwWhYY
*Inhuman Kiss* [แสงกระสือ] (2019)
    director: Sitisiri Mongkolsiri
*Insects in the Backyard* [อินเส็คส์ อิน เดอะ แบ็คยาร์ด] (2010)
    director: Tanwarin Sukkhapisit
*In the Night of the Revolution* (2007)
    director: Wathit Wattanasakonpan
*In the Realm of the Senses* [愛の コ リ ー ダ] (1976)
    alternate title: *L'Empire des sens*
    director: Nagisa Oshima
*In the Shadow of Naga* [นาคปรก] (2008)
    director: Phawat Panangkasiri
*Invisible Waves* [คำพิพากษาของมหาสมุทร] (2006)
    director: Pen-ek Ratanaruang
*I Remember* [ความทรงจำที่ไม่อาจลืมเลือน/ ผู้หญิงที่เจอผัวในวันที่ 10 เมษาฯ/ ย้ายถิ่น] (2011)
    director: Arthawut Boonyuang
*The Iron Ladies* [สตรีเหล็ก] (2001)
    director: Yongyoot Thongkongtoon
*The Island Funeral* [มหาสมุทรและสุสาน] (2015)
    director: Pimpaka Towira
*I Will Rape You With This Scissors* [sic] [หนังและกรรไกรในวันที่ 4 เมษา] (2008)
    director: Napat Treepalawisetkun
*I Wish the Whole Country Would Sink Under Water* (2014)
    director: Theeraphat Ngathong
    https://www.youtube.com/watch?v=xan81QREh64

# J

*Jan Dara* [จัน ดารา] (2001)
    director: Nonzee Nimibutr
*Jan Dara: The Beginning* [จัน ดารา ปฐมบท] (2012)
    director: Bhandevanov Devakula
'Jerry's Cousin' (*Tom and Jerry*, 1951)
    directors: William Hannah, Joseph Barbera
*Joking Jazz 4G* [หลวงพี่แจ๊ส 4G] (2016)
    director: Poj Arnon
*Joking Jazz 5G* [หลวงพี่แจ๊ส 5G] (2018)
    director: Poj Arnon
*Judgement* [ไอ้ฟัก] (2004)
    director: Pantham Thongsangl
*Just a Friend 2* [เพื่อน 2] (1991)
    director: Romeo Max

# K

*Kapi* [กะปิ ลิงจ๋อไม่หลอกจ้าว] (2010)
    director: Nitivat Cholvanichsiri
*Karaoke: Think Kindly* [คาราโอเกะ เพลงแผ่เมตตา] (2009)
    directors: Scene 22 (Chulayarnnon Siriphol, Chaiwat Tangtam, Weerasak Chaobol,
    Phurichaya Likhidakarananon, Ekaphop Duangkham)
    https://www.youtube.com/watch?v=slDFr4-X9ac
*Karma* (2015)
    director: Kannitha Kwunyoo
    original title: อาบัติ (*arbat*)
    revised title: อาปัติ (*arpat*)
    alternate title: *Arbat*
*Khan Kluay* [ก้านกล้วย] (2006)
    director: Kompin Kemgumnird
    alternate title: *The Blue Elephant*
*The King and I* (1956)
    director: Walter Lang
*The King of the White Elephant* [พระเจ้าช้างเผือก] (1941)
    director: Sunh Vasudhara
*KI SS* (2011)
    director: Thunska Pansittivorakul
*Krabi, 2562* [กระบี่ ๒๕๖๒] (2019)
    directors: Ben Rivers, Anocha Suwichakornpong

# L

*The Last Dictator* [อวสาน ร.ป.ภ.] (2020)
    director: Yuthlert Sippapak

*The Last Song* [เพลงสุดท้าย] (1985)
  director: Pisan Akaraseni
*The Legend of King Naresuan 5* [ตำนานสมเด็จพระนเรศวรมหาราช ภาค ๕ ยุทธหัตถี] (2014)
  director: Chatrichalerm Yukol
*The Legend of Suriyothai* [สุริโยไท] (2001)
  director: Chatrichalerm Yukol
*Letter from the Silence* [จดหมายจากความเงียบ] (2006)
  director: Prap Boonpan
*A Letter to Uncle Boonmee* [จดหมายถึงลุงบุญมี] (2009)
  director: Apichatpong Weerasethakul
  http://animateprojectsarchive.org/films/by_date/2009/a_letter_to
*Lice in the Wonderland* [เพลี้ย] (2014)
  director: Boonyarit Wiangnon
*Life Show* [เปลือยชีวิต] (2005)
  director: Thunska Pansittivorakul
*The Light of Asia* (1925)
  directors: Franz Osten, Himanshu Rai
*Liquid* (2017)
  director: Thunska Pansittivorakul
  https://vimeo.com/237712372
*The Love Culprit* (2006)
  director: Sanchai Chotirosseranee
*Love Destiny* [บุพเพสันนิวาส] (21 February–19 April 2018)
  director: Pawat Panangkasri
  broadcaster: Channel 3
*Lucky Loser* [หมากเตะ ... โลกตะลึง] (2006)
  director: Adisorn Tresirikasem

**M**
*The Macabre Case of Phrom Phiram* (2003)
  director: Manop Udomdej
  original title: คนบาป พรหมพิราม [sinners of Phrom Phiram]
  revised title: คืนบาป พรหมพิราม [night of sin in Phrom Phiram]
*Mae Bia* [แม่เบี้ย] (2015)
  director: Bhandevanov Devakula
*A Man Called Tone* [โทน] (1970)
  director: Somboomsuk Niyomsiri
*Meat Grinder* (2009)
  director: Tiwa Moeithaisong
  original title: ก๋วยเตี๋ยว เนื้อ คน [human meat noodles]
  revised title: เชือด ก่อน ชิม [slice before eating]
*Mercury Man* [มนุษย์เหล็กไหล] (2006)
  director: Bhandit Thingdee

*Middle-earth* [มัชฌิมโลก] (2007)
director: Thunska Pansittivorakul
'A Milhouse Divided' (*The Simpsons*, 1 December 1996)
director: Steven Dean Moore
broadcaster: Fox
*Mindfulness and Murder* [ศพไม่เงียบ] (2011)
director: Tom Waller
*Molding Clay* [วัฏสงสาร] (2018)
director: Watcharapol Paksri
alternate title: *All Done in the Opposite of Afternoon* [sic]
https://vimeo.com/415604183
*Monk and Motorcycle Taxi Rider* (2013)
director: Chulayarnnon Siriphol
https://www.youtube.com/watch?v=sD_8ZjKPo6A
*Monrak Luk Thung* [มนต์รักลูกทุ่ง] (1970)
director: Rungsri Tassanapuk
*Monrak Transistor* [มนต์รักทรานซิสเตอร์] (2001)
director: Pen-ek Ratanaruang
*The Moonhunter* [14 ตุลา สงครามประชาชน] (2001)
director: Bhandit Rittakol
*Motel Mist* [โรงแรมต่างดาว] (2016)
director: Prabda Yoon
*Mundane History* [เจ้านกกระจอก] (2009)
director: Anocha Suwichakornpong
*My Teacher Eats Biscuits* [คนกราบหมา] (1998)
director: Ing Kanjanavanit
*Myth of Modernity* (2014)
director: Chulayarnnon Siriphol

**N**
*19.09.2549* (2008)
director: Bopitr Visenoi
*Nang Nak* [นางนาก] (1999)
director: Nonzee Nimibutr
*Narayana's Arrow Spaceship: Between the Orbits of Mars and Jupiter* [ยานศรนารายณ์ ระหว่างวง
โคจรดาวอังคารและดาวพฤหัสฯ] (2014)
director: Thunska Pansittivorakul
*National Anthem* [เพลงชาติไทย] (2008)
director: Chai Chaiyachit
*Night Watch* (2014)
director: Danaya Chulphuthiphong
*Ninja 2: Shadow of a Tear* (2013)
director: Isaac Florentine

*Nineteen Eighty-Four* (1984)
    director: Michael Radford
*No Escape* (2015)
    director: John Dowdle
*Nymph* [นางไม้] (2009)
    director: Pen-ek Ratanaruang

## O

*100 Times Reproduction of Democracy* [การผลิตซ้ำประชาธิปไตยให้กลายเป็นของแท้] (2019)
    director: Chulayarnnon Siriphol
    https://www.youtube.com/watch?v=rjreWxDKJAk
*October 14 Thai Student Uprising 1973* [14 ตุลา] (1993)
    producer: Charnvit Kasetsiri
*October Sonata* [รักที่รอคอย] (2009)
    director: Somkiat Vithuranich
*Octoblur* [ลมตุลาคม] (2013)
    director: Patana Chirawong
*Official Trailer* [อนุสรณ์สถาน] (2018)
    director: Veerapong Soontornchattrawat
    https://www.youtube.com/watch?v=THhBOiMvAp4
*On Cemetery of Splendour* (2016)
    director: Nontawat Numbenchapol
*One Take Only* [ส้ม แบงค์ มือใหม่หัดขาย] (2001)
    director: Oxide Pang
    original title: *Som and Bank: Bangkok for Sale*

## P

*Parade of Golden Snail* (2019)
    director: Chulayarnnon Siriphol
    https://www.youtube.com/watch?v=o_oQFxDKUpo
*Paradoxocracy* [ประชาธิป'ไทย] (2013)
    directors: Pen-ek Ratanaruang, Pasakorn Pramoolwong
*Pattaya* (2006)
    director: Franck Gastambide
*Pee Mak* [พี่มาก ... พระโขนง] (2013)
    director: Banjong Pisanthanakun
*Persepolis* [پرسپولیس] (2007)
    directors: Marjane Stratapi, Vincent Paronnaud
*Pink Flamingos* (1972)
    director: John Waters
*Pirab* [พิราบ] (2017)
    director: Pasit Promnumpol
    https://www.youtube.com/watch?v=RjnprnAMgWc

*Planking* (2012)
    director: Chulayarnnon Siriphol
*Pleasure Factory* [快乐工厂] (2007)
    director: Ekachai Uekrongtham
*Ploy* [พลอย] (2007)
    director: Pen-ek Ratanaruang
*The Pob's House* [บ้านผีปอบ] (2011)
    director: Ukrit Sanguanhai
*Powder Road* [เฮโรอีน] (1991)
    director: Chatrichalerm Yukol
*Pret Arbut* [เปรต อาบัติ] (2017)
    director: Kanittha Kwunyoo
*Program Will Resume Shortly* (2020)
    director: Manit Sriwanichpoom

# R

*Rainbow Boys: The Movie* [เรนโบว์ บอยส์ เดอะ มูฟวี่] (2005)
    alternate title: *Right by Me*
    director: Thanyatorn Siwanukrow
*Rajprasong* [ราชประสงค์] (2012)
    director: Nil Paksnavin
    https://vimeo.com/53160365
*Reading for One Female Corpse* (1997)
    director: Araya Rasdjarmrearnsook
*'Red' at Last* [มนัส เคียรสิงห์] (2006)
    director: Suchart Sawasdsri
*The Red Eagle* [อินทรีแดง] (2010)
    director: Wisit Sasanatieng
*Red Movie* [แกะแดง] (2010)
    directors: Underground Office (Wachara Gunha)
*Reincarnate* [จุติ] (2010)
    director: Thunska Pansittivorakul
    https://vimeo.com/201547428
*'Remember'* ['วน'] (2019)
    director: Thunska Pansittivorakul
    https://www.youtube.com/watch?v=SKaW-ulMfHU
*'Remind'* ['บอกตัวเอง'] (2018)
    directors: Boyd Kosiyabong, Thep-ard Kawin-anan
    https://www.youtube.com/watch?v=5VrXPPKVb4g
*Re-presentation* [ผีมะขาม ไพร่ฟ้า ประชาธิปไตย ในคืนที่ลมพัดหวน] (2007)
    directors: Chai Chaiyachit, Chisanucha Kongwailap
*Respectfully Yours* [ด้วยความนับถือ] (2016)
    directors: Puangthong Pawakapan, Patporn Phoothong
    https://www.youtube.com/watch?v=ig2DCytG8_Y

*Return Happiness to the People* [คืนความสุขให้คนในชาติ] (6 June 2014)
  https://www.youtube.com/watch?v=uWw1ShLLFF0
*A Ripe Volcano* [ภูเขาไฟพิโรธ] (2011)
  directors: Taiki Sakpisit, Yasuhiro Morinaga
*River of Exploding Durians* [榴梿忘返] (2014)
  director: Edmund Yeo
  https://www.youtube.com/watch?v=6beD5YmmtQ4

## S

*Sai Tong* [บ้านทรายทอง] (1979)
  director: Ruj Ronapop
*Samui Song* [ไม่มีสมุยสำหรับเธอ] (2017)
  director: Pen-ek Ratanaruang
*Santikhiri Sonata* [สันติคีรี โซนาตา] (2019)
  director: Thunska Pansittivorakul
*SARS Wars: Bangkok Zombie Crisis* [ขุนกระบี่ผีระบาด] (2004)
  director: Taweewat Wantha
*Sathu* [หลวงพี่กับผีขนุน] (2009)
  director: Dulyasit Niyomgul
*Sayew* [สยิว] (2003)
  director: Kongdej Jaturanrasmee
*The Scar* [แผลเก่า] (2014)
  director: Bhandevanov Devakula
*Schindler's List* (1993)
  director: Steven Spielberg
*A Season in Hell* [ฤดูกาลในนรก] (2018)
  director: Thunska Pansittivorakul
  https://www.youtube.com/watch?v=NjLOFY02 WX8
*See How They Run* [โกยเถอะโยม] (2006)
  director: Jaturong Phonbool
*Serpico* (1973)
  director: Sidney Lumet
*Seven Boy Scouts* (2020)
  director: Yuthlert Sippapak
*The Shadow of History* [เงาประวัติศาสตร์] (2013)
  directors: Panu Aree, Kong Rithdee, Kaweenipon Ketprasit
*Shakespeare Must Die* [เชคสเปียร์ต้องตาย] (2012)
  director: Ing Kanjanavanit
*Shane* (1953)
  director: George Stevens
*Shooting Stars* [ดาวตก] (2010)
  director: Sutthirat Supaparinya
*Shut Sound* (2014)
  director: Joaquin Niamtubtim

*Sick Nurses* [สวยลากไส้] (2007)
    directors: Piraphan Laoyont, Thospol Sirivivat
*Sigh* [เมืองร้าง] (2002)
    director: Thunska Pansittivorakul
*Silenced Memories* [ความทรงจำไร้เสียง] (2014)
    directors: Patporn Phoothong, Saowanee Sangkara
    https://www.youtube.com/watch?v=JAbgvsDvkT4
*Silence in D Minor* (2006)
    director: Chalida Uabumrungjit
*The Silent Melody* (2018)
    director: Pimpaka Towira
    https://vimeo.com/300237259
*Sin Sisters 2* [ผู้หญิง 5 บาป 2] (2010)
    director: Sukit Narintr
*Sisophon* [ศรีโสภณ] (1941)
    director: Choti Prasit
    revised title: เลือดไทย [Thai blood]
*The Six Principles* [สัญญาของผู้มาก่อนกาล] (2010)
    director: Abhichon Rattanabhayon
    http://vimeo.com/18866840
*6ixtynin9* [เรื่องตลก 69] (1999)
    director: Pen-ek Ratanaruang
*Soi Cowboy* [ซอยคาวบอย] (2008)
    director: Thomas Clay
*Someone from Nowhere* [มา ณ ที่นี้] (2017)
    director: Prabda Yoon
*Somsri* [ครูสมศรี] (1985)
    director: Chatrichalerm Yukol
*The Sound of Music* (1965)
    director: Robert Wise
*sPACEtIME* [กาล-อวกาศ] (2015)
    directors: Thunska Pansittivorakul, Harit Srikhao, Itdhi Phanmanee
*Streaming* (2019)
    director: Thunska Pansittivorakul
'Sud-Swing Ringo Eto Bump' ['สุดสวิงริงโก้อีโต้บั้มพ์'] (2015)
    director: Udom Taepanich
    https://www.youtube.com/watch?v=uDQQncFBG8Q
*Sunset at Chaophraya 2* [คู่กรรม ภาค ๒] (1993)
    director: Banjong Kosallawat
*Supernatural* [เหนือธรรมชาติ] (2014)
    director: Thunska Pansittivorakul
*Suvarna of Siam* [นางสาวสุวรรณ] (1923)
    director: Henry MacRae

*The Sweet Gang* [ยกก๊วนป่วนหอ] (2005)
director: Niran Thamprecha
*Syndromes and a Century* [แสงศตวรรษ] (2006)
director: Apichatpong Weerasethakul

**T**

*2060* (2012)
director: Thunska Pansittivorakul
*246247596248914102516… And Then There Were None* (2017)
director: Arin Rungjan
*3-0* [สาม-ศูนย์] (2006)
director: Anocha Suwichakornpong
*13-04-2022 Tsunami* [13-04-2022 วันโลกสังหาร] (2009)
alternate title: *Death Wave*
director: Toranong Srichua
*Tang Wong* [ตั้งวง] (2013)
director: Kongdej Jaturanrasmee
*Taxidermia* (2006)
director: György Pálfi
*The Taxi Meter* (2014)
director: Natpakhan Khemkhao
*Tear of Child* [*sic*] (2014)
director: Weerachai Jitsoonthorntip
*Tears of the Black Tiger* [ฟ้าทะลายโจร] (2000)
director: Wisit Sasanatieng
*Ten Years Thailand* (2018)
'Song of the City' director: Apichatpong Weerasethakul
'Catopia' director: Wisit Sasanatieng
'Sunset' director: Aditya Assarat
'Planetarium' director: Chulayarnnon Siriphol
*The Terrorists* [ผู้ก่อการร้าย] (2011)
director: Thunska Pansittivorakul
https://vimeo.com/94874023
*Thai Contemporary Politics Quiz* [แบบทดสอบวิชาการเมืองไทยร่วมสมัย] (2010)
directors: Scene 22 (Chulayarnnon Siriphol, Chaiwat Tangtam, Weerasak Chaobol,
Phurichaya Likhidakarananon, Ekaphop Duangkham)
'Thailand's Tainted Robes' (*101 East*, 18 December 2014)
director: Pailin Wedel
broadcaster: Al Jazeera
https://www.youtube.com/watch?v=382VkLGpDaI.
*There Must Be Something Happen* [*sic*] [ต้องมีอะไรสักอย่าง] (1993)
director: Vasan Sitthiket
*Thibaan: The Series 2.2* [ไทบ้านเดอะซีรีส์ 2.2] (2018)
director: Surasak Pongson

*This Area Is Under Quarantine* [บริเวณนี้อยู่ภายใต้การกักกัน] (2008)
director: Thunska Pansittivorakul
*This Film Has Been Invalid* [sic] (2014)
director: Watcharapol Saisongkroh
*This House Have Ghost* [sic] (2011)
director: Ekarach Monwat
*This Way* [ทางออก] (2010)
director: Wasunan Hutawach
*Time in a Bottle* [เวลาในขวดแก้ว] (1991)
director: Prayoon Wongcheun
*Tongpan* [ทองปาน] (1977)
directors: Euthana Mukdasanit, Surachai Chantimatorn
https://www.youtube.com/watch?v=5JuCbWWTne8
*Tossaliam* [ทศเหลี่ยม] (2006)
director: Ittiwat Suriyamal
'To Whom It May Concern' ['ถึงผู้มีส่วนเกี่ยวข้อง'] (2019)
director: Kasiti Sangkul
https://www.youtube.com/watch?v=Ml1A1KUuVNI
*Transmissions of Unwanted Pasts* [วงโคจรของความทรงจำ] (2019)
director: Prabda Yoon
*The Treachery of the Moon* (2012)
director: Araya Rasdjarmrearnsook
*Tropical Malady* [สัตว์ประหลาด] (2004)
director: Apichatpong Weerasethakul
*The Truth Be Told (The Cases Against Supinya Klangnarong)* [ความจริงพูดได้ (คดีสุภิญญา)] (2007)
director: Pimpaka Towira
*Twilight Over Burma* [Dämmerung über Burma] (2015)
director: Sabine Derflinger
*The Two Brothers* [สองพี่น้อง] (2017)
directors: Patporn Phoothong, Teerawat Rujenatham
https://www.youtube.com/watch?v=KbQ9817ZZlI

**U**

*Uncle Boonmee Who Can Recall His Past Lives* [ลุงบุญมีระลึกชาติ] (2010)
director: Apichatpong Weerasethakul
*Undaunte Sons of Siam* [sic] [เลือดทหารไทย] (1935)
director: Wichit Wathakan
*Unseen Bangkok* [มหัศจรรย์กรุงเทพฯ] (2004)
director: Thunska Pansittivorakul

**V**

*The Vanquisher* [สวย ... ซามูไร] (2009)
director: Manop Udomdej

*Voodoo Girls* [หัวใจต้องสาป] (2002)
    director: Thunska Pansittivorakul
*Vous vous souviens de moi?* [วันที่ฝนตกลงมาเป็นคูสคูส] (2005)
    director: Thunska Pansittivorakul
    https://vimeo.com/92526606

## W

*We Will Forget It Again* [แล้วเราจะลืมมันอีกครั้ง] (2010)
    director: Napat Treepalawisetkun
*When Mother's Away* [*Khi mẹ vắng nhà*] (2018)
    director: Clay Phạm
'Which Is My Country' ['ประเทศกูมี'] (2018)
    director: Teerawat Rujintham
    https://www.youtube.com/watch?v=VZvzvLiGUtw
*The White Short Film/The Candle Light* [หนังสั้นสีขาว/ชั่วแสงเทียน] (2009)
    director: Prap Boonpan
*Woak Wak* [โว๊กว๊าก] (2004)
    director: Der Doksadao
    original title: ยอดชายนายโอ๊กอ๊าก [the top man, Mr. Oak-ak]
*Women in Democracy* [ผู้หญิงที่ผัวหายในวันที่ 14 เมษายน] (2009)
    director: Arthawut Boonyuang

## X

'Xnatta.soulless.nirvanA' ['นิพพาน'] (2019)
    director: Thanit Yantrakovit
    https://www.youtube.com/watch?v=h1pKRCgtMHo

## Y

*Ye … Dhamma…* [เย … ธมมา …] (2007)
    director: Watthana Rujirojsakul
*Young Bao* [ยังบาว คาราบาวเดอะมูฟวี่] (2013)
    director: R-Jo (Yuthakorn Sukmuktapha)

# BIBLIOGRAPHY

'ภาพยนตร์ไทยในยุค ๑๖ ม.ม.' [Thai films in the 16mm era]. 1997. *Feature Magazine* [สารคดี], vol. 13, no. 150 (August).

'สำรวจเส้นทาง พรบ. ภาพยนตร์ 2473 กับกรณีศึกษา' [exploring the path forward from the Film Act (1930), with case studies]. 1997. *Thai Film Journal* [วารสารหนังไทย], vol. 14 (November).

'จากเซ็นเซอร์สู่เรตติ้ง ทางออกที่เป็นไปได้' [from censorship to rating system: the way forward?]. 1997. *Thai Film Journal* [วารสารหนังไทย], vol. 14 (November).

'เลื่อนฉาย "สึนามิ"' ["*Tsunami*" postponed]. 2009. *Thai Rath* [ไทยรัฐ] (26 April). https://www.thairath.co.th/content/2004.

'ย้อนรอยเซ็นเซอร์หนังไทย ซ้ำซาก? ลักลั่น? ย้อนแย้ง?' [looking back at Thai film censorship: repeating itself? out of order? contradictory?]. 2013. *Thai Film Journal* [วารสารหนังไทย], vol. 18 (November).

Aekkachai Suttiyangyuen. 2018. 'Thai Films (Un)censored.' *GQ* (Thailand), no. 46 (July).

Aglionby, John. 1999. 'Thai Censors Ban "Insulting" Remake of *King and I* Film.' *The Guardian* (29 December). https://www.theguardian.com/film/1999/dec/29/world.news.

Anand Panyarachun. 1998. 'Getting to Know You.' *Outlook, Bangkok Post* (9 November).

Anchalee Chaiworaporn. 2001. 'Thai Cinema Since 1970.' *Film in South East Asia: Views from the Region—Essays on Film in Ten South East Asia-Pacific Countries* (ed. David Hanan). Manila: SouthEast Asia-Pacific AudioVisual Archive Association.

Anocha Suwichakornpong. 2010. 'Interview: Anocha Suwichakornpong—Mundane History.' International Film Festival Rotterdam (3 February). https://iffr.com/en/blog/interview-anocha-suwichakornpong-mundane-history-0.

Apichatpong Weerasethakul. 2007a. 'A Hidden Agenda That Deems Us Morons: The Folly and Future of Thai Cinema Under Military Dictatorship.' *Bangkok Post* (25 September). https://www.pressreader.com/thailand/bangkok-post/20070925/281840049293279.

———. 2007b. 'Who Can Save My Flying Saucer?' *Film and Music, The Guardian* (14 September). https://www.theguardian.com/film/2007/sep/14/1.

———. 2008. 'Influence: Today and Tomorrow.' *ArtAsiaPacific Almanac*, vol. 3.

*Apichatpong Weerasethakul: The Serenity of Madness* [阿比查邦・韋拉斯塔古：狂中之靜]. 2016. Hong Kong: Para Site. https://issuu.com/parasite_hk/docs/the_serenity_of_madness_-_exh_bookl.

Asaree Thaitrakulpanich. 2019. 'Thai-Farang Romance in "*Soi Cowboy*" Still Rings True: Producer.' *Khaosod English* (19 August). https://www.khaosodenglish.com/featured/2019/08/19/thai-farang-romance-in-soi-cowboy-still-rings-true-producer/.

Baker, Chris and Pasuk Phongpaichit. 2000. *Pridi by Pridi: Selected Writings on Life, Politics, and Economy*. Chiang Mai: Silkworm Books.

Barmé, Scot. 2002. *Woman, Man, Bangkok: Love, Sex, and Popular Culture in Thailand*. Chiang Mai: Silkworm Books.

Blake, Linnie. 2018. 'Ghost Game.' *Thai Cinema: The Complete Guide* (ed. Mary J. Ainslie and Katarzyna Ancuta). London: I. B. Tauris.

Boonrak Boonyaketmala. 1992. 'The Rise and Fall of the Film Industry in Thailand, 1897–1992.' *East-West Film Journal*, vol. 6, no. 2 (July). https://scholarspace.manoa.hawaii.edu/bitstream/10125/30702/1/filmjournal00602.pdf.

Boutigny, Guillaume. 2006. 'Thai Cinema and Censorship.' *Thai Cinema* (ed. Bastian Meirsonne). Lyon: Asiexpo Edition.

Brzeski, Patrick. 2013. 'Thailand's Pen-ek Ratanaruang on Risking It All to Film the Paradoxes of Thai Democracy.' *The Hollywood Reporter* (8 July). https://www.hollywoodreporter.com/news/thailands-pen-ek-ratanaruang-risking-581674.

Callahan, William A. 1992. *Imagining Democracy: Reading "the Events of May" in Thailand*. Singapore: Institute of Southeast Asian Studies.

Chalida Uabumrungjit. 2001. 'Cinema in Thailand: 1897 to 1970.' *Film in South East Asia: Views from the Region—Essays on Film in Ten South East Asia-Pacific Countries* (ed. David Hanan). Manila: SouthEast-Asia Pacific AudioVisual Archive Association.

———. 2007. 'Free Thai Cinema Movement.' PetitionOnline. http://www.petitiononline.com/nocut/petition.html.

———. 2008. '*Suvarna of Siam*: The Mindset of Censorship before the 1930 Film Act.' 10th International Conference on Thai Studies (9 January).

———. 2013. 'หนัง 14 ตุลาคม การเขียนประวัติศาสตร์ประชาชนด้วยกล้องถ่ายหนัง' [14 October films: writing social history with a movie camera]. *Thai Film Journal* [วารสารหนังไทย], vol. 18 (November).

Chanchana Homsap. 2013. 'ตำนาน "ดาวยั่ว" กับความโป๊เปลือยในสื่อบันเทิงไทย ช่วงปี 2500–2520' [the story of the *dao-yua* in Thai erotic entertainment 1957–1977]. *Read* [อ่าน], vol. 4, no. 3 (January–March).

Charnvit Kasetsiri. 1999. ภาพยนตร์กับการเมือง เลือดทหารไทย พระเจ้าช้างเผือก บ้านไร่นาเรา [film and politics: *Undaunte Sons of Siam, The King of the White Elephant*, our farmland] [*sic*]. Bangkok: P. K. Group.

Chulyarnnon Siriphol. 2018. 'My Biennale 006' ['เบียนนาเล่ของฉัน 006']. Facebook (7 November). https://www.facebook.com/chulayarnnon.siriphol/posts/10156186323563640.

———. 2020. *Give Us a Little More Time* [ขอเวลาอีกไม่นาน]. Bangkok: Bangkok CityCity Gallery.

Cicada Channel. 2019. 'Issue 3: *Monk and Motorcycle Taxi Rider.*' https://www.cicada-ch.com.

Connors, Michael Kelly. 2005. 'Hegemony and the Politics of Culture and Identity in Thailand: Ministering Culture.' *Critical Asian Studies*, vol. 37, no. 4 (December).

Constitution of the Kingdom of Thailand. 1997. http://www.oic.go.th/FILEWEB/ CABIWEBSITE/DRAWER01/GENERAL/DATA0016/00016936.DOC.

Cornwel-Smith, Philip. 2020. *Very Bangkok: In the City of the Senses.* Bangkok: River Books.

Cvikova, Ludmila. 2016. 'Tiger Talk: Prabda Yoon about *Motel Mist.*' International Film Festival Rotterdam (31 January). https://www.youtube.com/watch?v=4aU B1iY7iS0.

Daley, Dianne. 2008. 'In the Frame of Mind to Take Control: Politics Surrounding the Banning of Apichatpong Weerasethakul's *Syndromes and a Century.*' 17th Biennial Conference of the Asian Studies Association of Australia. http://artsonline.monash. edu.au/mai/files/2012/07/diannedaley.pdf.

*Dao Siam* [ดาวสยาม]. 1976. 'แผ่นดินเดือด!' [the earth is shaking!] (6 October).

de Souza, Alison. 2015. 'Shot in Chiangmai, but no Trace of Thailand.' *The Straits Times* (26 August). https://www.straitstimes.com/lifestyle/entertainment/shot-in-chiangmai-but-no-trace-of-thailand.

Dome Sukwong. 1996. หลงทางและคดีหลงทาง [how *Going Astray* lost its lawsuit]. Bangkok: Film House.

Dome Sukvong [*sic*]. 2013. *A Century of Thai Cinema Exhibition's Handbook* [*sic*] [คู่มือนิทรรศการ หนึ่งศตวรรษภาพยนตร์ไทย 2440–2540]. Salaya: Thai Film Archive.

Dome Sukwong and Sawasdi Suwannapak. 2001. *A Century of Thai Cinema.* London: Thames and Hudson.

Faulder, Dominic. 2018. *Anand Panyarachun and the Making of Modern Thailand.* Singapore: Editions Didiet Millet.

Film and Video Act. 2008. http://web.krisdika.go.th/data/outsitedata/outsite21/file/FILM_ AND_VIDEO_ACT,_B.E.2551_ (2008).pdf.

*Flashback '76: History and Memory of October 6 Massacre* [อดีตหลอน: ประวัติศาสตร์และความ ทรงจำ 6 ตุลา 19]. 2008. Bangkok: Pridi Banomyong Institute.

Foreign Correspondents' Club of Thailand. 2018. 'Programme Cancellation.' http://www. fccthai.com/items/2511.html.

Free Thai Cinema Movement. 2013. 'ย้อนรอยเซ็นเซอร์หนังไทย ซ้ำซาก? ลักลั่น? ย้อนแย้ง?' [looking back at Thai film censorship: repeating itself? out of order? contradictory?]. *Thai Film Journal* [วารสารหนังไทย], vol. 18 (November).

'*"Frienemies"*' สารคดีชีวิต ปรีดี-จอมพล ป. สะท้อนมิตรภาพและความขัดแย้ง จาก 2475 ถึง ปัจจุบัน' [*Frienemies*, a documentary on the lives of Pridi and Phibun, reflecting on their friendship and conflict since 1932]. 2017. BBC News (7 October). https://www.bbc.com/ thai/thailand-41558324.

Fuhrmann, Arnika. 2016. *Ghostly Desires: Queer Sexuality and Vernacular Buddhism in Contemporary Thai Cinema.* Durham: Duke University Press.

Gecker, Jocelyn. 2010. 'Thailand Bans Film about Transgender Father.' The Associated Press (24 December). https://archive.boston.com/ae/movies/articles/2010/12/24/thailand_ bans_film_about_transgender_father/.

Genova, Alexandra. 2019. 'The Director Speaks: Apichatpong Weerasethakul on the Future of Film in Thailand.' *Huck* (6 March). https://www.huckmag.com/art-and-culture/film-2/apichatpong-weerasethakul-interview-thailand-film/.

Goppong Khunthreeya. 2015. 'Critical Discourse Analysis of Thailand's Film Acts.' The Asian Conference on Media and Mass Communication (15 November). https://25qt511nswf i49iayd31ch80-wpengine.netdna-ssl.com/wp-content/uploads/papers/mediasia2015/MediAsia2015_19244.pdf.

Graiwoot Chulpongsathorn. 2009. 'Love Letters.' Criticine (15 December). http://www.criticine.com/feature_article.php?id=44&pageid=1277891554.

————. 2010. 'Thoughts on Contemporary Experimental Films in Thailand.' EX!T 2010. https://www.academia.edu/5023096/.

Gray, Carmen. 2012. *Mundane History*. Second Run DVD.

Green, Ronald. 2014. *Buddhism Goes to the Movies: Introduction to Buddhist Thought and Practice*. Abingdon: Routledge.

Grossman, Nicholas. 2009. *Chronicle of Thailand: Headline News since 1946*. Singapore: Editions Didier Millet.

Hamilton, Annette. 1993. 'Video Crackdown, or The Sacrificial Pirate: Censorship and Cultural Consequences in Thailand.' *Public Culture*, vol. 5, no. 3 (Spring).

Harrison, Rachel V. 2010. 'The Man with the Golden Gauntlets: Mit Chaibancha's *Insi Thorng* and the Hybridization of Red and Yellow Perils in Thai Cold War Action Cinema.' *Cultures at War: The Cold War and Cultural Expression in Southeast Asia* (ed. Tony Day and Maya H. T. Liem). Ithaca: Cornell University Press.

Herrera, Aliosha. 2015. 'Thai 16mm Cinema: The Rise of a Popular Cinematic Culture in Thailand from 1945 to 1970.' *Rian Thai: International Journal of Thai Studies* [เรียนไทย], vol. 8. https://firebasestorage.googleapis.com/vo/b/johnjadd-3524a.appspot.com/o/yS roOyFbNphMLJ9kMTSmDpxsJeX2%2Fpdf%2F1547097505328-RT8Ch02%20Thai%2016mm%20Cinema%20%20The%20Rise%20of%20a%20Popular%20Cinematic%20Culture%20in%20Thailand%20from%201945%20to%201970.pdf.

*Hotel Art Fair Bangkok*. 2019. Bangkok: Farmgroup.

Hunt, Matthew. 2012. 'Thai Movie Censorship.' *Encounter Thailand*, vol. 1, no. 7 (October). http://www.matthewhunt.com/portfolio/thaimoviecensorship.pdf.

————. 2013. 'Exclusive Interview with Apichatpong Weerasethakul.' *Encounter Thailand*, vol. 2, no. 13 (May). http://www.matthewhunt.com/portfolio/exclusiveinterviewwith apichatpongweerasethakul.pdf.

iLaw. 2013. 'Case #472: *Boundary*.' https://freedom.ilaw.or.th/yii/index.php/lawsuit/472.

Ing Kanjanavanit. 2011. 'Poses from Dreamland' ['ท่าโพสจากแดนช่างฝัน']. *Manit Sriwanich-poom: Phenomena and Prophecies*. Bangkok: Srinakharinwirot University.

————. 2014. Southeast Asian Film Festival 2014 (2 May). https://www.youtube.com/watch?v=0KVeo85RJvI.

Institute for Ideas and Information. 2019. Kembara Festival (7 February). https://www.youtube.com/watch?v=wcY8dndsBY8.

Issariya Praithongyaem. 2015. 'Thai Film Director Decries Censorship.' BBC News (15 October). https://www.bbc.com/news/world-asia-34540734.

Itthipol Waranusupakul. 2014. 'Film Regulation in Thailand' ['การกำกับดูแลสื่อภาพยนตร์ของ ไทย']. *The Journal of Social Communication Innovation* [วารสารวิชาการนวัตกรรมสื่อสาร สังคม], vol. 2, no. 2 (July–December). https://www.tci-thaijo.org/index.php/jcosci/ article/download/93071/72896.

Jablon, Philip. 2019. *Thailand's Movie Theatres: Relics, Ruins and the Romance of Escape*. Bangkok: River Books.

Jackson, Peter A. 2002. 'Offending Images: Gender and Sexual Minorities, and State Control of the Media in Thailand.' *Media Fortunes, Changing Times: ASEAN States in Transition* (ed. Russell H. K. Heng). Singapore: Institute of Southeast Asian Studies. https://www. academia.edu/20753768/.

Jit Phokaew, Kanchat Rangseekansong, Wiwat Lertwiwatwongsa, Chulayarnnon Siriphol, and Chayanin Tiangpitayagorn. 2012. 'Mysterious Object from Thailand.' *Experimental Conversations*, no. 9 (Summer). http://www.experimentalconversations.com/article/ mysterious-objects-from-thailand/.

Jolliffe, Genevieve and Andrew Zinnes. 2006. *The Documentary Film Makers Handbook*. New York: Continuum.

Jutatip Thitisawat. 2015. 'From Censorship to Rating System: Negotiations of Power in Thai Film Industry.' The Asian Conference on Media and Mass Communication (15 November). https://papers.iafor.org/wp-content/uploads/papers/mediasia2015/MediAsia 2015_14288.pdf.

Kittinun Klongyai. 2017. 'Love Missions: Junta's New Soapie Reflects Military Fantasy.' Prachatai English (22 June). https://prachatai.com/english/node/7226.

Knee, Adam. 2012. 'Scholarly Resources on Thai Cinema in English: A Bibliography in Progress.' *Thai Film Journal* [วารสารหนังไทย], vol. 16 (June).

Kong Rithdee. 2005. 'Underground Experience.' *Real.Time, Bangkok Post* (4 March). http:// w3.thaiwebwizard.com/member/thaiindie/wizContent.asp?wizConID=79&txtmMenu _ID=7.

———. 2006. 'Historical Inspiration.' *Outlook, Bangkok Post* (29 March). http://www. thaifilm.com/articleDetail_en.asp?id=79.

———. 2007a. 'Time to Move Forward.' *Real.Time, Bangkok Post* (4 May). https://www. pressreader.com/thailand/bangkok-post/20070504/282750582298565.

———. 2007b. 'Cat Among the Pigeons.' *Real.Time, Bangkok Post* (14 September). https:// www.bangkokpost.com/Realtime/14Sep2007_real001.php.

———. 2008. 'The Long Road Home.' *Real.Time, Bangok Post* (4 April). https:// pressreader.com/thailand/bangkok-post/20080404/282643208268471.

———. 2009. 'The Sad Case of the Bangkok Film Festival.' *Dekalong 3: On Film Festivals* (ed. Richard Porton). London: Wallflower Press.

———. 2010a. 'Robed in Controversy.' *Real.Time, Bangkok Post* (19 February). https://www. pressreader.com/thailand/bangkok-post/20100219/283648231053030.

———. 2010b. 'To Show or Not to Show.' *Real.Time, Bangkok Post* (27 August). https://www. bangkokpost.com/lifestyle/movie/193152/to-show-or-not-to-show.

Kong Rithdee. 2010c. 'The Red Eagle Has Landed … Again.' Real.Time, Bangkok Post (1 October). https://www.pressreader.com/thailand/bangkok-post/20101001/282458525303026.

—. 2010d. 'Insect in the Backyard.' Real.Time, Bangkok Post (26 November). https://www.bangkokpost.com/lifestyle/movie/208221/insect-in-the-backyard.

—. 2011. 'Monks in the Movies.' Outlook, Bangkok Post (9 February). https://www.bangkokpost.com/lifestyle/film/220543/monks-in-the-movies.

—. 2012a. 'Censors Ban "Shakespeare" Film.' Bangkok Post (4 April). https://www.bangkokpost.com/learning/advanced/287430/shakepeare-macbeth-banned-in-thailand.

—. 2012b. 'Never Mind Nipples, the Law Is an Ass.' Bangkok Post (29 September). https://www.bangkokpost.com/print/314609/.

—. 2017a. 'Massacre's Memory.' Life, Bangkok Post (20 July). https://www.bangkokpost.com/lifestyle/social-and-lifestyle/1290455/massacres-memory.

—. 2017b. 'The Inciting Incident.' Life, Bangkok Post (6 October). https://www.bangkokpost.com/lifestyle/film/1337603/the-inciting-incident.

—. 2019. 'Until the Abyss Stares Back.' Koschke, no. 2.

Kooiman, Mirjam. 2017. 'Infected Memories.' Foam, no. 47.

Kornkritch Somjittranukit. 2016. 'The Royal Anthem: Shaping Thai Political Views Through Cinemas Nationwide,' Prachatai English (22 November). https://prachatai.com/english/node/6732.

Lamb, David. 2000. 'Thai Movie Ban Shows Respect for King Supersedes Freedoms.' Los Angeles Times (12 February). https://www.latimes.com/archives/la-xpm-2000-feb-12-mn-63631-story.html.

Lim, Paige. 2018. 'In the Spotlight.' Tatler (Thailand), vol. 26, no. 320 (April). http://www.thailandtatler.com/arts-culture/arts/in-the-spotlight.

Linssen, Dana. 2017. 'Un/Folding: If Light Was the Measure of Time.' Apichatpong Weerasethakul (ed. Marente Bloemheuvel and Jaap Guldemond). Rotterdam: nai010.

Luckana Kunavichayanont. 2018. I Am You [ฉันคือเธอ]. Bangkok: Bangkok Art and Culture Centre Foundation.

Malinee Khumsupa and Sudarat Musikawong. 2016. 'Counter-memory: Replaying Political Violence in Thai Digital Cinema.' Kyoto Review of Southeast Asia, vol. 20. https://kyotoreview.org/issue-20/counter-memory-replaying-political-violence-in-thai-digital-cinema/.

Manit Sriwanichpoom: Phenomena and Prophecies. 2011. Bangkok: Srinakharinwirot University.

Manote Tripathi. 1998. 'The King and Us.' The Nation (29 November).

May Adadol Ingawanij. 2008. 'Disreputable Behaviour: The Hidden Politics of the Thai Film Act.' Vertigo, vol. 3, no. 8 (Winter). https://www.closeupfilmcentre.com/vertigo_magazine/volume-3-issue-8-winter-2008/disreputable-behaviour-the-hidden-politics-of-the-thai-film-act/.

—. 2013. 'กับดักของฉันทามติ' [the consensus trap]. Read [อ่าน], vol. 4, no. 4 (April–June).

McDaniel, Justin. 2010. 'The Emotional Lives of Buddhist Monks in Modern Thai Film.' *Journal of Religion and Film*, vol. 14, no. 2 (October). https://digitalcommons.unomaha. edu/jrf/vol14/iss2/9.

Melalin Mahavongtrakul. 2017. 'Redefining What's "Appropriate."' *Life*, Bangkok Post (27 November). https://www.bangkokpost.com/news/special-reports/1367627/redefining-whats-appropriate.

Monruedee Jansuttipan. 2016. 'TrueVisions Pulls Prabda Yoon's "*Motel Mist*" from Cinemas Straight After Premiere.' *BK* (17 November). https://bk.asia-city.com/movies/news/ prada-yoons-motel-mist-pulled-last-minute-screening-program.

Montlake, Simon. 2007. 'Making the Cut.' *Time* (Asia), vol. 170, no. 16 (22 October). https:// www.content.time.com/time/magazine/article/0,9171,1670261,00.html.

*Nation, The.* 2006. 'Film Brings Shame Upon Thai Society' (30 April). http://www.nation multimedia.com/2006/04/30/opinion/opinion_30002874.php.

Nattaya Chetchotiros. 2008. 'Sondhi Explains His "Final War."' *Bangkok Post* (26 August). https://www.bangkokpost.com/260808_News/26Aug2008_news11.php92.

Niwat Wattanayathanaporn. 2018. Facebook (1 November). https://www.facebook.com/ permalink.php?story_fbid=2277045905909578&id=100008125726542.

Nontawat Numbenchapol. 2013. '*Boundary* Banned by Censors, Screening Not Permitted in Kingdom of Thailand' ['ฟ้าต่ำแผ่นดินสูง / ไม่อนุญาตให้เผยแพร่ในราชอาณาจักรไทย']. Facebook (23 April). https://www.facebook.com/boundarymovie/photos/a.53918288 2780942/578122008887029.

Noy Thrupkaew. 2003. 'The King and Thai.' *The American Prospect* (20 August). https:// prospect.org/features/king-thai/.

Oradol Kaewprasert. 2005. 'The Very First Series of Thai Queer Cinemas: What Was Happening in the 80s?' Southeast Asian Cinema Conference: Cinema at the Borders (16 August). https://openresearch-repository.anu.edu.au/bitstream/1885/8671/1/Kaew prasert_VeryFirstSeries2005.pdf.

Panu Aree. 1997. 'ประวัติภาพยนตร์ทดลองในประเทศไทย' [the history of experimental films in Thailand]. *Bangkok International Film Festival*.

Parinyaporn Pajee. 2006. 'A New Spectre: Insensitivity.' *The Nation* (4 August).

Parinyaporn Pajee. 2013. 'Freedom on the Big Screen.' *The Nation* (6 June). http://www. nationmultimedia.com/life/Freedom-on-the-big-screen-30207685.html.

————. 2018. 'Where Equality Counts.' *The Nation* (16 March). http://www.nationmultimedia. com/detail/movie/30341028.

Parry, Richard Lloyd. 2014. 'Thailand's Big Brother Bans Orwell's *1984*.' *The Times* (11 June). https://www.thetimes.co.uk/article/thailands-big-brother-bans-orwells-1984-5snkwlx7xzt.

Pasuk Phongpaichit and Chris Baker. 2004. *Thaksin: The Business of Politics in Thailand*. Chiang Mai: Silkworm Books.

Pinkerton, Nick. 2020. '*Krabi, 2562*.' *Sight and Sound*, vol. 30, no. 5 (May). https://www.bfi.org. uk/news-opinion/sight-sound-magazine/reviews-recommendations/krabi-2562-ben-rivers-anoch-suwichakornpong-thailand-tourism-cinema-holocene-geology.

Piyanan, Gail. 2018. 'Interview with Arin Rungjang.' *Time Out Bangkok* (1 January). https://www.timeout.com/bangkok/art/interview-with-arin-rungjang.

Plate, Tom. 2011. *Conversations with Thaksin: From Exile to Deliverance—Thailand's Populist Tycoon Tells His Story.* Singapore: Marshall Cavendish.

Pokpong Chanan. 2013. *Paradoxocracy* [ประชาธิป'ไทย]. Bangkok: Matichon Publishing.

Pongsawee Supanonth. 2013. 'การควบคุมเนื้อหาภาพยนตร์กับสาระที่เปลี่ยนไป' [regulating a changing film industry]. *Siam Communication Review* [วารสารนิเทศสยามปริทัศน์]. https://tci-thaijo.org/index.php/BECJournal/article/download/54107/44909.

Pravit Rojanaphruk. 2013. 'Despair Over Move to Stop Film about the South Being Screened.' *The Nation* (30 April). http://www.nationmultimedia.com/politics/Despair-over-move-to-stop-film-about-the-South-bei-30205106.html.

Pulver, Andrew. 2016. 'Apichatpong Weerasethakul: "My Country Is Run by Superstition." ' *The Guardian* (12 April). https://www.theguardian.com/film/2016/apr/12/apichatpong-weerasethakul-cemetery-of-splendour-thailand-interview.

Rapeepan Sayantrakul. 2007. 'ตัด-เบลอ-ดูด-เตือน-เฉือน-ระงับ! "เซ็นเซอร์แบบไทยๆ" ยังน้อยไป หรือมากเกินพอ' [cut-blur-bleep-warn-slice-ban! Thai censorship: not enough, or too much?]. *Sarakadee* [สารคดี], vol. 23, no. 266 (April).

Reuters. 2007. 'Thailand Pulls Iranian Cartoon from Film Festival' (27 June). https://www.reuters.com/article/us-thailand-iran-film/thailand-pulls-iranian-cartoon-from-film-festival-idUSBKK1636620070627.

Rich, B. Ruby. 2013. *New Queer Cinema: The Director's Cut.* Durham: Duke University Press.

Richardson, Thomas. 2006. 'Interview with Chatrichalerm Yukol.' Medium (14 October). https://medium.com/@anticonsultant/interview-with-chatrichalerm-yukol-26d00b18c9b6.

Richburg, Keith B. 2000. 'Not Playing: *"Anna and the King."* ' *The Washington Post* (7 January). https://www.washingtonpost.com/wp-srv/WPcap/2000-01/17/021r-011700-idx.html.

Sakdina Chatrakul na Ayudhya. 1989. 'Direction Unknown.' *Cinemaya*, vol. 4 (Summer).

Sasiwan Mokkhasen. 2016. 'Lack of Competition Stifles Thai Film Industry.' Khaosod English (15 March). https://www.khaosodenglish.com/news/business/2016/03/15/1458032447/.

Satien Chantimatorn. 1972. 'Thai Cencorships and the "Ban Movies" ' [sic] ['เซ็นเซอร์กับหนังต้องห้ามในเมืองไทย']. *The Social Science Review* [สังคมศาสตร์ปริทัศน์], vol. 10, no. 3 (March).

Sayan Daengklom. 2011. 'ห' [or]. *Read* [อ่าน], vol. 3, no. 2 (January–March).

Schoonover, Karl and Rosalind Galt. 2016. *Queer Cinema in the World.* Durham: Duke University Press.

Sessons, Jesse. 2018. '*The Holy Man.*' *Thai Cinema: The Complete Guide* (ed. Mary J. Ainslie and Katarzyna Ancuta). London: I. B. Tauris.

Sinnott, Megan. 2004. *Toms and Dees: Transgender Identity and Female Same-Sex Relationships in Thailand.* Honolulu: University of Hawai'i Press.

Sirichai Leelertyuth 2012. 'ภาพยนตร์สนทนา ข้อสังเกตว่าด้วย "การเมือง" ในหนังไทย' [talking about politics in Thai films]. *Prachatai* (28 June). https://prachatai.com/journal/2012/06/41309.

Sonthaya Subyen and Morimart Raden-Ahmad. 2014. *Once Upon a Celluloid Planet: Where Cinema Ruled—Hearts and Homes of Films in Thailand* [สวรรค์ 35 มม.: เสน่ห์วิกหนังเมือง สยาม]. Bangkok: Filmvirus.

Soopsip. 2013. 'Stuck with a Troublesome Film, Yuthlert Builds His Own Cinema.' *The Nation* (18 November). http://www.nationmultimedia.com/life/Stuck-with-a-troublesome-film-Yuthlert-builds-his-30219715.html.

———. 2016. 'Poj Lines up Another Romp for His Monks of Mirth.' *The Nation* (17 March). http://www.nationmultimedia.com/life/Poj-lines-up-another-romp-for-his-monks-of-mirth-30281756.html.

Sopida Rodsom. 2017. 'The Evolution of Sex in Thai Movies.' *Time Out Bangkok* (1 February). https://www.timeout.com/bangkok/movies/the-evolution-of-sex-in-thai-movie.

Streckfuss, David. 2011. *Truth on Trial in Thailand: Defamation, Treason, and Lèse-Majesté.* Abingdon: Routledge.

Sucheera Pinijparakarn. 2004. 'Call to Limit Gay Presence on TV.' *The Nation* (5 June). http://www.nationmultimedia.com/search/page.arcview.php?clid=2&id=100073.

Sudarat Musikawong and Malinee Khumsupa. 2017. 'State Censorship of Thai Cinema: Right of Expression or Enemy of the State.' 13th International Conference on Thai Studies (17 July).

Surasak Glahan. 2016. 'Sex Scene Lands French Movie Film Fest Ban.' *Bangkok Post* (8 July). https://www.pressreader.com/thailand/bangkok-post/20160708/2816 85434171169.

Terwiel, B. J. 2011. *Thailand's Political History: From the 13th Century to Recent Times.* Bangkok: River Books.

Thai PBS World. 2019. 'Thai Politics Getting Faster and More Furious' (11 June). https://www.thaipbsworld.com/thai-politics-getting-faster-and-more-furious/.

'The Twelve Core Values for a Strong Thailand.' 2014. National News Bureau of Thailand. http://thainews.prd.go.th/banner/en/Core_Values/.

Thongchai Winichakul. 2020. *Moments of Silence: The Unforgetting of the October 6, 1976, Massacre in Bangkok.* Honolulu: University of Hawai'i Press.

Thunska Pansittivorakul. 2018. *Quasi una fantasia* [อัศจรรย์]. Bangkok: Linga Project 2018 [लिंगम् Project 2018].

Townsend, Rebecca. 2017. *Cold Fire: Gender, Development, and the Film Industry in Cold War Thailand.* Ithaca: Cornell University Press. https://ecommons.cornell.edu/bitstream/handle/1813/47725/Townsend_cornellgrad_0058F_10097.pdf.

———. 2019. 'The Adulterer: Censorship, Morality, and Foreign Films in Thailand.' *Journal of Women's History*, vol. 31, no. 1 (Spring). https://muse.jhu.edu/article/719495.

van Fenema, Joyce. 1996. *Southeast Asian Art Today.* Singapore: Roeder Publications.

*Vasan Sitthiket: Blue October* [ตุลาลัย]. 1996. Bangkok: Sunday Gallery.

Vaschol Quadri. 2013. 'Interview: *"Boundary"* Director Nontawat Numbenchapol on the Censorship Controversy.' *BK* (26 April). https://bk.asia-city.com/movies/article/interview-director-nontawat-numbenchapol-boundary-documentary-ban-controversy.

Veera Musigapong. 1978. ไอ้ข้าส์ ... จอมเนรคุณ [the leading betrayer]. Bangkok: Bhannakij Publishing.

Wassana Nanuam. 2014. 'Yingluck Saw the Coup Coming.' *Bangkok Post* (24 November). https://www.pressreader.com/thailand/bangkok-post/20141124/28.1505044526716.

West, Andrew J. 2011. 'Obsessive Compulsive.' *Fine Art*, vol. 8, no. 79 (May).

Wimonrat Aroonrojsuriya. 2000. 'หนังโป๊กับเสรีภาพหลัง 14 ตุลาคม' [freedom for pornographic films after 14 October]. *Thai Film Quarterly* [หนังไทย], vol. 2, no. 8 (April–June).

Winston, Curtis. 2009. '"*Quarantine*" Under Lockdown.' *Daily Xpress*, vol. 2, no. 450 (30 October). https://www.issuu.com/charoen_naeem/docs/20091030.

———. 2012. '10th WFFBKK: Victor Is Awarded.' Wise Kwai's Thai Film Journal (18 November). http://thaifilmjournal.blogspot.com/2012/11/10th-wffbkk-victor-is-awarded.html.

Yu Sen-lun. 2004. 'The 4th Taiwan International Documentary Festival: A Sweet and Sour Slice.' *Taipei Times* (13 December). https://www.taipeitimes.com/News/feat/archives/2004/12/13/2003214942/2.